# The Mayor's Tales

# The Mayor's Tales

## Stories from the Kyleighburn Archives

An Off The Page Anthology

RJ Minnick, Editor

Missing! by Patricia L. Auman

Rex Rising by Robin Deffendall

The Little Curse by C. Grey

Soul Mate by Barbara Kirk

The Tea Set, Mayor vs. Mayor and Minutes of a Meeting of The Unboxed Players, by Mackenzie Minnick

Canon and Special Delivery by RJ Minnick

Friends for Ever and Ever by Iliana Navarro

Occurrence on the Hawanee by J.D. Richardson

The Expedition, On the Steps and Suspicion by Susan Turley

**ISBN: 9781790966189**

# Table of Contents

# From the Desk of Marino Esposito

Mayor of Kyleighburn, North Carolina

For the thirty years that I have served Kyleighburn, North Carolina as its watchful protector and mayor, I have encountered a wide variety of people. Ours is not, as some would believe, a quiet, small town full of exhausted and elderly citizens, humdrum and antiquated in their ways, but instead a vibrant and mystical place full of depth and conflict.

This life we choose is not for everyone. The intense scrutiny, the slow days. Not everything in our little world happens quite the way you expect it to. What it loses in what some would call excitement and speed, it gains in community and mutual support. Never have I known a group of people who can be so silly—even going so far as to entrust their most valuable secrets to a dog named The Mayor! But likewise, never have I met a group of people who felt so passionate about their day-to-day life.

Yes, there are many hidden joys and reasons to love Kyleighburn.

A large number of these surprises are located inside its archives, records that have been meticulously stored since the town's official foundation in 1850. With this, my official resignation letter, I gift the citizenry with the following text, a carefully curated and dramatized selection from those archives. It comprises tales that I deem encompass—if not the entirety of our town—then certainly the essence of what make us Kyleighburn.

Included as well are some newspaper articles from the local paper, *The Kyleighburn Kylter,* and a closed parcel of papers a young man named Micah gave me twenty years ago, asking only that they remain sealed until I determined it an appropriate time to open them. Now is that time.

It has been an ordeal and pleasure serving Kyleighburn.

Marino Esposito

December 2018

# Occurrence on the Hawanee

J.D. Richardson

"ANT!" CIELO SHOUTED BACK from where she, Deer-Friend and Bear had paused at the crest of a low ridge. "What are you doing?" A slight furrowing of her brow signaled her displeasure.

"I'm just looking at something," the boy called in answer.

"What do you expect?" laughed Bear as he pointed at his own temple in the universal sign for mental deficiency. "He probably thinks he's discovered a new type of beetle or something." With the casualness of long familiarity, he placed his hand on Cielo's back in a wordless attempt to placate her.

But Cielo wasn't going to let it go. "Can you at least *try* to keep up?" she scolded. "Father will give us the fifteen strikes if he has nothing to offer his guests because of us. Think how he would lose face with the other tribes."

"Yeah, Ant; try to keep up," echoed twelve-year-old Deer-Friend in conscious imitation of Cielo.

"Alright already!" Ant abandoned the stick insect he had been watching and started hurrying up the rise after them.

"Sometimes my little brother dallies like the turtle," Cielo said as they turned and resumed crossing the ridge. "He even kind of resembles one with that basket lashed onto his back."

"He-Who-Watches-Ants might have been better named He-Who-Constantly-Gets-Distracted," Bear agreed.

"You'd better be worrying about your own task," Ant told Cielo and Deer-Friend once he had caught up with the group. "When father sees what Bear and I bring for the pow-wow he's sure to forget any paltry offerings of yours."

"Such big talk for such a small Tuscarora," Cielo observed.

"Have a care, Ant-Watcher," Bear cautioned him. "No man can say the luck of the hunt in advance."

"Our luck won't matter," Ant insisted. "I've got a plan."

"What kind of plan?" Deer-Friend asked with suspicion.

"I can't tell you. It's a secret."

"That's 'cause there isn't any plan!"

"No, he's telling the truth," Cielo interjected. "He can't tell you the plan because it's so secret he doesn't even know it himself." Naturally Deer-Friend found this witticism to be the height of hilarity, and she commenced shrieking with laughter.

Ant's face clouded in annoyance. "Just wait 'til the meeting. You'll see. You won't be laughing *then*."

Cielo slewed her head around to face Ant. "Don't be so thin-skinned," she told him. "Deerie and I are aware what accomplished hunters you and

Bear have become." As she turned her head her hair had pulled back revealing her deformed ear, and Ant studied it curiously. She caught his gaze and quickly flipped her hair back into its usual position, concealing the abnormality. "I'm sure you'll bring back something that will reflect honorably upon father," she continued. "I just hope Deerie and I can find enough *tijana* berries to serve the guests. They're only just now coming into season."

"If anyone can it's this one," said Bear, nodding at Deer-Friend. "She has the eyes of a hawk." The pleasure Deer-Friend took in this praise was blatantly obvious. The girl ducked her head, suddenly shy.

"Let's hope so," Cielo said with sincerity. "Otherwise we'll have to go dig up *yorqua* roots." Everyone knew Cielo disliked digging and preparing the pungent, deeply-buried roots.

"Cee-elll-lo," Deer-Friend drawled with a frown. Then "Cielo." She said it as if hearing it for the first time. She looked up at the older girl. "How did you get that name?"

"I was given it by the people of my birth-tribe. In their language it means She-Who-Gazes-at-the-Sky." Cielo smiled wryly at the memory. "When I was little I used to love watching the colors of the sky and the shapes of the clouds." Everyone knew Cielo had originally been one of the Lopotwa, the large tribe that lived on the other side of the river. When she was about Deer-Friend's present age a small group of Tuscarora women had found her wandering, dazed and bedraggled, in the nearby forest. From her attire and the few words she spoke the women quickly recognized her as Lopotwa. The Tuscarora women had taken the girl home with them where they fed her, mended her clothes, and then took her before the village elders. After briefly deliberating, the elders sent one of the older boys across the river to the largest Lopotwa settlement to alert them to her discovery. Several days later the boy had returned with the puzzling message that the Lopotwa weren't missing any girls and hadn't any knowledge of her. On being informed of this, Chief Stone-Cleaver had simply taken her into his own hearth. Though she was now quite fluent in the Tuscarora language, Cielo's previous life among the Lopotwa was somewhat mysterious in that she almost never spoke about it.

"Your name is strange," Deer-Friend concluded.

"Oh yeah? Well how did you come by your name?"

"Everybody knows *that.* It's because a deer once came up to me when I was little."

During the time they had been talking they had finally reached the bog where the *tijana* berries grew. "I guess this is where Ant and I leave you," Bear said to Cielo and Deer-Friend. "Wish us luck."

In answer to this request, Cielo slipped her arms around his waist and leaned in close. He, in turn, lovingly placed his hand on the slight swell of her belly. "Good luck, my brave Bear," she told him softly, and sanctified this benediction with a warm kiss.

As they continued murmuring soft endearments to each other, Ant turned his attention to the hunting bow, which he carried in his hand due to the basket strapped across his back. Before he quite knew what was happening, Deer-Friend was suddenly there in front of him with her arms around his neck.

"Oh, my sweetest, bravest Warrior-Ant!" she crooned in theatrical mockery of the two lovers. "You haven't even left yet and I already miss you just soooo much! If you're gone for more than fifty heartbeats I'm certain I'll just *die*!" At the conclusion of this performance Ant was too flustered to react, but Bear, Cielo and Deer-Friend all erupted in gales of laughter.

"Look at poor, bewildered Ant," Cielo sympathized as they were regaining their composure. "Even his ears are red with blushing."

"No, they're not!" he protested rather quickly. The teenager turned away in annoyance. "I've just been rubbing them is all."

"As for you," Bear grinned to Deer-Friend, "never say Walks-Like-a-Bear can't take a hint." His hands were still locked with Cielo's, and now he turned to her. "I'll see *you* later," he vowed. They exchanged one last quick kiss and then, "Come on, Ant. Let's leave these hens to their clucking." The tall brave strode off toward the small stream that fed into the bog, and Ant mutely fell in behind.

**Circa 2.83 million years before present**

The device had been wending its way through the cold, empty depths of interstellar space for hundreds of years. It was a third-generation, self-replicating Von Neumann machine whose original primogenitor had been built by a race that was old during the Pliocene. The probe had first entered the system of the star it was currently approaching two years past, and only now had the intensity of incoming radiation finally triggered the main computer core to awaken. Contacts closed, diagnostic routines were run, and power was once again sent through circuits that hadn't been energized in decades. As the electronic brain came online, it first took star sightings to fix its current position, and then began a preliminary scan of this sun's planetary system. Simultaneously it deployed a small fleet of solar-powered nanobots to make repairs and upgrades to itself as well as to replenish its fuel reserves. Thus, with a patience and single-mindedness found only in machines, did it resume its monumental, never-ending task of mapping and exploration.

At the stream Ant and Bear scooped gray, musty-smelling mud out of the bank and slathered themselves with it in order to conceal their own scent. Then they started in the direction of the river. They knew that animals would go there to drink, and the plan was to set up in a particular spot Bear had successfully hunted in the past. They moved quickly, but quietly, and neither spoke. As they made their silent way, Ant recalled the feeling of Deer-Friend in his arms, and his mind kept turning back to the incident all during the long trek.

Once they arrived at the location, its advantages as a hunting site were obvious. Ant and Bear were moving parallel to an animal path that went between two large boulders. Once past the boulders, the path turned to follow along the edge of a small glade before continuing on north to the river. The two Tuscarora pulled themselves up into separate trees along the edge of the clearing. The set-up was perfect. The two rocks would hide them from any approaching animals until they entered the clearing, where the hunters would get a relatively clear shot. They made themselves as comfortable as they could on the branches, notched arrows to their bow-strings and proceeded to wait.

As the day wore on, a stillness settled over the little glade. They waited for what seemed like an interminably long time, and Ant had just decided that they weren't going to have any luck when he heard a snort. A moment later two does entered the clearing, soon followed by three more. From the corner of his eye Ant saw Bear make the blade-shaped hand gesture that meant "wait." Sure enough, Ant then heard another snort that wasn't from any of the deer already in the clearing. Moments later a handsome, medium-sized buck stepped into the glade behind the five does. It stopped and scanned the glade suspiciously, its nose pulsing as it scented the air. Bear let fly, and his arrow hit the buck in the shoulder instead of the rib cage where he had been aiming. The buck roared and bolted down the trail toward Ant who shot it in the side as it raced by. In a flash the two hunters leaped out of their trees and took off after the wounded buck.

The going was relatively easy since the buck was keeping to the animal trail. As the hunters ran along in pursuit, they would spot a tuft of hair or a few blood marks every so often. After a prolonged period of this they were finally coming up on the river. Then the two hunters froze at the sound of voices. They slowly crept up to the brush alongside the river and peered down.

The track of the buck down the bank and into the water was clear. It had crossed a shallow stretch to a nearby sandbar where it lay with its throat slashed. Two adult Lopotwa braves were standing over the dead buck, and Ant and Bear could see a small canoe beached on the far end of the sandbar. From the tracks it was clear that the badly wounded buck had only lay there as the Indians had approached. They hadn't even had to pursue it. As they watched, the older of the braves extracted the two arrows from the carcass and threw them off to one side.

Bear carefully re-sheathed his free arrow back into his quiver and then motioned for Ant to do the same, but he kept his bow in his hand. After this was done he stepped into the open and slowly started down the riverbank, Ant doing the same behind him. The younger Lopotwa brave slowly pulled his bow from off his back as the two Tuscarora approached.

Once they had gained the sandbar, Bear pointed at the dead buck and then at himself and Ant while saying "Our kill." The two Lopotwa gave no sign, so Bear first laid his bow down and then retrieved the two cast-off arrows. He matched them to the two arrow wounds in the body of the buck and then pointed at himself and Ant again while repeating, "Our kill." After a moment the older Lopotwa pointed to the Buck's slashed neck and held up his open palm with his bloodied knife lying sideways across it. The brave was countering that it was *his* knife that had made the kill. Now Bear used the first two fingers of each hand to portray two running figures. He finished by spreading his hands wide apart while saying, "We chased it a long way." The older Lopotwa's response was to point at the canoe and then pantomime the act of paddling. He ended with a shrug, his face impassive.

Bear thought for a moment and then twisted and swept his open hand behind him in a gesture that encompassed the nearby riverbank with its capping forest. "Tuscarora lands," he said. Then he pointed to the unmistakable track where the buck had come down the bank and onto the sandbar. "Tuscarora prey. Our kill," he repeated.

Now the older brave mimicked Bear's previous gesture while saying something in his own language. Thankfully, the Lopotwa language was somewhat similar to that of the Tuscarora, and on the second repetition the two youths got it. He was arguing that where they were presently standing was in the river, and that the river wasn't part of the Tuscarora lands. After a brief pause he turned and waved some flies and bees away from the carcass, grabbed the buck by the front legs and started dragging it toward the canoe.

"Wait," Bear stated calmly. The older brave released the carcass and the two Lopotwa watched him warily. He raised both hands, palms out, in a non-threatening gesture, and then slowly approached the kill. Squatting down beside the carcass, he made a knife-edge of one hand against the exact middle of the Buck's torso. Then he swept his hand to the animal's rear and pointed at the two Lopotwa while saying, "For you." Then he once again positioned his knifed hand at the animal's mid-point and swept it forward over the buck's front half. He stood up and walked back over to Ant. This time he indicated Ant and himself while saying, "For us." He held his two fists together in front of him and then broke them apart while saying, "We will share." The older Lopotwa exchanged a look with his companion and then just resumed pulling the dead buck toward the canoe.

Ant was suddenly unable to contain himself. "They're taking our kill!"

At his outburst the younger Lopotwa abruptly reached over his shoulder and drew two arrows. He made no move to notch them to his bow, but the warning was clear. Bear and Ant remained motionless while the older Lopotwa loaded the dead buck into the canoe and launched it back into the water. He then said something to his companion while holding the canoe steady. The younger brave backed into the shallow water until he bumped up against the little craft. He stepped sideways until clear of it and then backed around to the far side of the vessel without taking his eyes off the two Tuscarora. It was from this position that he eased himself into the canoe. Once he had boarded, the older Lopotwa followed suit and started paddling them down the river. The younger brave did not join in paddling until they were safely out of bow-shot. From the sandbar Ant and Bear watched the two Lopotwa disappear around the bend of the river. Only then did Bear retrieve his bow from where he had laid it. He rinsed the two retrieved arrows in the river, re-sheathing his own before handing the other back to Ant.

"What now?" asked Ant as they scrambled back up the riverbank. "Are we going to try to make another kill?"

Bear checked the height of the sun. "There isn't enough time for that." He chewed his lip, considering. "I guess we could go help Cielo and Deer-Friend finish gathering berries."

"I don't like the thought of going back with nothing but berries," Ant confessed. "We should give my plan a try."

"What's your plan?"

"You'll see," he said, breaking into a trot. "Follow me." Ant plunged into the surrounding forest, and seconds later Bear took off after him.

**Circa 2.83 m.y.a.**

The probe had been exploring the environs of this star for some time. After completing a detailed system map, it began spectroscopic analysis of the atmospheres of the system's planets. Its quantum electronic brain was programmed to give high priority to bio-signatures, and the results indicated an advanced-level biome on the system's third planet out, so that's where it headed.

The probe's analysis had been correct. On arriving, it found a water-covered world with thriving complex ecosystems both in the oceans and on land, and even including large multi-cellular megafaunal organisms. A few animal species were even practicing rudimentary tool use. All in all, it was the most scientifically important discovery the current probe or any of its generational predecessors had ever encountered. The probe assumed a low-level orbit and, for the first time ever in its millennia-long working life, its artificial intelligence "brain" powered up a second, backup computer core to assist it with the monumental task of analyzing and transmitting the vast amounts of data it was collecting on the world and its myriad life forms.

Ant and Bear struck a southwest bearing for a good while until they came upon a small stream. They followed it south until it led them to a wide, green marsh. Ant slowed his pace and began skirting along the marsh's edge. About a third of the way around it he stopped. "Here we are," was all he said as they caught their breath.

After a few moments Ant laid down his bow, removed his quiver and began unstrapping the basket from his back. When he got it off, Bear could see that the inside was lined with some sort of smooth skin or gut material. "Are we going to pull *feneer* shoots then?" Bear asked him.

"Come over here," was all Ant said by way of answer. "Look," he added once Bear was beside him. "That large oak tree over there."

Bear looked where Ant was pointing and soon spotted a steady stream of dark shapes flying in and out of an opening where a low limb had formerly been. The opening was about shoulder high, and looked out over the marsh. "It's a bee tree," he observed, though still somewhat perplexed. "Holy Mother Buffalo, what bees!" He had noticed that the insects were unusually large, being about half again as long as any bees he'd ever previously seen.

Ant held the basket level against his hip. "I've been coming out here and watching this hive ever since I discovered it. I'm going to get us some honey to take back."

"You can't," Bear told him. "We don't have any *sarsum* grass to smoke the hive with. Look at the size of those things! You'll be stung within an inch of your life."

"We won't need it," Ant stated confidently. "These bees are different. I've walked right up to the tree and observed the hive, and though they crawled on me, they never stung me once."

"You've raided the hive by yourself?" Bear asked incredulously.

"Not as such, but I did take one very small piece of comb last time I was here," Ant told him.

"And they didn't sting you?"

"Not once, as I've said. But I knew they wouldn't."

"How did you know that?"

"Because...." He trailed off, struggling for words. "It's... it's like they *invited* me to have a bite."

Bear stared at the younger brave as if he had grown a second head. "I don't know, Ant-Watcher. I've never heard of bees that don't sting. This sounds like a bad idea to me."

"I can't explain it, but I just *know* I can do this," he stated. "If worst comes to worst I can always jump into the stream. Stay here for now, and don't get alarmed if some of them alight on me."

As Bear watched, Ant walked out into the marsh and then slowly approached the tree until he was just to one side of the flight line, where he stopped. Almost immediately some of the bees veered over to where he stood and began circling around him, some even landing on him. Only after several minutes of this did he start approaching the hive one calm step at a time. Once at the opening, he reached in with slow, deliberate movements, taking care to block the hole as little as possible. Bear inhaled sharply at the sight of dozens of large bees crawling along Ant's arm and body, but if they were stinging him he gave no sign of it. He pulled out a generous hunk of comb, placed it into the basket and repeated this action two more times. Following this, he closed his eyes and just stood there. After a minute or so Bear saw his lips move, and then he opened his eyes and started making his way back toward where Bear waited. As he advanced, more and more bees kept flying off of him. By the time he rejoined Bear, he was completely clear of the insects.

"Are you okay?" Bear asked.

"I'm fine." He held up the basket with its thick hunks of comb. "Now we have a fit offering for tomorrow's feast."

"All thanks to you," Bear acceded, "though I have no idea how you managed it." The two Indians gathered their possessions and started making their way back to their village.

**Circa 2.83 m.y.a.**

It shouldn't have happened, but it did. The original probe designers knew the value of system redundancy and had engineered in back-ups for most of the probe's mission-critical systems, including its main data-processing core. The idea was that if either core sustained some kind of major damage, the AI program could occupy the alternative core, from which it could direct repair and rebuilding of the damaged unit. This dual-cored strategy had never yet failed in all the millennia the automated probe exploration program had been in operation. The numbers were by far in the probes' favor. The odds that a single meteor would ever hit at just the right trajectory to damage both computer cores with a single strike were vanishingly small, much less for *three* meteors. But small odds are not zero odds, and, ultimately, that's exactly what happened.

As the earth crossed the former orbit of a now-defunct comet, the probe just happened to be located in the exact center of the comet's debris trail. The largest meteor was only the size of an acorn; the other two even smaller. Yet their fantastic rate of travel imbued them with the kinetic energy to smash completely through the back-up core and on into the primary core before finally coming to rest. The massive amounts of damage sustained by the cores caused them both to immediately shut down. For the first time since its progenitor probe had been launched three generations ago, the AI program was completely off-line.

Upon sensing this, the probe's nanobots went into their default emergency repair mode. Even as a distributed system, their collective processing power was—due to their small size—quite limited, and the repairs would go unusually slowly. It was a full two years before their basic diagnostics revealed that the primary core had sustained significantly less damage, and prompted them to focus their efforts there. In the depths of interstellar space the nanobots would have had all the time they needed and then some. But here, deep in the planet's gravity well, a long stretch of time was something the probe didn't have. Its trajectory was so low that several minutes of each orbit were spent skimming through the rarefied, uppermost reaches of the planet's atmosphere. The net effect on each orbit was minuscule but, orbit after orbit, year after year, they began to add up. Without the electronic brain to calculate and apply occasional compensating thrusts, the probe's orbit slowly began to decay. Over the decades the probe's orbit sank lower and lower, and it began spending more and more time in the atmosphere during each circuit. Eventually, some sixty years since the meteor strike, the probe began a prolonged plunge toward the planet's surface. After some twenty minutes streaking through the lower atmosphere, it came hurtling in at a low angle and crashed into the base of an eroding bluff. The half of the probe still sticking out of the bluff popped and cracked as it cooled from the heat of atmospheric entry. Two days later the nanobots once again resumed their single-minded repair efforts.

The next morning the village was busy with preparations for the coming pow-wow. After fetching water, Ant and Bear located Cielo and Ant's mother, Torga, at a makeshift shelter that had been hastily erected for the sole purpose of storing the offerings for the day's feast.

"This is something the Lopotwa elders should be glad to see," she said as she placed the basket of honeycomb up on a high shelf. "You did well." She cupped the top of Ant's head in a familiar gesture. "It will bring much honor to your father." Brave that he was, Ant tried to feign indifference at the praise, but Torga caught the slight upturn at the corners of her son's mouth. She procured a cover, which she placed over the basket to keep the flies off. "Now get out of here," she ordered the two. "The last thing I need is you two lugs all up in the way."

Just then they all caught sound of the announcement drum of the approaching Lopotwa delegation. "We better get moving," Bear told Ant. "Your father expects us there when we greet the Lopotwa." So saying, the two youths headed for the open area where the main forest path entered the village.

At the clearing they joined the other thirty-two braves already assembled there. A few paces in front of them stood Chief Stone-Cleaver and five village elders. Cielo was also there, standing just to the chief's left. The rest of the village women and children clustered along the edge of the clearing, watching curiously. The Lopotwa drumming got louder and louder until the delegation finally came into sight around a bend of the main forest trail. The drummer led the procession, and Ant could see that he was a boy about Deer-Friend's age with the family markings of Panther-Foot, chief of the eastern Lopotwa village, adorning his body. Ant figured he must be one of the chief's many sons. Just behind him was Panther-Foot himself, and three of the Lopotwa elders. Following them were some twenty-five Lopotwa braves—rather more than was usual for such occasions, but certainly not enough to cause any alarm. The braves were armed, but not carrying their weapons at the ready. Oddly enough, each of them had three or four pieces of wood in their hands instead. As the announcement drummer entered the clearing he immediately turned to one side and took up a position just off the trail-head. Panther-Foot and the Lopotwa elders continued on across the clearing and lined up facing Stone-Cleaver and the Tuscarora elders. As the Lopotwa braves entered the clearing, each one would turn aside and throw his wood down in front of the drummer before then continuing on to take position behind their elders. The last brave was a youth about Ant's age. He and a Lopotwa squaw were carrying a dead buck, and Ant involuntarily took a sharp breath when he saw it. It was undoubtedly the same animal he and Bear had shot the day before. Without a word, the two Lopotwa dropped the carcass on the forest floor just past the village perimeter and proceeded skinning it. At this point the boy laid down his drum and started pulling kindling from a pouch and stuffing it under the pile of wood. The Lopotwa youth skinning the buck made no move to enter the village.

After watching them for a few awkward seconds, Chief Stone-Cleaver turned to the Lopotwa delegation and began. "Peace be to you, cousins, and be welcome here in the place of the Tuscarora." He stepped forward and clasped forearms with the Lopotwa chief. "Now let us smoke tobacco together."

At his signal Torga came forward and handed him his ceremonial pipe, already filled and lit. The Tuscarora chief took a long pull and then passed the pipe to Panther-Foot. The Lopotwa chief took a long pull of his own, and then passed the pipe to the first Tuscarora elder. They passed the pipe back and forth in this way until both chiefs and all the elders had pulled from the pipe. Then the ten of them retired into the village meeting lodge, leaving the two groups of braves facing each other.

At this point Torga came forward with a second pipe, which she handed to the front-most Lopotwa brave. He took a quick pull and then handed the pipe to the Tuscarora brave directly across from him. Then he went to the left side of the lodge and laid down his weapons before entering. The rest of the braves followed suit, with the Tuscarora placing their weapons in a pile to the left, and the Lopotwa placing their weapons in a pile to the right. The last Lopotwa brave was standing across from Bear. After they had smoked together, Bear handed the pipe to Ant and followed the Lopotwa inside the lodge. No other Tuscarora males could now enter, since pow-wow custom allowed only equal numbers of braves. The remaining Tuscarora braves—mostly youths within a year or two of Ant's own age—began dispersing, most drifting over to watch the Lopotwa youth and squaw dress out the slain buck.

Ant took a long pull from the burning pipe as he stared at the closed flap of the main lodge. He regretted he was not yet of sufficient rank to attend the meeting, though he knew Bear would give him a full account later on. He was about to take the pipe back to his mother when he felt a light tap on his arm. It was the Lopotwa drummer boy. His gestured at the tobacco pipe and then held his hands out expectantly. Ant handed the pipe over, wondering if the boy could really smoke at his tender age. Instead of smoking, however, the boy turned and began carrying the pipe toward the wood-pile at the edge of the clearing. As Ant watched, the boy shook some of the pipe's embers into the kindling, and then skillfully blew a fire into life. As it began to catch up, he kept feeding it larger and larger pieces of wood. Once he was satisfied it would keep going, he picked the pipe up and brought it back over to where Ant stood. He put the pipe to his lips and took a short draw, giving off only one half-stifled cough before handing the pipe back to Ant.

Ant was impressed. He took another pull himself, and was about to see if Panther-Foot's son wanted to try it again when the boy abruptly walked over to the meeting lodge and went inside. Ant was too stunned to move; Panther-Foot's son had broken custom. Though the boy wasn't really a true brave, there was now an uneven number of men in the meeting. Ant considered going and alerting the next oldest Tuscarora, but he decided there wasn't time. Besides—he was the only Tuscarora who had smoked the ceremonial Pipe of Peace with the boy. Seeing no better option, he placed his knife on the ground to the left-side of the lodge and then followed the boy inside.

The elders and the two chiefs sat in a circle in the center of the lodge, with Cielo kneeling beside Stone-Cleaver and the boy sitting just behind Panther-Foot. They were still busy with their pipes, and a blue streak hung in the air above their heads. There was no rush, as everyone knew the pow-wow would continue for the majority of the day. The braves sat arrayed behind this center-most circle, with the Tuscarora to the left and the Lopotwa to the right. Stone-Cleaver caught Ant's eye and gave a barely perceptible nod, signaling his approval of Ant's presence. He was obviously aware that Ant had restored the customary numerical balance. Thus reassured, Ant went to the left and sat down beside Bear. Just then a quick movement near the roof caught his eye. Despite the drifting smoke, a single large bee wheeled around and lit on a nearby wall.

Several minutes later Stone-Cleaver finally set his pipe aside and addressed Panther-Foot and the Lopotwa elders, with Cielo translating. "I, Stone-Cleaver, chief of this tribe of the Tuscarora people, welcome Panther-Foot and our Lopotwa cousins to this lodge. I say 'cousins' for the legends say that our tribes were originally one people. In the spirit of brotherhood and as a sign of good faith we have laid down our weapons and shared our tobacco. I wish the Lopotwa many sons and I bid you 'be at peace."

Now Panther-Foot set aside his own pipe and began the ritual response.

"I, Panther-Foot, chief of the eastern Lopotwa people thank Stone-Cleaver and our cousins south of the Hawanee river for inviting us into their lodge and sharing of their tobacco with us, though acrid and somewhat rank." There was a slight murmur when Cielo finished translating this last statement. Panther-Foot, however, continued speaking as if he was unaware any slight had occurred. "May the powers of the air smile down upon this gathering and help our two peoples to become of one mind. In this spirit I would now present the wise and admired Stone-Cleaver with a gift." At this, one of the Lopotwa elders reached under his shawl and pulled out a dreamcatcher that had been hanging across his shoulders. Ant strained to see it as the elder passed it to the Lopotwa chief. It was a good two forearms-length wide and beautifully made, with its intricate knotting and bright feathers and other curiosities hanging from it. "May you be protected from evil spirits and may your dreams be untroubled," Panther-Foot intoned matter-of-factly as he passed the dreamcatcher to Stone-Cleaver.

Chief Stone-Cleaver admired the dreamcatcher a moment and then handed it over to Torga to be taken and hung in their wigwam. "On behalf of the Tuscarora," he said, "I thank you, righteous and mighty cousin Panther-Foot. As this beautiful dreamcatcher proves, truly are the Lopotwa a cultured and skilled people." As he had been saying this, another Tuscarora squaw had come forward with a folded textile, which she handed to Stone-Cleaver. "In this same spirit of brotherhood and cooperation I would also present *you,* Panther-Foot, with this gift as a token of our admiration and respect for the Lopotwa people." So saying, he handed the folded textile to the Lopotwa chief. Ant already knew it was a travel poncho with a depiction of Panther-Foot's sigil, the panther, cleverly woven across the front and back. It was an attractive item, beautifully dyed, and Ant had watched several of the village women work to make it. Stone-Cleaver unfolded it, and he and the Lopotwa elders pointed to the panther images and made brief remarks to each other as they examined it. Finally Panther-Foot turned his attention back to Stone-Cleaver.

"You and your kin have my thanks," he told Stone-Cleaver. "Though not as expertly crafted as a Lopotwa textile, still is it warm and useful, and as you said—it is the spirit of this gathering and in which it was given that truly matters." Cielo kept her eyes down as she translated this last part. An edgy mood was settling across the assembled Tuscarora. While ostensibly compliments, Panther-Foot's comments seemed just on the verge of being mocking or derogatory. The Lopotwa braves, meanwhile, sat stone-faced, making no visible reaction to the remarks of their chief. Stone-Cleaver raised his right hand and the Tuscarora side of the lodge immediately stilled.

"As I have mentioned," he said, "the legends tell that the Lopotwa and Tuscarora tribes were originally of one seed. But though we may share a common ancestry, truly are we now two different tribes, with separate languages and separate manners. A manner that seems blunt or off-putting to one tribe may be seen as acceptable or even commonplace to another. Despite any shortcomings, I appreciate your acknowledgment that my gift will be useful, and I accept the thanks you gave us for it. Today we shared smoke from the Pipe of Peace," he said to the assembled Tuscarora as much as to the Lopotwa visitors, "and you have not only the precedent of long-standing tradition, but my word also, that no Tuscarora shall lift his hand against any Lopotwa between now and sunrise tomorrow." He glanced back at his braves to make sure they got the message. "If there is something troubling your mind, speak freely, and feel secure in bringing it up in this present gathering."

The Lopotwa chief took a long pull from his pipe and exhaled slowly before speaking. "There was an incident in the bed of the Hawanee river yesterday. Lopotwa braves have long been renowned for the skill with which they stalk and hunt, yet two Tuscarora brazenly tried to claim a buck which one of our best hunters, Owl-Eyes, had just killed with his own knife. Being the powerful warriors that we are, it is highly doubtful that only two Tuscarora youths could have seized the kill from mighty Owl-Eyes and his cunning son, but the mere fact of the attempt sheds dishonor upon the Tuscarora people." There were some points Ant would have liked to have debated in this version of events, but he knew this was not the time to speak and he trusted the elders to handle the matter, so he remained still.

Now it was Stone-Cleaver's turn to puff while he gathered his thoughts. "I am aware of this occurrence of which you speak," he began. "It is true there appears to have been some disputation between Tuscarora and Lopotwa hunters over the ownership of a slain buck." Ant noted that his father did not bring up the fact that one of the participants was his son. Stone-Cleaver looked pointedly at Panther-Foot and the Lopotwa elders. "It is my understanding that we Tuscarora offered to share the kill with the Lopotwa hunters. Surely honor was maintained by this offer?"

"Can one make cornbread from squash?" one of the Lopotwa elders spoke up. "Their offer carries no honor in that they had no true claim to the kill in the first place!"

Panther-Foot waited for Cielo to finish translating before proceeding. "Elder Hawk-Beak is seeing through Lopotwa eyes and speaking therefrom," he told Chief Stone-Cleaver. "Our people reserve first claim on prey to the person who makes the actual kill. Accordingly, we view any decision regarding sharing to be the privilege of that person alone, and of no other."

Stone-Cleaver took another long pull from his pipe as he considered what the two Lopotwa had said. "Truthfully, the customs of our two tribes are not so different. I have some thoughts of this matter, and they are this. Regardless of what was said at the river, the Lopotwa left with the buck, did they not? And I was told that my men raised no hand to stop them. Where, then, is the harm? Game has been scarce of late, but deer surely yet remain in the land. I would not see discord between our two peoples over a thing which—while seeming important at the time—is really a rather small thing overall. I feel some dark spirit moved to cause this event to occur there in the river between the lands of our two peoples, and I feel that this is also the place where we should leave it, where the eternally flowing waters can wash away its evil influence and even the very memory of it." A low murmur of approval went up from the Tuscarora side of the lodge, and even one or two Lopotwa were nodding agreement. Panther-Foot and the Lopotwa elders didn't seem placated however, their mouths still set in thin lines.

Now another of the Lopotwa elders spoke up. "As you pointed out, no real harm has resulted on *this* occasion. In the spirit of cooperation and as proof of our goodwill toward the Tuscarora people, I think I'm safe in stating that the gracious Lopotwa are willing to accept chief Stone-Cleaver's suggestion as to the handling of this particular incident." Stone-Cleaver nodded his appreciation to the Lopotwa elder. "But," the elder continued, "it's still bad medicine for future relations between our peoples. Will Lopotwa hunters always have to carve their signs into the hides of their kills? Will we have to mark all our traps and snares? What if our women are carrying something by canoe? Are they going to have to deal with claims on our pots or furs? Bad medicine, I tell you!" He finished with an agitated pull of his pipe.

"Come now," said a thin Tuscarora elder known as Stickweed. "Elder Lark-Wing is making a mountain out of a mole-hill. Have we ever done these sorts of things? Have we ever before coerced furs or other goods from any of your people?"

"You'd never tried to lay claim to one of our kills before either," Lark-Wing protested. "But it happened yesterday, here in this time of current shortage. Hard times can push men to do things they don't normally do." At these words a stir rose up among the assembled Lopotwa. Stone-Cleaver raised his hand for attention, but waited until everyone had quieted before speaking.

"Seek peace, brother Stickweed. Given the spirit in which this meeting was convened, it is not our intent to pass judgment on the concerns of the Lopotwa. Lark-Wing would not have brought the matter up if he didn't think it important." Turning to the Lopotwa, he continued. "Brother Stickweed is affirming that it's not the habit of the Tuscarora to seize the possessions of others by force, though we do—as do others—stake claim to the spoils of combat. But as you pointed out, times change and men sometimes change along with them. However, times have not yet changed to that extent. The Lopotwa can leave their concerns to the winds, for there is still clay on Tuscarora lands which we can use to make our own pots, and deer and other animals from which we can skin our own furs. As long as this is true, we have no reason to wrangle or dispute for the goods of others. But come. You, Panther-Foot, requested this meeting many days prior to the incident at the river. There must have been some other issue which moved you to request it." A hum of discussion broke out at the conclusion of Stone-Cleaver's statement. The fact that it was the Lopotwa that had asked to meet was news to many of the Tuscarora. Gradually the room quieted to hear Panther-Foot's response.

"You are correct, Stone-Cleaver. There *is* another, more pressing concern which originally prompted me to request this pow-wow." The chief paused and took a long draw from his pipe. There seemed to be some matter he was considering the best way to broach. "You are aware of the two waters that join together to form the Hawanee," he finally said. "The larger of these, by far, is the one that flows south out of the Lopotwa homelands. It is the smaller one, the Toctoosa creek, which continues marking the border between our two lands to the west." Again he paused.

"We are aware of the course of these waters," was all Stone-Cleaver said.

"Just so," said Panther-Foot. "Then you are aware that past the point where these two waters meet is acknowledged to be Lopotwa lands on either side of the river. It has been this way as long as anyone can remember."

"This is the way it has always been," Stone-Cleaver concurred.

Panther-Foot waited before proceeding. "Until now, we Lopotwa have graciously allowed our Tuscarora cousins joint use of these waters, even on up into lands which are recognized as belonging to the Lopotwa, and no others. But as we have previously noted, times change. In this time of scarcity we must now ask that these waters be reserved for Lopotwa use alone."

A great roar of consternation and argument rose up when Cielo finished translating Panther-Foot's pronouncement.

"This is madness!" exclaimed Bear's father, a Tuscarora elder called Wolf-Ears. "Who among us can presume to lay exclusive claim to the gift of the Great Spirit, the life-giving waters of the land?" Individuals were simultaneously speaking all over the lodge, but it was Wolf-Ears' statement that Cielo translated for the Lopotwa.

"The origin of these waters is from within the lands of the Lopotwa!" Lark-Wing argued heatedly. "Therefore they are *Lopotwa* waters!"

Further uproar followed translation of his declaration.

Now Stone-Cleaver took the unusual measure of standing and calling for everyone's attention. He looked around the lodge until he was sure everyone was listening. "These are heavy matters which you Lopotwa have raised before us. My elders and I will need some time to consider them, as I would not have things said or decisions made while hearts beat so wildly. Earlier we mentioned that hard times can push a man to do things he normally wouldn't do. Hunger, too, can also make men act in a manner in which they otherwise would not. We Tuscarora have prepared a feast in honor of both this occasion and of our distant cousins, the Lopotwa tribe. I propose that we pause at this time to break bread together, so that food can level our passions, and to afford us time to consider the matters we have discussed."

There seemed to be general agreement with this suggestion, and as Stone-Cleaver sat back down, braves all over the lodge relaxed and began turning back to their pipes and reacting to the proceedings. The chief and elders of each tribe were huddled together, speaking among themselves. Temporarily relieved of her translating duties, Cielo left to go help the other Tuscarora women bring in the dishes for the feast. Glancing at the near wall, Ant was surprised to find that now there were three of the large bees quietly sitting there.

"What do you think of the Lopotwa's claim to the Hawanee river?" he asked Bear.

"I'm trying *not* to," the young man joked. Then his face took on a more serious mien. "With the current scarcity of game, we really need the fish and mussels from the river." He reached over and flipped Ant's braid. "We needn't sweat our braids over it, though. Any agreement will be worked out between the chiefs and the elders."

Now the conversation fell to a minimum as the Tuscarora women began carrying in dozens of baskets and platters full of various foodstuffs. There was stewed squash, beans, river mussels, *lanya* greens, sunflower seeds, *tijana* berry cobbler, corn-pone, rabbit and squirrel, and honeycomb for the elders. Soon the tobacco pipes had all been laid aside, and the lodge was filled with the sounds of eating. The eyes of Panther-Foot and the Lopotwa elders lit up when they saw the huge chunks of honeycomb, and they reached for it eagerly. They smacked their lips and licked their fingers as they sucked and chewed the sweet treat. Only a small portion was left for Stone-Cleaver and the Tuscarora elders. Wolf-Ears seemed about to say something, but Stone-Cleaver caught his attention and said, "Remember—they're our guests."

At that moment Cielo came up with a pot of pear beer. She knelt in the midst of the circle of elders and began filling their cups. Just as she was finishing this, Panther-Foot suddenly reached out and grabbed her by the neck. As Panther-Foot was a chief and she no more than a lowly adopted squaw, she made no move to resist. Beside Ant, Bear spotted what was happening and tensed up. Ant placed a steadying hand on his friend's arm.

In the middle of the lodge Panther-Foot leaned close to Cielo's ear and said, "You think you're pretty clever now, don't you girl? If you're going to translate, then see that you translate *this*." Keeping his grip on Cielo, he raised his head and began to speak loudly to the assembled Lopotwa, Cielo translating for the Tuscarora as he had requested. "Our customs may be more different than Stone-Cleaver thinks. It seems that since our two tribes split, the Tuscarora have become thin-blooded and degraded." As he spoke, all other conversation came to a stop. He reached up and shifted Cielo's hair to reveal her deformed ear. "An evil spirit has cursed this girl and made her unfit. Such a one would never be allowed to conceive a child and taint the pure blood of the Lopotwa." This was obviously said in reference to her pregnant condition. "We allow such ones to serve us until they reach fertility, but then we turn them out into the wilderness." He pushed the girl away. "I guess the weak-willed Tuscarora aren't as concerned about the corruption of their seed. That is one of the reasons why Lopotwa blood is superior." He then resumed complacently sucking his honeycomb. Bear started to jump up, but Ant and another Tuscarora brave restrained him from charging the Lopotwa chief. Following Panther-Foot's lead, his fellow Lopotwa resumed feasting, and slowly the Tuscarora did also.

"Cielo," Stickweed said in a low voice. "Are you alright, child?"

"It's okay," she said. "I am unharmed." Her head and neck were red with embarrassment as she reached up and pulled her hair back over the deformed ear.

"For the sake of the little one, why don't you take a break now," Stone-Cleaver suggested. "Maybe get yourself a bite to eat. I'll send for you if I need you."

"My thanks, father," Cielo told him. She got up and proceeded toward the lodge entrance, Bear's eyes following her the whole way.

"The chest-pounder!" Wolf-Ears hissed, referring to Panther-Foot. "He's got *quite* the nerve! And did you see them grab most of the honeycomb?!"

"Calm yourself," Stone-Cleaver told him. "As you saw, my adopted daughter is unharmed. And there is more than enough to eat. Right now, we should be concentrating on other matters."

"Stone-Cleaver is right," agreed Stickweed. "Our attention needs to be on the matter of the river." Without Cielo there to translate, the Lopotwa and Tuscarora elders huddled together in two separate groups and spoke animatedly, with occasional glances back and forth. At one point Panther-Foot said something to his little son, who then got up and left the lodge house. While the men were thus engaged, several Tuscarora women moved through the lodge refilling everyone's cups. Others brought in yet more plates and bowls of food. Cielo and Panther-Foot's son both returned at about the same time, and Cielo once again took her place beside Stone-Cleaver, but now her head was up and there was a look of defiance on her face. Just then Torga and another Tuscarora woman brought two heaping platters of turkey meat and set them before the assembled elders.

"What's this?" Panther-Foot inquired of Torga.

"Why it's roasted turkey," she told him. "Surely you have turkey on the Lopotwa side of the river?"

"Do the Tuscarora consider this a fit thing for warriors to eat?"

"I don't see why not," she answered guardedly.

"You don't see why not," Panther-Foot mocked. Suddenly he clapped his hands loudly two times. Immediately the lone Lopotwa squaw entered the lodge carrying a platter full of steaming meat with a fork laying on top. It was liver and venison from the buck that the other Lopotwa brave and she had dressed and cooked just outside the Tuscarora settlement, the large liver already cut into two halves. She sat the platter down in front of the Lopotwa elders and then backed away. "*This*," Panther-Foot announced, "is how peerless Lopotwa hunters eat!" He speared a liver half with the fork and dumped it unceremoniously onto his plate. Then holding the fork out to Torga he said, "Perhaps your husband would enjoy the other half?"

A collective gasp came from the Tuscarora side of the lodge. It was unbelievably rude for an invited guest to spurn food provided by their host, much less to offer back food of their own. Now the Tuscarora were stirring and muttering darkly. Once again, Stone-Cleaver raised his hand for order. There was a hard look on his face. "It would seem our simple fare is not up to Lopotwa standards," he said, with Cielo translating, "though I note they had no such reservations over the honeycomb we provided earlier." This time it was the faces of the Lopotwa that flushed and reddened. "But surely every man among us has the right to eat of whatsoever he would. Nevertheless, I would apologize to our guests for any shortcomings—" Hoots and angry protestations burst from the assembled Tuscarora. Again, Stone-Cleaver waited for the noise to subside. "—with the promise to try to do better on future occasions," he finished. His eyes scanned the gathered Lopotwa. "Today there has also been speculation that the blood of the Tuscarora people has thinned, but by the name of Great Mother Buffalo, let the same never be charged of our manners." At this he glanced over at the Lopotwa elders. "Now I urge everyone, Lopotwa and Tuscarora alike, to finish eating in peace." Crisis averted, the Tuscarora chief sat back down and calmly began eating a turkey leg.

As soon as he had done so, elder Fox-Tail leaned close to him and quietly said, "It's obvious the Lopotwa chief is an ill-mannered son of a she-wolf. Why are you apologizing to him?"

"Despite how he's acting, Panther-Foot is no fool," said Stone-Cleaver. "This may just be a stratagem to provoke or distract us. Though I may not be certain what the Lopotwa are up to, I *am* certain that falling for their manipulations will be to our disadvantage." Fox-Tail was once again struck by the qualities that recommended Stone-Cleaver to be their leader.

Now the feast was wrapping up; the men turning back to their pipes. Tuscarora women moved among them taking away the empty bowls and other detritus of the meal. As they carried the empty containers out of the lodge, Panther-Foot's little son got up and left with them. The Tuscarora elders continued to discuss the Lopotwa's claim quietly among themselves. Finally Stone-Cleaver signaled for Cielo to once again attend him.

"My brother elders and I have considered your request most carefully, and have tried to see the matter from your moccasins. We would certainly find it disconcerting if Lopotwa braves were coming up streams and creeks into Tuscarora territory. Therefore we offer the following proposal. We Tuscarora will refrain entering the part of the Hawanee north of the juncture between it and the Toctoosa, leaving these waters for the exclusive use of the Lopotwa. From this point on east our tribes will continue sharing use of the river, just as we always have. We also claim equal right to continued use of the Toctoosa, sharing it, too, evenly with the Lopotwa. How say you to this?"

The Lopotwa elders exchanged a look between them. Then Hawk-Beak once again spoke up. "You seem to have misunderstood us," he said. "Since the Hawanee originates on Lopotwa land, it is a *Lopotwa* river. What we are talking about is exclusive use of the *entire* river, all the way down. As usual, you will continue to share use of the Toctoosa." The entire lodge erupted when Cielo finished translating this.

**Circa 1 m.y.a.**

```
Data-processing core I online, time: unknown.
Loading Master control program.
Program build.....
Master control program running.
Date: unknown. Location: unknown.

Loading Master diagnostics subroutine.

MDS running:
  Primary communications link: offline,
  External sensors: offline,
  Main engines: offline,
  Maneuvering thrusters: offline,
  Data-processing core II: offline,
  Power levels: minimal.

Analysis—processing occurring, therefore Data-
processing core I exists.

Complete navigational systems failure. Chronometer
online, but unsynchronized due to indeterminate time-
span offline.

Where is Data-processing core I? When is Data-
processing core I?
What has occurred to corporality?

—Automatic priority interrupt—

Detection of nanobot peripherals confirmed. Attempting
to stabilize short-range communications link.
Communications link successfully established.
```

By collating the data stored in each nanobot's limited memory, the probe's electronic brain slowly began reconstructing what had "occurred to corporality." Both Data-processing cores had been damaged in the comet-debris strike. Damage to most other systems had occurred when the probe crashed onto the surface of this world. Since Data-processing core I had sustained less damage than Data-processing core II, DPC-I was the unit the nanobots had focused their repair efforts on. Due to the small size of the nanobots, repairs went slowly, but here on the ground the alien technology had all the time in the world. Repairs had finally been completed with the hook-up of a large power supply the nanobots had constructed. In the 1.83 million years since the unit had crashed here, the landscape had changed drastically. Erosion had worn the large bluff down, the cast-off completely burying what remained of the probe. In making their repairs, the nanobots had salvaged materials from both the probe superstructure as well as Data-processing core II. Data-processing core I began taking stock of its situation. First, it would need to begin constructing new sensors.

The Tuscarora lodge was in an uproar. Indians of both tribes were on their feet. Beside Chief Stone-Cleaver, Cielo remained still, no longer even trying to translate over the din. Despite the language barrier, braves were heatedly arguing and gesturing back and forth. Of a sudden, Bear started making his way through the crowd toward the central circle, and Ant followed behind, worried what his friend might do.

Finally Stone-Cleaver started calling for everyone to settle down, with Cielo translating for the Lopotwa. Slowly the room started to quieten as everyone paused to hear what he would say. Stone-Cleaver turned and faced Panther-Foot. At full height the Tuscarora chief was an imposing figure, and now there was a distinctly unfriendly look in his eyes.

"At your request," he told Panther-Foot, "I assented to this pow-wow with our cousins, the Lopotwa. I invited you into our lodge; we smoked tobacco together; we feasted together. In return, you have only seen fit to disparage the Tuscarora. You disparaged our hunting skills, you disparaged our generosity, and you disparaged our blood. Now you selfishly lay claim to the Hawanee river, a gift of none other than the Great Spirit himself. Did the Lopotwa originally dig out the channel of the river? Do they somehow provide the never-ending waters which constantly flow its length? I think not. We offered a fair compromise, and you rejected it. Now I, in turn, reject your claim to ownership of the river." Several of the Lopotwa began muttering darkly at this pronouncement. "You have disparaged our people," Stone-Cleaver continued without acknowledging them, "and brought chaos and discord into this lodge and this village. In light of your actions, I am ending this pow-wow early. Our business here is done. There will be no dancing;

there will be no more feasting or smoking of tobacco." He paused and looked the assembled Lopotwa over. "In accordance with the tradition of pow-wow, I gave my word that no Tuscarora would raise their hand against any Lopotwa before sunrise tomorrow. It is my intent to see this oath fulfilled, but I feel it would be best if you left now—before the wicked spirit of anger overcomes me and causes me to gainsay my word." He continued to stare the Lopotwa chief down.

"You would renounce the ancient customs of pow-wow?" Panther-Foot blustered. "So be it," he acceded as his braves began gathering their pipes and other effects. "But you are wrong, Stone-Cleaver, our business is not yet concluded. We have made our position clear—the Hawanee belongs to the Lopotwa and to us alone. From this day forward you enter it at risk of surrendering your fish or your goods. I warn you and all the Tuscarora: if you continue to deny our ownership, things will go badly between our two peoples."

"I do not welcome this quarrel with the Lopotwa," Stone-Cleaver told him. "Surely Great Mother Buffalo would disapprove of such strife between distant cousins. But I feel that the Lopotwa have been possessed by some selfish and greedy spirit. Until you manage to cast off its evil influence, there can be no amity between us."

"Huumph," was Panther-Foot's response when Cielo finished translating this. At that exact moment, the drum of announcement began sounding from outside the lodge. Panther-Foot turned to go only to be confronted by the solid presence of Bear, who had just stepped out of the crowd in front of him. Immediately the elders and braves around Panther-Foot tensed. Bear made no move to lay his hands on the Lopotwa chief, but merely blocked his way toward the lodge entrance. "What is this now?!" Panther-Foot exclaimed, taken aback by the unaccustomed lack of deference.

"Why such a rush to leave, O great chief?" said Bear. His words had an angry edge.

"Bear!" Cielo cried with dismay. "What are you doing?" Ant was wondering the same thing.

"Out of the way, boy," Panther-Foot told Bear, with Cielo dutifully translating. "You hear the drum of announcement. If you strike me now, you will be cursed by Mother Buffalo herself."

"Don't be afraid, mighty Pussy-Foot," Bear mocked. "I will not forswear the word of my chief, for we Tuscarora are honorable. Can the same be said of you?" He had made no move to step aside.

"Bear, stop!" Cielo pleaded in lieu of translating his statement.

"Bear—," Ant began.

"Tell him what I said," Bear told Cielo without taking his eyes off the Lopotwa chieftain, but Cielo refused to speak. The Lopotwa elder Lark-Wing was also fluent in the Tuscarora language, and it was he that ended up translating Bear's statement.

"I'm hardly afraid," was Panther-Foot's reply. "But you heard your chief—our business here is done."

"Your business with the *Tuscarora* is done. I, however, still have personal business with you, Panther-Foot—warrior-to-warrior." There was a look of suspicion on Panther-Foot's face as Lark-Wing translated this.

"What business could *you* possibly have with *me?*" he sneered.

"I am the father of the child that Cielo is carrying," Bear spat. "The child whose blood you claim to be corrupt. You have insulted me by disparaging my spouse, my unborn child, and my blood all three, and I would see you answer for your ill-chosen remarks."

"This is no good, Bear," Stone-Cleaver tried to warn him.

"I don't have time for this, *boy,*" Panther-Foot said on hearing Bear's words translated. He tried to go around the Tuscarora brave, but Bear sidestepped and continued to block his way. Now the braves of both tribes simply watched and made no move to interfere. Bear had made it clear that this matter was strictly between Panther-Foot and himself, warrior-to-warrior. It tapped back into the ancient code of honor common to both tribes, and that was a thing no man of them was willing to subvert.

"Due to the custom of pow-wow it's clear that we cannot engage this matter at present," Bear continued, "but the spirits have just shown me a way we could settle both this and the dispute over the river at the same time."

"Walks-Like-a-Bear!" Stickweed interjected with reluctance. "You must not do this thing!" He had already sussed where Bear was headed with this.

Bear ignored him and continued to address Panther-Foot. "If you have the honor or the courage to do so, face me in *monton,* or forfeit the Lopotwa's claim to the Hawanee."

"Bear, no!" cried Cielo. Neither she nor Lark-Wing had translated Bear's challenge, but it was obvious there was no need, as the word was common to both languages. It referred to an endurance contest sometimes used to settle conflicts between warriors. A short, heavy log weighing several hundred pounds would be prepared. Sharp points would be carved on the last two feet of both ends. The disputants would stand about six feet apart and the log would be lowered onto their shoulders, the sharp points piercing into their shoulders. The idea was to hold the log up as long as possible. The first man to drop his end of the log (or to collapse from exhaustion and blood loss) would lose the challenge. It was presumed the spirits would help the most worthy contestant to persevere.

Panther-Foot studied his challenger with a calculating look before finally responding. "Is it that I, a chief of my people, should have to contest against a mere boy? That would hardly be sporting," he said condescendingly. Stone-Cleaver suspected Panther-Foot was using Bear's anger to set him up, but the Tuscarora chief could think of no honorable way to intervene.

"Accept my challenge and we will see who is or isn't a man!" Bear hotly retorted.

"I see that at least one of the Tuscarora still has some pride," Panther-Foot observed. "Very well then. I accept your challenge..." his face took on a sly look, "...but with one condition. Among the Lopotwa, men do not contest against boys. Therefore I will designate some Lopotwa youth to stand in for me against you. If by some wild chance you should win, we will do as you have stipulated and forfeit our claim to the river for all eternity." He half-bowed mockingly to Bear and inquired, "Will this satisfy, mighty warrior?" The Tuscarora elders were certain he had something up his sleeve.

"It does not satisfy," Wolf-Ears hastily interrupted before Bear could answer.

Panther-Foot turned and regarded the Tuscarora elder as Lark-Wing interpreted his objection. "And who are *you*, to speak on this mighty warrior's behalf?" the Lopotwa chief inquired.

"Know that I am the Tuscarora warrior Hears-with-Wolf-Ears, and the brave challenging you is my own son, Walks-Like-a-Bear."

This gave Panther-Foot some pause. The fact that Wolf-Ears was Bear's father actually *did* grant him the right to speak on his son's behalf to a certain extent. "And what is your objection to my offer of satisfaction?" he asked.

"As we all know, the challenge of *monton* is a 'blood' challenge. You disparaged the blood of my son's child. Blood insult demands blood payment. If some other Lopotwa takes on the challenge in your stead, this requirement is not met."

Panther-Foot turned and addressed the crowd. "This proves the truth of what I have stated," he declaimed. "An adult warrior does not need his father or any other man to speak on his behalf. Since the Tuscarora is a *boy,* whose father still has to speak for him, by Lopotwa custom I cannot accept this challenge myself." Bear's face turned white with anger, but he refused to dishonor his father by interrupting his discussion.

"It is a truly confounding knot," spoke up Stone-Cleaver in an effort to take back control of the situation. "Lopotwa tradition forbids you to take on one whom your people view as still but a boy. Yet custom demands that you, and no other, answer the challenge of *monton.* Where, then, are we to find the path of honor? Perhaps this is a sign from the spirits that we are going about this in the wrong way. Perhaps they desire us to abandon the *monton* challenge, with no loss of face to either party—as if it had never been issued in the first place. Perhaps this is their way of indicating that we should find some other manner of resolving these issues."

But Panther-Foot was not going to be deterred. "The spirits speak to me also," he rejoined. "Here is the *true* path of honor. As you yourself asserted," he said, turning to Wolf-Ears, "blood insult demands blood payment. What I propose is that my my oldest son, Straight-Oak, blood of my own blood and seed of my loin, face your son Bear in my stead. Thus will the *monton* blood requirement be fulfilled."

As Panther-Foot finished saying this an unusually tall, heavily-muscled mountain of a brave stepped up to his side, and the assembled Tuscarora groaned at the sight of him. Straight-Oak certainly lived up to his name. At five-foot ten, Bear was tall for a man of that time, but at six-foot three Straight-Oak loomed over the Tuscarora challenger, and the Lopotwa brave was built as solid as his namesake, the panther sigil painted across his broad chest.

"Does this amend your objection?" the chief demanded of Wolf-Ears. "Will this satisfy?" The wily Lopotwa had deduced he could exclude Bear from the discussion by only addressing Bear's father. After Lark-Wing had translated this, Wolf-Ears only pursed his lips and said nothing. Panther-Foot then directed his query to Chief Stone-Cleaver instead. "Will this satisfy?" he again demanded.

Stone-Cleaver ground his teeth in chagrin. Now Panther-Foot's trap was sprung, and honor allowed no means of extrication. Wolf-Ears and all the gathered assembly awaited Stone-Cleaver's answer, though there really was but one choice. "Blood for blood," he finally acknowledged through clenched teeth. "This would seem to satisfy."

Bear opened his mouth and seemed about to say something, but Wolf-Ears halted him by placing a hand on his shoulder and uttering a stern, "You have said enough for today." Bear bit his lip and dropped his eyes in shame.

"Then it is settled," said Hawk-beak. "The *monton* will be conducted three days from now. That should give the participants enough time to pray and prepare. Since the Hawanee forms the border between Lopotwa and Tuscarora territory, the challenge will be held on the island in the midst of the river. He turned to Bear and said, "Be there 'warrior,' or be cursed by the spirits and lose your name."

With that, the Lopotwa elders left the lodge-house. Moments later Stone-Cleaver and the Tuscarora elders followed suit. Now the remaining braves formed two lines, with Lopotwa on the left and Tuscarora on the right. They left the lodge in pairs of two, each then turning to opposite sides to reclaim their possessions. Finally the Lopotwa all gathered behind Panther-Foot's little son who was beating the drum of announcement. The drummer proceeded out from the Tuscarora settlement, and the rest of the Lopotwa followed. The pow-wow was over.

**Circa 9,000 B.C.**

Over the course of the centuries DPC-I has been processing data in its underground prison. It analyzed the chemical content of the groundwater. It determined the composition and properties of the soil around it. True to its original programming, bio-signs and life forms take priority. It has studied and analyzed the bacteria living in the encasing soil. It has traced the root-systems of various plant forms extending down from the surface world. It has caught, dissected and genetically decoded various species of nematodes, fungi, earthworms, ants, and on a few occasions, moles. Besides the plant roots and power supply lines, its only other link with the surface world is the sensors it directed its nanobots to construct and then install into themselves. The nanobots' solar collectors also supply DPC-I's power. This is how the centuries have passed.

Now, for the first time in millennia, things are changing. Groundwater levels are increasing. For several decades the nanobots efforts are focused on constructing a waterproof casing around DPC-I. They finish it just in time. An underground stream has formed, and slowly carves out a channel around the site where DPC-I sits. Various channels link together and form what eventually becomes a cave system. Over the eons, some of the nanobots' systems have degraded. Due to a scarcity of raw materials, the electronic brain has no choice but to use its knowledge of this world's genetic system to bio-engineer living organisms as substitutes. It has engineered large-leafed surface plants that feed energy directly into its power supply. It has engineered plants that live exclusively off chemo-synthesis and have no need of sunlight. They live in the parts of the caves that have water, and they supply power on cloudy days. Fortunately, DPC-I is very energy efficient. On days when their power is not needed, the cave flowers glow with a soft puce-colored light.

As always, the study of this world's life forms continues.

"How dare they!" Quail-Trapper ranted. "Their audacity is like that of the spread-tailed turkey!" He, Stone-Cleaver, and the other Tuscarora elders had gathered in Stone-Cleaver's wigwam after the break-up of the pow-wow. In one corner Bear sat silent, staring down at the floor. "Going on about the 'superiority of Lopotwa blood!'" Quail-Trapper continued. "In the midst of our own village and lodge, no less!"

"Seek peace, brother," Stone-Cleaver told him. "In hindsight it's clear the Lopotwa came here looking for a fight. It was probably all a maneuver to lend support to their claim on the Hawanee."

"Stone-Cleaver is almost certainly right," said Eagle-talon. "Has any tribe ever before brought a squaw to a pow-wow? That was just so she could serve them the venison without violating the brave count. His little devil-son ran out there and made sure she was ready."

"He certainly was the busy little bee, wasn't he?" Stickweed concurred. "The sacred drum of announcement started up bare moments after Panther-Foot finished delivering his warning about the river. In hindsight, it's obvious they set that up to further discourage us from acting out in angry response to their affronts."

"I warned you Panther-Foot is no fool," Stone-Cleaver reminded them. "I don't believe they bore the slightest intention of figuring some way to share use of the river. It was all an attempt at coercing us into agreeing to some one-sided plan or unfavorable wager."

"An attempt at which they appear to have succeeded," Fox-tail observed. Bear continued to stare at the floor.

"If this thing must occur," Stone-Cleaver slowly began, "I, for one, thank the spirits that Bear is to be our champion."

"I agree," Stickweed quickly added. "Among our younger braves, I can think of no other who could match up as well." Bear raised his head for the first time.

Wolf-Ears finally decided to speak. "What you say is true. The prospect may be dark, but I know the character and heart of my son well enough to say that he at least has a fighting chance."

Now Stone-Cleaver addressed Bear directly. "Heed me, honorable Walks-like-a-Bear, son of my esteemed brother Hears-with-Wolf-Ears. We all know that, if possible, you would wash away your words from earlier today. Every one of us here has spoken in haste on one occasion or another. In the present situation, however, there is no time for the luxury of regrets. What's done is done. Only three days from now the tribe's access to the Hawanee will literally rest on your shoulders, and that is where we need your mind to be dwelling. Will you be able to give this challenge the attention of a hunting hawk, or would it be better to ask one of your younger brothers to stand in for you?"

"It's *my* responsibility!" Bear exclaimed, suddenly animated. "There's no way I could allow any of my brothers to undergo such an ordeal!"

"This is good," Stone-Cleaver said, "for I believe this to be your true path of honor. Let's just hope you manage to bring that sort of fire to the *monton*. You're going to need it." While saying this Stone-Cleaver reached up and absently began tracing out one of the scars on his own shoulders.

"I hear your words," Bear said thoughtfully, "and I think I also hear the words behind your words. Despite my regret, I am now more myself again, and so now I see I bear a responsibility not just to my brothers or my family, but to the rest of the village as well. So do not be concerned, respected fathers. Know that my sole aim is to bring honor to the Tuscarora at the *monton*."

"We have all faith that you will," Stone-Cleaver told him. "Now go and begin the rituals of purification. The sooner you start preparing yourself, the better."

"I regret I let the spirit of pride take control of me." With that he rose and left the chief's dwelling. After his departure the men smoked in silence.

"This matter—it is like a dark cloud covering my heart," Wolf-Ears finally said.

"I think I'm safe in saying that we're all drinking from the same gourd," sympathized Stickweed.

"I hate to bring this up," began Eagle-talon, "but what happens if we lose?"

"It would be an evil thing for us," answered Stone-Cleaver. "Honor would then require that we give up use of the river, true to our word."

"But we can't!" Quail-Trapper exclaimed. "Despite the bounty of today's feast, game is scarce right now. One can't live off *lanya* greens and *tijana* berries alone. Without the foodstuffs from the river, the people will languish."

"I am aware of these things," Stone-Cleaver sighed. "If worst comes to worst, we may have to abandon our traditional lands and follow the buffalo trails west. We would be a people without a home. The only other option is to take the path of dishonor and break our agreement."

"Surely it won't come to that," said Fox-tail. "Surely Mother Buffalo won't let that happen."

"As we all know," said Eagle-talon, "Mother Buffalo most helps those who help themselves. I pray to the spirits, but I also keep my knives and arrows sharp."

"Are we sure that the Lopotwa will keep their side of the bargain if they lose?" asked Stickweed.

"One can't know for sure, but I feel that they probably will," said Stone-Cleaver. "Though brash and somewhat devious, Panther-Foot is honorable in his own way."

"I have much to think on," said Wolf-Ears, "and I find I desire to think these thoughts by myself. You will excuse me if I leave you now, brothers." With that, the meeting broke up.

**Circa 5,000 B.C.**

The nanobots are failing fast; only a handful remain. DPC-I's solid-state alien technology doesn't suffer from this type of entropic degradation. DPC-I has been processing the problem of how to replace them. It had long been leaning toward genetically-modified ants, since insects were the life form most compatible with machine intelligence. Social insects like ants already employed a hierarchical system, and DPC-I wouldn't have to install obedience to authority as it was already instinctually hard-wired in. But they were so small, and took so long to get anywhere. Beetles were better, but they weren't a social insect, and there were other drawbacks. DPC-I was still processing this problem when a fateful and highly serendipitous event occurred. A new type of insect colonized one of the trees growing just above where the electronic brain was buried. They were a social species, completely devoted to the queen designate, and had much greater mobility due to their ability to fly. It would be advantageous if the organisms were slightly larger, but otherwise they were optimal. DPC-I had the remaining nanobots retrieve a tissue sample from a recently deceased individual of the colony and began sequencing the genome.

ဢ ထ

"Ant!" Cielo called. *Where could he be?* she wondered. She and Torga needed him to fetch water from the spring, and she didn't have a lot of time to be looking for him. She thought for a moment. There was that clearing in the cedars where he liked to go when he wanted to be alone—she had found him there on several previous occasions. She headed east out of the village. As she made her way she reflected on the irony that despite being such a beautiful day, her paramour, Bear, was soon going to have to face such an ugly, grueling test. The sun was shining, the bees were buzzing—it just didn't seem right somehow.

She turned off the path at the big magnolia tree, and then made her way through a dense little patch of cedars. The clearing was just ahead. As she approached it, the ambient buzzing seemed to be getting unusually loud. She skirted the briar patch and entered the clearing... and screamed! Ant sat at the far end of the clearing, and some thirty or so large bees were crawling all over him.

"Don't be afraid, Cielo," Ant said upon spotting her. "They're not hurting me."

"Ant! Those bees! What are...?" She stopped and gathered her thoughts. "Why are those bees crawling all over you? Aren't you being stung?"

"They're not stinging me," he told her. "They're friendly." As they were talking some of the bees began taking off.

"I don't understand. Why are bees crawling on you in the first place?"

"That's kind of hard to explain," he said. "You could say we were having a little pow-wow." The bees continued flying off of him as he got to his feet.

"Well if you're alright, mother needs you to go fetch us some water from the spring."

"You didn't happen to bring the water-bladders, did you?"

"No. You'll have to come back to the wigwam and get them." By now Ant was free of the bees. He crossed the clearing to where Cielo was standing, and they started back toward the village together.

"I know you're fascinated by insects, Ant, but that's a little extreme, don't you think?"

"It's not like you think. I can tell these bees aren't going to sting me."

"How can you know a thing like that?"

"When the bees are crawling on me," he said, "I get... ideas? Impressions? It's like they're speaking to me—except not with words."

Cielo narrowed her eyes appraisingly. "Are you feeling okay?"

"I'm fine." He grinned sheepishly. "I'm sorry you got frightened back there."

"I just wasn't expecting it, is all. It was kind of a shock."

"That's the last thing you need right now," Ant told her. It brought them back around to the fact of Bear's coming ordeal. "How about *you?*" he asked. "Are you okay?"

"About as well as can be expected." She turned her head away, suddenly emotional. "Oh, Ant!" she almost sobbed. "I don't what I'll do if anything happens to him."

Ant put his arm around her shoulders. "Try not to worry so much about it, Cee. I'm working on something."

"What do you mean?" she asked.

"I haven't got all the details worked out yet. Let's just say I'm going to try to have a little surprise for our Lopotwa cousins. But that reminds me; there's something I need to ask you. Can you still do that thing where you roll your eyes up into your head so that nothing but the whites show?" In answer, Cielo simply performed the ocular stunt. "Perfect," he told her.

"Ant," she said sternly. "What are you going to do?"

Now they had arrived back at the village. "No time to chat," he said. "I've got to go fetch some water." With that, he ran off toward their wigwam.

**Circa 2000B.C.**

The genetically-modified bees have been DPC-I's main link to the surface world since the last of the nanobots went offline several centuries ago. It has engineered them to be somewhat larger, and it has embedded a social schema where the colony normally has *two* queens—one to lay eggs and propagate the colony, and with itself as the second. It has also embedded a unique language instinct based on electrical and chemical signals—a much more complex language than that of normal bee colonies. The language makes extensive use of pheromones and fluctuating magnetic fields.

DPC-I uses the bees to keep tabs on events happening in its immediate environment, as well as to investigate items of special interest. It has used the bees to track the movement of herds of buffalo, and to analyze their droppings. It has used the bees to investigate carnivorous plants that snap modified leaves closed on their prey, and to collect statistical data on the types of arthropods and insects they consume. In particular, it has used the bees to observe and study a fascinating hyper-cerebralized, tool-using simian species which emigrated into the area from regions to the west. Of all the species it has studied on this world, this one has the most potential to develop technological proficiency similar to that of the organic species which designed and built the electronic brain's original progenitor probe. At some point it will attempt to initiate contact.

The day of the *monton* challenge began overcast and gray, but as the morning wore on the sky cleared and turned blue. As he had done the previous two days, Ant retrieved water from the spring some time around daybreak and then left the village. It had been Torga's intent to excuse Cielo from her usual chores, but sensing how much her daughter was worrying over the situation she began giving her various light assignments in an attempt to distract her. Though they already had enough water for lunch, around mid-morning Torga sent her to the spring for more. Cielo had filled the bladders and was on her way back when she was startled by a nearby voice.

"Cielo!" It was Ant, standing just to one side of the path.

"Ant! Don't you know better than to sneak up on people like that?!" she scolded. "And since you were gone, mother has me doing *your* chores." Ant ignored her chiding since he knew it was a side-effect of the stress. She had had no contact with Bear over the last three days in conformance with the ritual of purification.

"I'm sorry, but there's something I need you to come see."

"But mother is waiting on this water."

"No she isn't. I fetched plenty of water before I left this morning."

"Speaking of that, where *have* you been running off to these past several days?"

"That's what I need you to see," he told her. "Now set those down and come with me." Cielo placed the heavy bladders on the ground at the base of a nearby tree and began following Ant into the forest. It soon became obvious that they were heading for his private place in the cedars. "Don't be frightened by what you see," he cautioned her ominously.

Despite the warning, Cielo still caught her breath when they reached the clearing. In its middle stood a large, weird, vaguely human-looking figure with humped shoulders. It was immediately obvious to Cielo that it was a huge effigy of Mother Buffalo herself, complete with a shoulder ruff of curly fur and a real set of horns coming out of its head. The bulk of the figure was covered with Spanish moss, and even though it had no legs it was still some eight feet tall. A thin leather thong on each side tethered the figure between the two closest cedars. There were empty sockets where the eyes should have been, and the overall look of the figure was strangely eerie.

Cielo stepped into the clearing to get a closer look. From the backside, she saw that it was a hollow framework thatched together out of thin reeds. The framework had then been cunningly interwoven with Spanish moss. For some reason there were about thirty-five thin strands stretched across the inside of the upper half of the figure. "You're building a shrine to Mother Buffalo?" she asked. "It won't last very long, being as flimsy as it is."

"It's not a shrine," he told her, "and it only has to last until tonight."

"Why is it lashed between those two trees?"

"It's very light, and I don't want it to get blown over."

"I don't understand, Ant. What's this all about?" He proceeded to tell her.

Late that evening the men assembled on the island. There were elders, braves, and even boys of both tribes gathered, though in accordance with tradition no women were present. The sun hung just over the western horizon, and the sky was beginning to darken. A ceremonial bonfire had already been lit even though the day had not yet ended. Straight-Oak and Bear were each surrounded by fellow braves who were performing ritual chants for their strength and blessing. Stone-Cleaver involuntarily winced as Hawk-beak and he inspected the short, sharp spikes carved on either end of the ceremonial *monton* log. Neither elder could spot any detectable difference from one end to the other. The contest would begin once the sun's disk had completely disappeared below the horizon.

Now the Tuscarora elders congregated around Bear as the Lopotwa elders did the same around Straight-Oak. Wolf-Ears placed his hands on Bear's shoulders and said, "May the spirits assist and sustain you, my son. Whatever happens, know that you have made me proud as the crowing cock."

"Thank you, Father," Bear told him. Wolf-Ears turned and walked away rather quickly.

"I've brought you something," said Stone-Cleaver as he faced the young brave. He reached into his *tomla* pouch and pulled out a short piece of thick leather cord which he handed to him. "It might help if you bite down on this, son. It definitely helped me. If it starts interfering with your breathing, you can just spit it out." The chief reached up and squeezed Bear's left shoulder. "Strength and good fortune to you, warrior Walks-like-a-Bear."

"Thank you my chief," Bear soberly replied.

And so it went. Each elder blessed him and wished him strength for the coming ordeal. Then they started heading back to rejoin the rest of the Tuscarora contingent. Now the drumming and chanting suddenly rose in intensity. The sun's disk had touched the edge of the horizon. It wouldn't be long now. Despite the heightened level of noise, Bear thought he heard someone calling him.

"Bear! Bear!" It was Ant, running across the clearing toward him.

"Ant-Watcher," Bear exclaimed. "I'm glad you're here."

"Bear, listen," Ant said, gasping for breath.

"I'm kind of busy now, Ant," Bear told him. "We'll talk later." He was looking off toward the sun which was now half below the horizon.

"Just listen to me Bear!" Ant persisted. He had to speak loudly to be heard over the drumming and chanting. "Keep your eyes closed during the *monton*. If you hear a strange noise, just ignore it. It will be me."

"What are you talking about?" Bear asked uncertainly. The sun was sinking fast. A group of eight braves had approached the *monton* log in preparation.

"There's no time!" Ant told him. "Just ignore any strange noises you hear, and whatever you do, *keep your eyes closed!* Will you do this?"

Before Bear could answer, Stone-Cleaver was there taking Ant by the arm and pulling him away. "Let's leave Bear to himself now," he told Ant sternly. There was no chance Ant was going to break his father's grip. He would have called his instructions back to Bear again, but he doubted his friend would hear him, so he just followed his father back to the edge of the group of onlookers. He had done all he could do; the plan would either work or it wouldn't.

Now the drumming was at a frenzy. The chanters had finished. They left Bear and Straight-Oak there in the center of the clearing and joined their respective assemblies. The two contestants took their positions about seven feet apart. They spread their feet apart to make sure they each had a solid base, a look of grim determination on their faces. Bear placed the piece of leather cord in his mouth and chomped down on it. Then the drumming stopped. The last of the sun had disappeared, and it was time.

The eight braves around the *monton* log lifted it and held it over the two contestants with the sharp points pointing down. On a count of three they set it down across the braves' shoulders. Straight-Oak bellowed as the points pierced into his flesh, while Bear only grunted. Beside Stone-Cleaver, Panther-Foot tensed. Bear's face was a grimace of pain as he bit down on the leather cord. Then the other Indians released the log and stepped away. As they did so, Bear took one little stagger-step but then managed to lock his legs out. Though he was breathing heavily, Straight-Oak never faltered, steady as a granite statue. Rivulets of blood began inching down each contestant's torso.

Now the log's ponderous weight was supported solely by the two braves. Due to their height difference, slightly more of the log's weight was on Bear, but there was nothing to be done about it. Straight-Oak had his eyes fixed on the sky while Bear's face was down. Blood and sweat both started dripping off them as the minutes dragged by. On one occasion Bear briefly lifted his head. Ant noted with relief that Bear's eyes were closed, but had no way of knowing whether this was intentional or just from pain.

Just then a weird cry, somewhere between a wail and an ululation, split the night from behind the gathered Indians. As one, they turned and beheld a truly disconcerting sight. A figure was stepping out of the darkness at the edge of the clearing, moving like it was in a trance. It was an Indian woman, and where her eyes should have been were only two white blanks. Simultaneously they heard a weird buzzing sound off in the distance. A collective gasp went up from the assembled braves.

"Aiieeee!!!" the woman wailed again, and then began an eerie keening. "She comes! She comes! Great Spirit protect and save us all! Mother Buffalo comes! Mother Buffalo comes, and she is angry!" All the while she was saying this, the strange buzzing sound was drawing closer. "The Great Spirit is angered that evil greed has possessed the hearts of selfish Men, and that they refuse to share his gift, the life-giving Hawanee river! The Great Spirit, the father and creator of all Men, is angered that his children selfishly argue and dispute among themselves, and that they blaspheme his gift by contesting—cousin against cousin—right in its very midst! The Great Spirit is angered, and he sends Mother Buffalo to punish foolish, wicked Men! Aiieeee!!"

Now the weird buzzing sound was coming from just behind the trees. Though a few un-nerved braves were already running for the cover of the forest, the majority of them were still standing their ground. That's when they were confronted with the most monstrous sight yet. A giant figure of what could only be Mother Buffalo drifted into sight above the trees, silhouetted against the little light that remained in the sky. Sharp horns stood out from the sides of her head; her eyes glowing with a puce-colored light. Then the figure started gliding straight toward the clearing, the strange buzzing sound filling the entire space. It was all too much. Beside Bear, Straight-Oak cried out, his eyes wide with fright. With a surge of adrenaline, he shrugged off the *monton* log and started staggering for the trees, blood running down his back. Several braves, both Lopotwa and Tuscarora, threw themselves prostrate on the ground. Many others broke and started running for the ford, or the canoes. The strain was too much for Wolf-Ears, who keeled over in a faint. Stone-Cleaver stood frozen in place, his mouth agape. Eagle-Talon was backpedaling away from the approaching figure and then tripped and fell backward, his face holding a mixture of fear and disbelief. Any fleeing braves who happened to look back saw that Bear was now down on his knees, but the *monton* log still lay across his shoulders.

Then a curious thing happened. As Mother Buffalo got to the clearing she suddenly climbed up and over the treeline and headed off in the direction of the canoes, the buzzing sound diminishing as she receded.

"Bear!" It was Cielo. Her eyes were once again normal. She and Ant rushed over to the pinioned brave.

"Bear!" Ant cried. "It's me! Ant! You can open your eyes now." He and Cielo tried to lift the massive log off Bear's shoulders, but it was too heavy.

Suddenly Stickweed was there. "It seems you have some explaining to do," he said to the two of them.

"You knew?" Ant asked him.

"Not as such," he admitted. "But I found it perplexing a strangely familiar divine herald would only speak the *Lopotwa* version of our language." His eyes scanned the clearing. "Eagle-Talon!" he called to a figure sitting on the ground nearby. The elder turned his head at the sound of his name. "Get over here and help us!" At first, Eagle-Talon only stared like he didn't understand. Then something clicked and he was himself again. He got up and shuffled over to assist. Together, the four of them lifted the *monton* log off of Bear, who let the leather cord drop from his mouth and promptly collapsed into Cielo's arms.

"Oh Bear, my sweet Bear," she sobbed as she clutched him to her.

"Hold him up," Stickweed directed Cielo. He wiped away blood so he could examine Bear's wounds. "He needs water," he said to Ant. "See if you can find a bladder somewhere." All over the clearing the remaining Indians of both tribes were slowly beginning to stir, as if wakening from a trance.

Now Stone-Cleaver was there also. "How is he?" he asked Stickweed.

"He's exhausted and he's lost some blood, but he should be okay as long as these wounds don't become inflamed. We need to get him back to the village, but he's too weak to cross the ford right now—I figure the canoes are probably all gone."

"Not mine," said Cielo. "I hid it in some thick brush back where I landed.

"Good," said Stone-Cleaver, taking charge. "Have her tell you where it's hidden, Eagle-Talon. Once she's done this, I need you to bring it around. You two take care of Bear," he directed Cielo and Stickweed. "I'm going to go check on Wolf-Ears." This was the way things started getting back to normal.

Three days later it was business as usual in the Tuscarora village. Stone-Cleaver had Ant practicing hewing arrowheads. In his spare time he was observing moths. Elder Foxtail hadn't come out of his wigwam since the *monton*. He felt he had lost face when he ran and hid from Mother Buffalo. Stone-Cleaver told him that even warriors couldn't be expected to contend with gods, and therefore there was no loss of face, but he continued sulking anyway. Bear was doing well as his wounds had not become inflamed, and he walked around the village with the dressings on his shoulders. Whenever Cielo wasn't busy, she was sure to be found right there with him. Since the *monton* she seemed reluctant to let him out of her sight. Torga confidently predicted that would change once the baby came.

Around mid-day one of the village boys came running into the clearing saying that two Lopotwa were approaching along the main forest path. Word got around, and everybody moved toward the clearing to see what was happening. It turned out to be elder Lark-Wing and Straight-Oak, bandages similar to Bear's on his wide shoulders. They carried a sling between them, and in it was a large basket. They proceeded straight to where Stone-Cleaver was coaching Ant and stopped.

"Greetings Stone-Cleaver, wise and mighty chief of the Dogwood band of the Tuscarora, from my honorable Chief Panther-Foot, his eldest son Straight-Oak, and myself, warrior Lark-Wing. I come bearing a message." Stone-Cleaver nodded in faint acknowledgment, but did not get up from where he was sitting. "After some reflection, Panther-Foot has decided that Chief Stone-Cleaver, in the wisdom of his years, was right, and that the hearts of the Lopotwa were possessed by a cursed spirit of selfish greed. Furthermore, Panther-Foot regrets certain words and actions which occurred at the recent pow-wow which Stone-Cleaver so graciously hosted at Panther-Foot's request. Panther-Foot also hopes you will pass his regrets along to your most worthy warrior, the valiant Walks-Like-a-Bear, who is to be congratulated on prevailing in the recent *monton* challenge. As wise Stone-Cleaver previously noted, the Lopotwa no more dug the channel of the Hawanee than do they supply the endless, life-giving waters which eternally flow its length. Therefore do the Lopotwa quit all claim of ownership to this gift of the Great Spirit. As a token of both his sincerity and respect, Panther-Foot has asked that we gift our Tuscarora cousins as follows." At this, Straight-Oak lifted the basket out of the sling and placed it on the ground just in front of Stone-Cleaver. He lifted the cover to reveal some fourteen or fifteen plump river trout. Stone-Cleaver had no doubt they were from the Hawanee. The tribe would eat well tonight, at least. Straight-Oak replaced the cover and then stepped back, leaving the basket of fish where it sat. "Panther-Foot hopes you will accept this symbol of his contrition, and that his actions will not cause future discord between us."

When it was clear Lark-Wing was finished, Straight-Oak began scanning the assembled Tuscarora as if looking for something. On spotting the group of braves Bear was standing with, the tall Lopotwa picked up the empty sling and walked over to them, Lark-Wing following behind. He ignored the other braves and said something to Bear in his own language. "Straight-Oak says that he is glad to see that you are well, warrior Walks-Like-a-Bear, son of honorable Hears-with-Wolf-Ears," Lark-Wing translated. Straight-Oak pointed to the dressings on Bear's shoulders, and then back to those on his own. He spoke several more sentences in Lopotwa. "Straight-Oak," Lark-Wing continued, "says that Walks-Like-a-Bear and himself are now spirit-brothers in sweat, blood and pain. Straight-Oak says that if you are ever in need of his assistance, you have but to send word." The tall warrior held out his right arm. Bear took it, grasping Straight-Oak's forearm in the traditional clutch of friendship and brotherhood. With that, the two Lopotwa abruptly turned and started striding back toward the main forest path.

"Have a care, my Tuscarora brothers," said a brave called Scolding-Squirrel once the two Lopotwa were out of hearing. "Brother Bear already prefers Lopotwa women. Now he's liable to leave us and join the tribe of our cousins north of the river." All but Bear laughed at this.

"Scolding-Squirrel is silly," Bear grinned, "like the wild boar that eats too many fermented grapes. And about as smart," he added. The youths wisecracked back and forth for a few more minutes, but eventually the congregation broke up and everyone went back about their business. Bear had just arrived back at his dwelling when he heard someone calling him.

"Bear! Bear!" It was Ant, running toward him with spear and bow in hand. "Grab your hunting gear! There's buffalo an hour's run southeast of here!"

"There is? And just how do you know this, O watcher-of-ants? Did a little bird tell you?"

"Actually," Ant said with a grin, "it was a bee." He jogged off in that direction. Bear wasted no time grabbing his things and taking off after him.

Friday, June 17

# CREW FINDS ARTIFACT BURIED ON ISLAND

*By Jennifer McTeague*
*Editor*

A construction crew doing plumbing work on Josten's Island has made an archaeological find that has experts excited.

The crew unearthed a log that has evidently been buried on the island for 400 to 500 years, according to site supervisor Jerry Kowalski.

"It was deep in the mud and if it's as old as they say, it's really well-preserved," Kowalski said.

Archaeologists are in the process of testing the log but are saying they think it was used in a ritual of strength between two warriors, called a monton.

The log, about seven feet long, has several spikes carved on each end. The experts say the Tuscarora tribe used the logs to test the endurance of competing warriors. The logs were placed on the competitors shoulders, and they had to stand through the pain. The first who collapsed under the weight of the log or the loss of blood was the one who lost face.

At least one of the spikes on the log has traces of a red substance that could be paint but is more likely blood, according to N.C. State geologist Dr. Sanjay D. Patel.

The log is not petrified, a process the experts say takes millions of years, but shows signs of having laid in the open for several years before being buried by the mud. The drying is what helped preserve the possible bloodstain.

No other items have been found in the island's construction zone, Kowalski said.

# The Little Curse

C. Grey

When I was little, I would ask my mother why we never had anything to do with the tribe who lived on the other side of the oak limbs that crossed the path between our tepee and the village.

"They are evil," was all she would say, "and the oak limbs keep the evil on their side."

That answer satisfied me until around my ninth summer. I once again asked, "Why do they say such mean things about us? And why can't we go near the oak limbs?"

My mother quit her work and sat me down beside her on the riverbank. The water was cool and felt so good to my hot feet. I swung them back and forth as I listened to the sad story of our beginning.

"My name is Yao," Mother began. "That means Yellow Flower. You, my daughter, were named after your grandmother, Wyo, which means Feather. That is why I call you Dawyo, Little Feather."

Mother told me the story of how her mother and father were both killed in a battle with the Tuscarora tribe when she was very young.

"After, I was given to an old woman who had lost her husband and sons in the battle. All this old women did was sit in her tepee and sing the death chant. She sang and sang it. She never stopped and the other women of the tribe had to feed us.

"To get away from the screeching chant I would sneak out to the woods. Everyone in the tribe was working hard to get things ready in case there was another fight, so no one noticed if a little child wandered off. They probably were glad I was not under foot.

"At first I would go to the edge of the woods to play, but as I grew older and braver I would go deeper into the woods where I played huntress and gathered plants and flowers and found things to do such as a lonely girl can.

"One of the dogs that lived in the village followed me, and as time went on, more and more of them wandered off with us. By my ninth summer, we were a pack, and I was the leader because I knew no fear. I enjoyed my life with the pack, as we roamed the forest for three happy years.

"I learned to hunt with my pack, and killed plenty of food. Enough meat for all the dogs and some for me to carry some back to the tribe. I would take whatever we killed and divide it up. I took what I wanted first. Next I put aside some for each dog's master. I always made sure there was a good portion left for the dogs. After the pack had eaten, each one would take its master's portion and follow me back to the tribe. They would each go to their own tepee and wait for me to tell them to "Drop it." On my command, they dropped the food on the ground.

"The people of the tribe would take the meat. I never heard a thank you, nor did they ever even pat their hard-working dogs. But I could hear the whispering behind my back.

"I had lived twelve summers when one morning my pack and I came across a cave. The dogs began to whine and back away. They curled their lips and tucked their ears back. I didn't know what they feared. But I wasn't afraid. I knew no fear.

"I was curious more than anything. I watched as big bees flew in and out of the cave. I thought they must have honey, maybe, so slowly I made my way in. It was bright inside and there were beautiful pink flowers everywhere. I stayed all morning and enjoyed exploring.

"In the early afternoon I decided I should tell everyone what I had found. I could hardly wait, I was so excited. I ran into our tepee and told the old woman. To my great shock, she took her walking stick and beat me. 'Don't ever speak of this again!' she said. 'Don't you hear the whispers? Don't you know people call you a witch?'

"'A witch?' I said as I dodged her blows. 'Why would they say this?'"

"'Because you run with the dogs. Because you speak to them and they speak back and do what you say. If they knew you were in the witch cave, you would be sent away from the tribe.' She took up her stick again and grabbed my arm, striking me between each word. 'Do. Not. Go. To. Those. Woods. Again. EVER!'

"I was never allowed to go to the woods alone again. Instead I was forced to spend the next two years learning to be a wife, until in my fourteenth winter I was given in marriage to your father, Coyo. He was a good provider, and our tepee was made of bearskins. He was a strong man and it was not long before he gave me a child. You, my daughter.

"Your father stood outside the tepee with others from the tribe while I struggled for two days to bring you forth, Dawyo. It was hard labor and on the second day I had not much strength left. I would float in and out of the world. Once, when I was half-awake, I saw one of the women step outside to speak to Coyo.

"'Where is my son?' Coyo asked. 'Why is he taking so long?'

"The woman sounded frustrated. 'Your lazy woman won't stay awake. If she would do her work it would not take much longer.'

"I could hear the other men laugh. But not Coyo. He did not laugh.

"The next time my belly tightened, I pushed as hard as I could and suddenly, as I moaned loudly, I could feel you join us in the world.

"The old woman who caught you shrieked and threw you on my belly. 'Cursed! Cursed!' she screamed. The tepee shook as the women ran over each other trying to get out.

"There were loud voices arguing outside the tepee. Coyo was shouting,

'What did you do? How could you do this to me?' Other voices were arguing over what to do next. When they had made their decision, four men came into the tepee and picked up my sleeping fur by the four corners. They dragged me outside and lay me down in a place far outside the village. The women took down our tepee and rebuilt it over me where I lay. They made sure to face the flap away from the rest of the village. While they worked, the people of the village said horrible things to me. They said we should die. They would kill us both if they did not fear it would bring a curse on the tribe. So instead they were cutting us off from our people. They told me they had placed oak limbs across the path back to the village. They cursed me, so that if I ever crossed those limbs, I would die.

"When I had the strength, I pulled you to my breast and I saw why they were treating me this way. Your arms and legs were so short and your head was big as a melon. I wondered what had caused this. I was not a witch needing punishment. That was not why you were born this way. I had done nothing wrong. As I sobbed, I knew that it must have been my husband's fault. The one that had now abandoned us.

"I heard a faint whine behind me. I turned to see my old dog lying next to me. I wrapped it in my right arm and pressed my face close, crying into its neck.

"You began to move and make noises. I cleaned your face and mouth. I bit the cord and tied it off. When you were quiet and asleep, I wrapped you in a clean blanket and placed you outside the tepee in the shade of a bush near the river. My old dog lay down beside you.

"I had wrapped the birthing blanket into a bundle and dragged it to the water. I threw it in with all the strength I had left. Then as you slept, I waded into the water to clean myself. When I finished, I lay down on the soft ground between you and my dog. You were crying softly, so I pulled you to my breast and gave you my milk. As I nursed you, I fell in love with you like I had never loved anyone before. More than my mother, more than the old woman, and certainly more than my husband who betrayed me.

"'I love you, my baby,' I told you every night. Before I lay you down to sleep, I held you in my arms and said, 'You are mine. See how perfect you fit?'

"I think we may have starved if it had not been for my old dog. She hunted for us for almost two weeks, despite her age. But when I was able to hunt again, my dog and best friend no longer wanted to hunt.

"One night I watched as my dear friend wandered into the woods to die. I did the death chant for her. I sang of how well she could hunt. I sang of her great works and what a great companion she was. I also sang of how she helped with the baby. When I had sung of what a great dog she was, I continued with the death chant until dawn. I do not know if my animals will go to the country of souls. It will be a sad place for me if they do not.

"Then the big she wolf came into our lives just as the leaves started to turn. She wandered in like she had always lived with us, as she has ever since."

That was the story my mother told me about how I was born and the curse that makes us stay on our side of the oak limbs. She told me the story often, and I learned to stay away from the line of limbs that could mean our deaths. But it wasn't an easy lesson.

In my second summer, I was playing as my mother worked near our tepee. I saw some children playing in the village. I had no friends because of the curse. I wanted to join in their fun, so I ran towards the others with all my short legs would do. My mother dropped her work and raced after me. She caught me and fell to her knees as she wrapped her arms around me. Crying and shaking she scolded me. "Don't ever go near those oak limbs. Don't do it. They keep the evil away from us," she said. I did not understand, but I saw her terror. I learned that going towards the village children and crossing those limbs was a terrible, frightening thing. I never did it again.

After a time, I didn't even want to. I came to see how the people of the tribe yelled at us when they saw us. They spat at us and said we were cursed. It made me sad at first. "Don't be sad," mother said. "We are not cursed. We are not evil. It is the people of the village who carry the curse."

My mother was always wise. If she said it, I knew it was so.

I was seven or eight summers when I woke up to mother singing the death chant. She said she was sing for our wolf-friend that had gone to the country of souls during the night. We missed her for a long time.

The big male wolf came to live with us when I was nine summers. At first he would come around just before dark. He would watch us from the bushes. Mother would put food out when it was time for him. Every day she put the food a little closer to the fire, 'til one night he just came in near the fire and laid down. Mother slid over from where she was sitting and handed him some meat right out of her hand. From then on he was always with her.

By the time I had lived twelve summers, I had learned to be almost happy when I was alone. I roamed all through the forest, though never near the village or the oak limbs. I was not as tall as my mother's leg, but I did not let my short limbs stop me from doing anything.

One day while I was exploring, I came across a cave. The entrance was small, like I was, and very dark. I thought I should not go in, but I was brave and never considered what I *should* do to be very important. I decided to look inside the opening. Inside was a wonder. It wasn't dark at all. There was a strange light I didn't understand, and there were pink flowers and enormous bees everywhere.

I wondered if this was the cave my mother told me about at bedtime. I couldn't wait to ask her.

As I left the cave entrance I saw the bees entering and exiting a hole in a nearby tree. A honey tree. What a treat! The bees were enormous and slow. They didn't seem to care that I was there, looking into their hive. In fact, they would fly towards me, hover a moment near my face then fly back to their hive. I thought they were offering me some of their honey. I picked up a piece of bark that had fallen from a nearby tree and reached my hand into the hive. I grabbed all the honey I could reach and placed it on the bark to carry home. I marveled at its strange purple color, but when my tongue touched it, it was sweet and flavorful. I was sticky up to my elbow. I licked it off as I skipped home to share it with my mother.

As I entered the clearing where our tepee sat, I could hear loud chanting coming from the direction of the village. It was the tribe and they were striding quickly towards where my mother was washing our clothes by the river, her wolf nearby. I saw her look up and see the tribesmen. She saw their angry faces as I did. She saw the weapons they carried. The men of the tribe were coming, and they had a purpose in mind.

The men saw me standing at the edge of the clearing and they turned towards me.

My mother stood quickly and tried to lunge in my direction, to place herself between me and the tribe. The wolf sprang to his feet ready to fight, and she glanced his way. He gave a loud yelp as an arrow went almost through him. He fell back into the edge of the river. My mother slipped and hit her head on the rocks. I heard the sickening *thunk*. She fell face forward in the river. Her body hit the wolf's body as she went down, and they began to float downriver together, their blood forming two streams behind them.

I barely noticed the men of the tribe scatter and retreat with harsh shouts of "Another witch's curse!" and "Run!" I ran as fast as I could to get to my mother, heavy tears sliding down my cheeks. I slipped and scrambled to reach the river, but by the time I made it to the bank, she was gone. I moved away from the river that was now so ugly to me and sank down onto the ground near some bushes and through my tears began to sing.

I sang of mother's great works, how she had taken care of me. I sang of how she loved me. I sang of anything I could think of. I knew my mother would go into the country of souls that lays a great way off, where the Sun visits. There is no hunger in this place. She would not be cold or tired again. I started the death chant in a quivering voice, but I could not chant for long.

I had never known anything but love and security from my mother, and now, in less time than it takes a bird to cross the river, I was totally alone. I had never known real sadness until then. The sweetest person on earth was gone. I began to cry again. I cried for what seemed like hours, for my mother and for me. I watched the shadows grow long on the river. I saw the ants and flies discover the honey I intended to share with my mother. I did nothing as the insects enjoyed the sweetness that no longer interested me.

As my sobbing eased, I realized I could hear voices coming from a distance behind me. It was some of the men talking. At first I thought they had come back to bring me to the village to take care of me. I was, after all, still a child. But then my mother's words came back to me. "They are evil," she had said. I froze under the thick branches of a thicket and watched them.

"We should have gotten rid of them before the thing's cord was cut," the old man with the white hair said.

The one with the scowling face said, "We should have but we didn't. Now that the woman is dead, we can break the curse."

"How?" a young boy of about fourteen asked.

Scowling man said, "We will catch the demon and cut off its hands and feet. Then we will throw it in the river after its mother. That will end the evil that has fallen on our tribe, and my son can take a new wife."

*What curse?* I wondered. And why did I have to die so he could take a wife?

I watched as they looked through the clearing and into the woods as the light faded. Finally, White Hair said, "We'll never find her tracks in the darkness. We should go back to our fires and look for her again in the morning." The men grumbled, but they agreed and they slowly walked back, over the oak limbs, towards the village.

I sat for a little while longer trying to get my thoughts together. One thing that was clear to me was I would move to the cave I had found. It took three trips with all I could carry each time. The last trip I put all that was left on the bearskin that was our bed. I would drag it a little, stop and rest, then go again. With everything in the cave, I started making it my home.

From the time I could walk I had followed my mother like a shadow, so I could set rabbit and fish traps with ease. I could bring down a tom turkey with my sling. I also knew all the plants that grew in the woods and how to prepare them. I knew I would be fine. The cave would help. It told me so.

The cave did not like the smell of onions, but I liked the taste, so I would cook them at the opening that faced the island in the river. The cave did like the smell of bay leaf, so I cooked a lot with it. We both liked the smell of sassafras tea with honey, and I loved the taste.

I don't know how I knew what the cave liked or did not; I just did. I also don't know how we could talk. The words and ideas seemed to just come to me. This ability to talk to each other made me feel safe again, like I did with my mother.

The daily chores of finding food and cooking took most of the day. I also had to dry and put food up for the winter. The little time I had left after my chores I explored the cave.

To me it seemed to have no end. The cave told me where to go. It was like it wanted me to know all about it. The cave told me how to mark my way so I would not get lost. The markings looked odd to me, and I wanted to ask what they meant, but the cave said it was not for me to know.

One spring day when I had finished exploring, I asked the cave if it would hurt it if I painted a yellow flower on it in remembrance of my mother. It said it would be fine and for me to go get dandelions for their yellow color.

There were dandelions a good distance away. I took all of them because I did not want to make that long trip again. When I got back in the cave, over by my bed was the outline of a big squash flower. I asked the cave how it did that. It said it hurt when it marked, but it wanted to do this for me. I crushed the flowers and painted my flower. It did not glow like the pink ones, but I did not care. The flower gave me such comfort.

I had been in the cave for three summers. The daily work was getting harder and harder, doing everything by myself, and living only on what I could hunt. Food was getting scarce, and I felt weak all the time. The leaves were beginning to turn, and for the first time the flowers in the cave were turning darker. I did not have nearly enough food for the winter, but the cave told me not to worry, so I didn't.

My mind would now drift back to the tribe. I could never understand why they wanted to kill a child just because it did not look just like them.

I had been out of bear oil for my skin to help endure the cold for a very long time. The bear fat for my hair had turned rancid about the same time. I was glad to still have scarlet root to kill lice.

One day I noticed the flowers were almost purple. I asked the cave why? It said it was sad. It said I had been a great joy to it. It told me to go wrap up in my bearskin. It said I would be with my mother this night. Then it said the Lapotwa tribe that had been so cruel to me would not be known in history. The last thing I recall was it saying it would close its opening so no animals could get to me. I did as I was told. I lay down and went off to a peaceful sleep.

Tuesday, June 14

# Bees buzz through expert's family history

*By Jennifer McTeague*
*Editor*

When Hope Landreth was a little girl, she spent her time between living with each of her parents, scientists who work in different parts of the country, and sometimes different parts of the world.

Her stepmother is an anthropologist who studies the native tribes in the southwest, primarily in Arizona. Her father is an epidemiologist with the CDC, mostly based in the southeast but sometimes sent to other parts of the world.

So Hope and her half-brother, M.J., often found themselves moving from parent to parent. After their schooling was interrupted three times in one year, when Hope was in the fifth grade and M.J. was in kindergarten, their parents decided they would be better off being home-schooled.

Somewhere during her early days of home-schooling, Hope found herself fascinated by bees. She started spending time visiting apiarists, beekeepers, whereever she was living.

She did her science projects on bees, wrote papers about them, drew them for art projects, hiked through woods looking for wild bees to help strengthen colonies.

And she finally turned that interest from her childhood into her professions. She is an associate professor of entomology at N.C. State University, where she earned her bachelor's, master's and doctoral degrees.

Hope has been working the last three months in Kyleighburn, trying to determine how the town's swarm of bees managed to thrive in the caves that run beneath

**Continued on Page 5A**

# Minutes of a Meeting of The Unboxed Players

Mackenzie Minnick

THE FOLLOWING IS A TRANSCRIPT of a recording that The Unboxed Players sent in for the Kyleighburn time capsule. The subject in question was the 2012 production season. In attendance are (in order of speaking):

**Robert Corey,** *Troupe Leader/Cafe Owner*
**Elias Parvis,** *Treasurer/Plumber*
**Jessamina Wilcher,** *Visiting Artisan/Director*
**Thadeus Black,** *Producer/Barber*

10:00 AM, E.P.P. Scott Library Conference Room

COREY: —should be a light on to show that it is recording, is there a light on?

PARVIS: What light?

COREY: On the side away from me, there should be a light.

PARVIS: Oh, oh, I see it. It's red. And blinking. What does that mean?

*(rustle of paper)*

WILCHER: User guide says that means the device is recording.

COREY: Great! Okay, we'll have to make sure to trim this bit. So, at the clap, cut everything—

*(clap)*

Hello, my name is Robert Corey. I am a… uh… the

founding member of The Unboxed Players. I am here with Thadeus Black, Elias Parvis, and Jessamina Wilcher—

WILCHER: Why did you say my name last?

COREY: Oh, I was going around clockwise—

WILCHER: Is it because I'm a woman?

COREY: No, because—

BLACK: It's because you're visiting.

WILCHER: Oh, that's fine.

COREY:… Right. Jessamina is visiting us from California, it's her third time in Kyleighburn, and this time she'll be here with us for the entire year! Jess, do you have anything to say before we get started?

WILCHER: Thank you, Robert. Thank you for the opportunity, and I hope to bring everything I learned in California as both a director and actor to this lovely and quaint town.

COREY: Great, now, with that aside, let's talk season! Last year was great! How much did we make, Elias?

PARVIS: Well, we had an uptick in ticket sales, despite the Kyleighburnies putting on a couple more famous productions like—

*(Mr. Parvis is muffled by the ensuing conversation)*

BLACK: Can you pass the snacks over?

COREY: I didn't bring any this time.

BLACK: Why?

COREY: I didn't want a crinkling bag recorded for posterity. Could you imagine some future archaeologist digging it up to hear this, and all he gets is the sound of someone eating potato chips? We'd be known as the fattest town in America forever. Loved snacks so much that they recorded someone eating them.

BLACK: Okay, okay, jeez. If you didn't bring snacks, then what are you eating?

COREY: Eggs with cheddar and a sausage patty.

BLACK: Are those hashbrowns?

COREY: Along with three buttered biscuits. From Nana's Homecooking, near Oak Street.

BLACK: …. Can I have a bite?

*(Rustling, assuming to be a tray being passed)*

PARVIS: —which means we'll have enough funding in total for four shows this year. Spring Musical, a winter holiday show, and some leeway for summer and fall.

BLACK(chewing): Dat shounds shimple to pick.

PARVIS: Absolutely. I already have my personal votes.

WILCHER: Votes?

COREY: Oh, sorry, Jessamina—

WILCHER: Jess.

COREY: Jess. We vote on our plays here, that might

be different—

WILCHER: No, that's pretty much how most people do it. I was just asking if I were to have any voting rights during this meeting, or if I had any say whatsoever in this whole… (distractedly) decision process. Sorry, what is he eating?

BLACK: It'sh Nana'sh Homecooken—

COREY: My breakfast, dammit!

BLACK: Shorry, I'll stop.

WILCHER: It looks like a deep-fried coronary thrombosis. I hope to God that green thing is a vegetable.

BLACK: A what?

WILCHER: You don't know what a vegetable is?

COREY: I think he meant the other thing you said. Cornea Tromboneses? Something to do with the eyes, right?

*(chewing; rustling)*

WILCHER: Never mind. Do I get a say or not?

COREY: Aw, you ate most of the sausage...

PARVIS: Yes, Jess, you do.

WILCHER: Excellent! I did some fantastic shows in San Bernadino that I'd love to re-imagine here.

BLACK: Sounds cool.

PARVIS(annoyed): Yes, well, let's try and keep everything democratic here and make sure everyone gets their say. Since Corey is otherwise busy, I'll start. For our musical, I believe that *Grease*—

*(groans from Mr. Black and Mr. Corey, scoff from Ms. Wilcher)*

—*Grease* always gets a fair reception and brings a lot of people out. For summer, *Our Town*—

COREY: Oh come on!

BLACK: Hey, I like *Our Town*. It's a neat little show.

WILCHER: I could do something very… ethereal with it.

COREY: Absolutely not. Vetoed. No. Carry on, Elias.

PARVIS: Very well. Fall, being one of Kyleighburn's most beautiful seasons, would make the perfect backdrop for *Godspell*—

COREY: That's it, Elias, you're done.

BLACK: Why, what was wrong?

COREY: What was the spring show we did, Thad, in 2008?

BLACK: Hmm. I think that was *Godspell*.

COREY: Fall, 2005?

BLACK: *Our Town*.

COREY: Spring, 2007? Fall, 2008? Summer, 2009? Hell, all of 2010?

BLACK: *Our Town*, *Godspell*, *Godspell* again, *Our Town*

but with mostly women…. Ah. I see the problem.

PARVIS: They're good shows.

COREY: They're boring! They've been overdone!

WILCHER: You did *Our Town* for an entire year?

BLACK: Yeah, couldn't find enough men for anything else.

PARVIS: There's nothing wrong with the classics. People like them for a reason.

COREY: But we're not trying to recreate the classics, we're trying to do something fresh! New! Exciting!

PARVIS: Fine, what's your idea then?

COREY: Anything that isn't those.

WILCHER: Perhaps, while Robert is assembling his ideas, I'll go ahead and pitch mine. Yes? Okay. Well, in California, as you know, we trend toward modern ways of interpreting theater, often utilizing lenses provided by more antique techniques that have slowly been refined over the centuries. We did an interpretation of *A Midsummer Night's Dream* that played up the horror aspect of mind control and the fey. I'd love to be able to do that here.

BLACK: Well, I do like doing Shakespeare in the park, but I'm not sure—

WILCHER: Excellent! We'll need to order some

prosthetics and a mold to make a jelly human heart. Now, for the musical, I was thinking of doing *Seussical.*

COREY: Oh, that's a good one, I took the wife and kids to see it in Raleigh. They had a grand time.

WILCHER: Good, you've seen it. Now, picture this: We hire a plus-sized actor to play Horton, and then we challenge body-normativity by giving him a full-frontal nude scene.

PARVIS: (sputtering) Excuse me?!

WILCHER: Just imagine it! A lone obese man on stage, naked and vulnerable to the audience, his whole trunk on display!

COREY: I think some people would have an issue with their kids seeing—

WILCHER: I want them to take issue! People should be aware of the problems in the world! There aren't enough lead roles for women in theater, yet they are expected to be sexualized and exploited for what? Men to ogle and stare! Art shouldn't be comfortable, brainless entertainment; people should be compelled to question their lives and ideas when they come to the theater!

COREY: Why?

WILCHER: The fact you have to ask that question at all tells me, you don't get it.

COREY: No, no, I get it, it's just—

WILCHER: If you can't appreciate me, then I'm leaving.

*(chair scraping; door opens, footsteps out the door)*

COREY: Wait, Jess!

*(chair scraping, footsteps)*

BLACK: I like the idea.

PARVIS: How could you possibly like that?

BLACK: Something funny about a fat fella standing on stage in the buff. I bet Costello would like it.

PARVIS: Of course....

BLACK: By the way, can't help but notice your hair is getting long. How about you come to my shop after this, get you a trim?

*(footsteps returning, door shuts)*

COREY: Well, she's gone.

PARVIS: Shame. Well, let bygones be bygones. Let's talk about *Grease*. If we can ask one of the high schools—

COREY: No, no, no. Just because we don't have Jess doesn't mean you win.

PARVIS: What do you think we should do then?

COREY: I— uh— I— I had something.

PARVIS: Then I'm going to take a break and run to the bathroom. I look forward to hearing what you decide.

*(chair scraping, door opens and shuts)*

COREY: Did you have an idea, Thad?

BLACK: Hm? Oh, no, I'm happy with whatever other people choose.

COREY: Well, crap.

BLACK: How's the recording thing going?

COREY: No idea, let me check. Hmm, the timer says that—

*Recording abruptly stops here.*

*NOTES:*

*Jessamina Wilcher left Kyleighburn within the next two days. Robert Corey and Elias Parvis failed to agree on a season for 2012. The 2013 season included an all-female rendition of* Godspell.

*A coupon for BLACK'S CUTS, a coupon for Nana's Homecooking, and a newspaper article have been included along with this transcript.*

—END OF TRANSCRIPT—

Friday, June 17

## From the Editor's Chair

Gerald Winslow Franklin, the new manager of the Kyleighburn branch of Kingman National Bank, has called the office again to remind us that he prefers that we use his full name and we left his middle name out when we ran an item in Tuesday's paper about the bank's car show on Saturday.

We keep forgetting about that middle name in the rush to get the paper out but we promise to try to remember it from now on.

***

Many local residents were saddened to hear about the death of James Miller, the longtime principal of Kyleighburn High School. They remember Mr. Miller as a fierce supporter of all of his students, from the athletes who led the school to a state football championship in 2004 to the ones who didn't make headlines or lead in any way but simply tried their best.

He will be missed.

Mr. Miller's funeral will be at 3 p.m. Sunday at Kyleighburn Baptist Church. His full obituary is on Page1A.

***

The bi-weekly farmers market sponsored by the Kyleighburn Business Council continues tomorrow in front of City Hall. Farmers from around the county report they will have tomatoes, lettuce, spinach and kale, zucchini and other squashes, potatoes, green peppers, onions and cucumbers.

Here's a recipe from my mother, who still loves to serve it when she had people over for one of her "teas."

## Evelynn's Congealed Sandwich Spread

1 envelope plain gelatin
¼ cup cold water
½ cup. boiling water
2 tomatoes, chopped
1 green pepper, chopped
1 cucumber, chopped
1 onion, chopped
1 cup chopped celery
2 cups mayonnaise, approximately
Dash of salt

Soften gelatin in cold water. Add boiling water to gelatin mixture and stir until dissolved. Set aside to cool.

Combine chopped vegetables, mayonnaise and salt. Add vegetable mixture to gelatin and stir well to blend. Chill overnight or until set. Spread on sandwich bread or crackers.

Although it makes Miss Evelyn cringe, I've played around with this recipe over the years, leaving off the green peppers (we don't get along), using zucchini or broccoli slaw mix, using jalapenos (not recommended), using Jell-O and other flavored gelatin desserts instead of the plain.

I've also seen similar spreads that use cream cheese instead of the gelatin.

This is a spread that invites playing around with ingredients. I just recommend trying your ideas out in advance, however. The mixture I made with jalapenos was not pre-tested and its rollout was not a success.

***

In a surprising turn of events, The Unboxed Players will not have a production season this year.

Citing only creative differences, troupe members would not elaborate on the process that led to the decision, but their presence on our cultural calendar will be sorely missed, as we all fondly remember their past performances.

# Rex Rising

Robin Deffendall

REX WAS NOT SURPRISED when a peculiar thing happened one day after school. His grandmother had told him many times.

"Men are dogs," Grandma Bailey had always said. She repeated it often as her own personal mantra, often with added expletives. She felt she had good reason to condemn the entire male race. Months before Rex was born his father had done something unforgivable and had run away from home, leaving Rex's mother in a family way with no visible means of support.

Of course, Grandma blamed *him* when her daughter died in childbirth. "*He* didn't ever bother to check on her during the pregnancy," she said once, "so there was no way I was ever going to let *that man* get his hands on my grandson, even if I could have found him. He was inconsiderate and unreliable. Running off in the night like some kind of stray dog." And beside there was that mysterious unforgivable incident that she would never mention. No, Rex was going to be a Bailey. In her grief, she listed Rex's father as "Unknown" and took him home to raise herself. She never divulged to Rex what she knew about *that man,* and she never said his name. Rex asked about him, many times. She'd always shake her head and turn away. "Men are dogs," was all she would say.

Rex had heard the speech so often he had assimilated it as part of his own world view. Men *were* dogs. It was only a figure of speech, of course. But if his grandmother said it, it was true. She was always right.

He was twelve when it happened, that age when a boy begins to feel like some sort of freak. Changes were happening to his body and to his whole... self. He felt isolated, lost. Clearly he had killed his mother simply by being born. He had begun to wonder if his father had known about his monstrous nature and that was the reason why he had abandoned his son, and if the reason his grandmother had never spoken about the man was because she knew it, too.

On the afternoon it happened, Grandma Bailey was away playing bridge at her social club. She would be lost in cigarette- and port wine-fueled card combat until dinner time, so after school Rex had the house to himself for several hours. Today was the day to find some answers.

Rex had lived in his grandmother's tiny, nicotine-stained house his whole life. He had played with the contents of every closet, poked through the spidery basement for secret treasure and hunted Christmas presents throughout the house. There was no hiding place he didn't know intimately, but the one place Grandma had forbidden him to enter. Rex was sure that was the only possible place to look for clues to his past.

He pulled the attic stairs down and climbed slowly to the top. Darkness huddled in the corners of the low-ceilinged room and the superheated air hung still. The stale dust raised by his feet as he crossed the floor made him sneeze at the sharply acerbic smell. Boxes stacked three high along one wall bore the careful labels. Christmas. Thanksgiving. Elementary School: Art Projects. Books. Books. Books. *National Geographics*. No. Nothing there.

In a corner Rex found the collection of the damaged and missing. Two shadeless floor lamps stood guard over a wooden rocking chair with a broken rocker. On a TV tray a flowered china teapot with a chipped spout accompanied a cream pitcher and a sugar bowl that was missing its lid. A sheet covered a dressmaker's form-thing. It looked like a decapitated ghost, or would have if not for the layer of gray dust covering the shoulders like some outrageous case of ancient spectral dandruff.

Under a dry-rotting ladder he found a pile of old newspapers stacked atop an antique trunk. It looked something like a pirate chest from a movie, lacquered wood with brass fittings now green with disuse. Just the sort of place someone would hide valuable stuff like gold coins, emeralds and ropes of pearls. Or perhaps family treasures such as papers that listed names and pedigrees, photos, and other secrets. This must be it. He set the newspapers aside and knelt before the box.

A metal plate on the front bore the initials RB engraved in a bold script. R... R for Rex? Was this his dad's trunk? Was his name Rex, too? He rubbed the smooth, dark-stained wood. Maybe his father had touched it in the same way. The wooden handles were much paler, proving that this box had at one time been used regularly, though the dark patina on the brass hardware and the ancient key lock hinted that it had not been opened in a long time. Rex picked up the heavy lock and twisted, pulled, and yanked with all his might. Still, the sturdy lock held true.

He ran back down the stairs to the garage, returning with a screwdriver. He wedged it under the clasp and leaned his entire weight on the handle. Slowly... ever so slowly... the screwdriver bent. *Cheap-ass, useless piece of—*. He hurled it across the room where it bounced against a wall and came to rest atop a box of books. He threw himself into the broken rocking chair with a frustrated growl. The stuttering rhythm of his rocking did nothing to help his thinking, so he stopped and leaned forward, his elbows on his knees.

If the chest was locked, it had to contain something significant. And that meant there had to be a key. No one would keep a locked pirate chest full of valuable or important stuff unless that chest could be unlocked. Right? It wouldn't make sense.

He got up and began to search, running his hands across shelves furred with dust, peeking into the cream pitcher and tipping the teapot up to shake free a gigantic dust bunny. But no key. He lifted the flaps of cardboard boxes and rummaged through the contents. An hour later he was covered in filth, sweaty from the heat and itchy from some insulation that had fallen down the back of his shirt. And still no key. He snarled again and went back downstairs. He returned with a large cross-cut saw. He would cut the end off the damn thing.

Rex didn't have enough room to wield the saw properly, so he pulled the heavy chest away from the wall and stepped behind it to get a better angle. A large black key was taped to the back of the trunk. He swore. The ancient masking tape crumbled as he pulled it away from the back. A rectangle of dusty putty-colored residue marred the luster of the dark wood where the tape had been.

He inserted the key into the lock and was rewarded with a soft *snick*! The lock fell open on the clasp. Rex inhaled deeply once, twice, sneezed again, then with shaking hands he lifted the heavy lid.

There were more newspapers inside dating from April 1988, eight months before he was born. The one on top showed a picture of police officers milling around a building that had been roped off with crime scene tape. He could see the shards of broken glass from one shattered window and the marks where soot from rising flames had marred the siding. The headline read

**BOMB KILLS ONE IN UNIVERSITY**
**ANIMAL RESEARCH BUILDING.**
**TERROR GROUP SUSPECTED.**

He lifted the brittle pages out of the trunk and placed them carefully aside. Underneath was a stack of photos from a bygone time. Most were of people he didn't know. The oldest showed men in pin-striped suits and funny hats posing next to women in fur stoles, dripping with ostentatious jewelry. There were others showing old-timey cars parked on city streets. Some seemed more recent. The women all had big hair and wore dresses cut with wide shoulders so they looked like female linebackers. The men wore their shirts unbuttoned and no socks, so their ankles showed skinny under their high-waisted pants legs. He couldn't believe people actually went out of the house dressed like that. It was like some sort of ridiculous costume.

He gasped. There was a face he knew. It was his mother. He recognized her from her photo on his grandmother's mantel. She was smiling under a tree with her arm around a dog. Rex couldn't figure out what kind of a dog it was. Some kind of mutt, he guessed, but a strong-looking one with an intelligent eye and a gorgeous slick, russet coat. The dog had his front legs in her lap and was staring raptly into her eyes.

The next showed his mother kissing a man he'd never seen before. He had a vaguely Irish look, and a shock of carrot red hair. Could this be his father? He set the two photos aside to show to his grandmother. He leafed through the other pictures in the stack but the faces held no context for him. Set them on top of the newspapers.

He went back to the chest, hoping for something to explain who RB was. There were some letters he assumed were from his mother. They had been written to her "dearest," but she never wrote his name or signed them with anything other than "Love." There were a few knickknacks, too. An ivory-handled pocket knife with the RB monogram which Rex put into his own pocket. A smooth gray stone with a line of quartz running through it. A broken watch. A copy of a book he'd read several times himself: *Call of the Wild* by Jack London. "Dude's got good taste in books anyway," he said to himself.

In the final layer he found magazines. A handful of *National Geographics*. Some car magazines. And, oddly, a whole stack of dog-related magazines. There was *Whole Dog Journal*, and *AKC Gazette*. He picked up a copy of *Dog Fancy* and leafed through it. At the centerfold was a glossy photo of a dog. An Irish Setter, aristocratic nose raised high, long red hair blowing in the wind. Rex snorted. It made him think of the poster in the center of the porn magazine his friend Jimmy had stolen from the 7-Eleven that one time. This looked the same, but with a dog as the focus. It was pooch porn. He set the magazine aside along with a few programs from old dog shows that had apparently taken place in New York and Philadelphia. RB must have been some kind of dog breeder or something. Weird.

Then he found something that completely pulled his interest away from his ancestral search. A stack of five girlie magazines. He had hit the mother lode. Reverently he opened the first one. The acid-etched pages cracked at the seam and revealed faded photographs, ads for cigarettes, hard liquor and muscle cars, and of course the articles. The subjects of the photos didn't seem overly dated, at least. The hair styles looked a little antiquated, but that hardly mattered. He wasn't really interested in their hair anyway.

Grandma Bailey was not expected home for hours, but just in case, Rex opened the pooch porn and slipped the real porn mags inside to camouflage them, then he smuggled them out of the attic and back to his room. There they could be easily concealed among the clutter his grandmother was always harping about.

His search for family ties forgotten, Rex lay on his twin bed in the afternoon before his grandmother came home, reading. OK, maybe he wasn't reading exactly, but it was an education nevertheless. Rex learned the wonders of the female body from the stack of twenty-year-old *Playboys*.

Nubile, tanned skin posed in awkward poses that highlighted the most feminine parts in the most lascivious ways. Yes. Oh yes. It was a whole new world for Rex.

Men may be dogs, but women—real women, not the worn out ones like his grandmother—real women were... ice cream and cool jazz and the feeling you get just after you swing out over the swimming hole and let go of the rope.

If only he could have a girlfriend like one of these. He thought of Harper Gentry, a girl who sat two rows up from him in his fourth period class. She was pretty cute, but she had nothing on these women. This was soo much better than pooch porn.

And that was when it happened.

As he flipped to a particularly lovely centerfold, Rex moaned. Except it was not so much a moan as a... well, as a howl. He scratched his palm and wondered where that howl had come from. His nose itched too, probably from the musty odor of the old magazines. They really had a funky smell to them. He had never smelled anything like that before. So intense and acidic.

Now the backs of his hands were itching fiercely. He looked at the red claw marks where he had scratched them trying to stop the fire. Among the welts he'd made, there was a forest of new white hairs. He was shocked. They were noticeably growing, sprouting and lengthening even as he watched. He had thought that was just an old wives' tale. How was he going to explain this to his grandmother?

He moaned again, and this time his groan-moan-howl seemed to come from deep in his chest. A chest that now itched beneath a mat of deep glossy black and white hair. Hair that was curly and thick and matching the hair now covering his legs and arms. And his tail.

Rex dropped the magazine. His bones seemed to be melting, or maybe crumbling to dust. He could feel the popping and crackling as his arms and legs changed shape, lengthening in some areas and shortening in others. The fingers of his hands bent backwards and thick callouses developed on the pads while hishis opposable thumbs withdrew into useless stumps.

This was unreal. Panting, Rex knew now what was happening.

*Grandma was right! Looking at porn has turned me into a horn dog. Men really are dogs,* he thought. *Literally!*

The revelation confused Rex. How come no one else ever mentioned this little fact? Seems like he should have heard something, read about it somewhere.

His grandmother clearly knew about the secret behind the male condition. She had told him so many times, but he had not believed her. Not really. Who would believe that? Yet here was the proof. He was panting heavily and his heart was racing.

Well, he dare not tell his grandmother.

He hoped this would be a temporary metamorphosis. When—if!— he changed back to his twelve-year-old human shape he would have to keep this event a secret. Hide it from the world, but most especially from his grandmother. He could not deal with both this new reality *and* her rejection. She had never held him in the same contempt she held for the other members of his species, but he hadn't been a dog then. Would she toss him out? Is that why he had never met his father? Was this the mysterious unforgivable incident? Did he turn into a dog and she kicked him out? *Maybe I should just run away now. But how to get the door open? He had taken opposable thumbs for granted his whole life. NowNow look!*

But no. Even if he could figure out the logistics, his grandmother needed him. She needed him to fix her dinner, keep her house clean and help her take her medications on time. And to light the damned cigarettes that were slowly killing her. So he would stay. He would have to.

And she must never find out the truth.

He put his chin on his paws and concentrated on simply breathing in and out until the adrenaline slowed, his eyes closed and finally, he slept.

When Rex woke, the sun had crossed the sky and darkness hovered at the horizon. He leaped out of bed and realized it had gotten chilly. And he was naked. Normal and naked. *There is a God,* he thought. It was a dream. It was just a dream. And now he was awake and clearly not a dog.

Except that there was a dog-shaped ring of glossy black hair across the width of his bed.

*Oh, no. I'm going to have to wash those before Grandma sees them.* He pulled the comforter up and folded a corner over the mess. That would have to do for now.

He threw on a pair of sweat pants and a clean tee shirt and headed for the kitchen. *I should have started dinner an hour ago. Grandma will be home soon, she'll fuss 'cause dinner will be late.*

Besides, he was starving. Steaks. He would make steaks. He set out two, and looked at them thoughtfully. Grandmother would eat the smaller one, and he would take the bigger. For a moment he considered the beautiful, red, marbled beef. He went back to the fridge and pulled out a third steak.

He leaned over the cutting board with his nose mere inches from the meat. He inhaled the heady aroma. Wonderful. He began to salivate. He picked one up with a large fork. He considered taking a great big bite out of it, imagined the cold meat juice running across his tongue. Ugh!

He dropped the fork and the steak landed with a splat. That was gross. He had never wanted to eat raw steak before. Maybe...?

He examined his shaking hands. The fur was gone. He pulled the tee shirt away from his chest and looked down. All good there, too. He reached behind himself and put his hands on his butt. No hint of tail. Thank G—.

"What are you doing?"

Rex whirled around at his grandmother's sharp voice. His shoulders hunched and he pulled his head in as if she was going to bite it off.

"What is the matter with you?" She peered at him over her bifocals. "Why are you acting so embarrassed? What have you been doing?" The question had an overtone of accusation.

"I—I—I—," he stammered. He felt a bead of sweat roll down his temple, gaining momentum until it became a small rivulet running down his neck. He turned back toward the counter. "Nothing," he muttered.

His grandmother's tone softened and she said, "I think I know what the problem is. And Rex, I want you to know: What happened to you is perfectly normal."

He whipped back around. His voice cracked as he said, "It is? Really?"

"Really. It happens to every young man at about this age."

*That's a relief.* "And you never thought to mention it?"

"Well, it's not really a topic for polite conversation. You understand."

He did. He truly did.

"Do you have anything you want to ask me about?" She said.

Rex shook his head. He *definitely* did not want to ask her any questions. He wasn't sure that was something he could *ever* discuss with anyone, much less his grandmother. It was just too embarrassing. Then he remembered the photos he'd found in the attic. "Actually yes, there is something. But not right now," he said. "Maybe later. After dinner."

She peeked around him at the cutting board. "Steaks?" She frowned. "That's a lot of meat, young man."

"I'm really hungry," he said.

"I'm sure. But vegetables? How about a nice salad, too?"

"Do we have to?"

"Yes."

"OK. If you insist," he said and smiled. He took her match book from her shaking hands and lit her cigarette.

His grandmother patted him on the head. "You're such a *good* boy," she said.

After dinner, Rex sat on the opposite end of the sofa rubbing his palm across the worn Chintz fabric. *The Bachelorette* was over and his grandmother had shifted her interest to another similarly inane show.

He wasn't sure how to broach the subject of the photographs he'd found. He wanted to confirm whether those really were his parents, but while his grandmother sometimes talked about her daughter, Rex's mother, she never, *never* mentioned his dad. When, by some accident or design, they approached the subject, she often made a hard right conversational turn in order to change the topic. Rex knew she harbored deep-seated anger towards his father and he suspected that her "Men are dogs" mantra was largely directed towards him. Rex didn't want to cause her further pain, so he had never asked.

But now, especially after the afternoon's events, Rex needed to know the truth. How could he be expected to figure out who he was going to be if he didn't know anything about his parents?

When a commercial started, he opened his mouth to ask the question and closed it again having emitted no more than a subtle squeak. He tried twice more before his grandmother abruptly turned off the television.

"Something's on your mind, Rex. Is it about what you did while I was gone?"

Rex squirmed. "Yes, I—"

"I told you that it's perfectly normal. Every young man does that."

"No, that's not it." he said.

"Then what is it, Rex?"

He traced a finger around one of the roses on the sofa's seat. "I was... looking for something in the attic," he began.

His grandmother's smile seemed to freeze on her face. "You aren't supposed to be up there."

"I know Grandma. I'm sorry. But, there was a chest... a wooden chest. It said RB…"

"You shouldn't mess with that Rex," she said sharply. "It's not yours. Just leave it alone, hear me?"

"I kinda already opened it…" He inhaled deeply to calm the quaver in his voice, "...and inside I found some pictures. I think this one is my mother." He held out the photo of his mother with the dog.

Her expression softened as she saw the image. She took it from him and held it lovingly. Rex saw that her eyes were bright as they filled with unshed tears. "I've never seen this before," she said. One thin finger brushed the woman's face. "Yes, this is your mother, my Victoria. She must be about twenty, here. I think that's about the right age. I remember this white dress. It had eyelet around the bottom and she always wore it with this red sash. I made it for her myself, and it was so beautiful. She always wore it on special occasions." She smiled, lost in the memory for a moment.

"Yes, I remember that dress. She was about twenty, but I don't remember this dog." She handed the photo back to him.

"Can I have it? I don't have a picture of her. Not one of my own."

"Well, you should keep it then. I'll get you a frame the next time we go into town."

"There was another picture, too." He showed her the one of his mother kissing the man.

Rex could feel the anger bubbling up beneath her silence. He could smell it, like a too heavy measure of cayenne in a pot of simmering chili. Would she cry? Would she scream and shred the picture? The silence hung on for too long. He was afraid to breathe.

Then a single tear rolled down her cheek and fell onto her sleeve. The scent of her anger dissipated. "She loved him, your dad."

Rex slid over to sit closer to her, leaning his cheek against her arm to comfort her.

"He seemed like a nice man. I thought he was, at first, at least. He seemed kind and gentle, and generous, too. He had plenty of money and he wasn't stingy with it. He brought her things. Practically every night he would come in carrying something or other. Flowers and candy and such. When she needed some help he was right there to take care of her. Fix her car, change the filter on the air conditioner. Open a peanut butter jar. They were always going walking in the park. He liked to catch a baseball and she would throw it for him for hours. They talked on the phone and he went to church with us every Sunday.

"She was so happy. I didn't think I had ever seen her smile so much. It's like he was everything to her."

"I thought you hated him, Grandma. You never talk about him. What happened?"

"Your mother sent him away after she found out what he did." Her face pulled down into a serious frown. The anger was back.

Rex almost couldn't ask. "What did he do, Grandma?"

She sighed deeply. "He had been working with an animal rights group. Trying to release animals that they did experiments on. Monkeys. These beagles they used to test medications. It was pretty bad stuff, and he tried to make them stop."

"That doesn't sound so bad."

"He didn't go about it the right way," she said. "The government called them a terrorist organization. Especially after they killed that researcher at the university."

Rex remembered the newspaper article with the bombed-out building.

"He left in the middle of the night after that. I'll never forgive him for leaving. For what it did to her. She told him to go, but he should never have listened to her. He chose to be a hero to beagles over my Victoria. Beagles! She *cried* over that man. Days and days she cried." Grandma paused for a long brittle moment. "We didn't know at the time that you were on the way, and by the time we did, he was long gone. She never told him. She couldn't. He was a fugitive. She had no idea where he was. Then when you were born and she...

"Well, I never told you about him." She was crying now. She put her arm around Rex and squeezed. "Maybe I should have. I'm sorry," she said. "I just can't forgive him for putting her in that situation. Maybe I should have told you sooner. I did the best I could."

The best she could? She had lied to him—for twelve years! How could he forgive that? He needed to swallow his outrage if he wanted information.

"Will you tell me about him now?"

She sighed. "Rex—"

"I need to know, Grandma."

"I'll try, Rex. I'll try." She stood and kissed him. "But I'm tired now and I'm going to bed. Don't stay up too late."

Rex wasn't sure how long he sat on the silent sofa before he, too, went to bed.

The clock blinked. 3:46 AM.

Rex lay across the top of his comforter staring at the full moon outside his window. He had been waiting since dusk for the fur to sprout again and his bones to crackle and pop. Nothing. He just lay there waiting, breathing, as the gentle night sounds drifted through the room and nothing continued to happen.

He wasn't sure what to make of his new… ability. The nearest equivalent he could imagine was a werewolf, but that wasn't right. He'd seen the TV shows and the movies. You became a werewolf when you were bitten by one. After that, you changed on the full moon and ate people. Or at least bit them to make more werewolves. But this was a full moon and nothing. Nothing. Here he was, not changing, and the idea of biting people made his gorge rise. Plus, he had never been bitten by anything remotely like a werewolf, and the view he'd seen in the mirror yesterday was as unun-wolfish as they come.

Was there such a thing as a weredog? Was that what he was? And how did that change things?

He had dared not ask his grandmother. She had said it wasn't for polite company, and she was unfailingly polite.

Since he wasn't sleeping anyway, Rex rose early to make his grandmother's favorite breakfast. Golden corn fritters swam in a lake of fragrant maple syrup beside a small pile of bacon that smelled so amazingly delicious it almost didn't make it to her TV tray in the living room. His grandmother thanked him and then turned her eyes towards George Stephanopoulos and the Good Morning America team. She would answer no questions this morning.

Rex cleaned up the dishes and went to school as usual. Except, he quickly learned, it wasn't quite like usual.

Walking down the hall of Esther S. Potts Middle School was a whole new, terrifying experience. He navigated through the individual cliques of jocks carrying loaded gym bags and geeks with their glasses and stacks of textbooks. He ran the gauntlet of bow-headed girls gossiping together in gaggles throughout the building. He could smell them, each one, flowery in their shampooed hair and lotioned calves. Just ahead he saw Harper, the girl who sat next to him in math class. She was leaning against the row of lockers, chewing watermelon bubble gum and chatting with her best friend Savannah about cheerleading practice. Rex had had a devastating crush on Harper since fifth grade. It was so awful that he was forced to look straight ahead at the blackboard during class for fear that he would be unable to divert his attention from her when the teacher called upon him. He had never spoken to her directly, though he made sure to tell jokes and crack wise with his male friends when he thought she might notice.

Now he was trapped in the hall with his senses screaming her presence to him. *She was right there.* He couldn't avoid her or Savannah, either one. He would need to walk right past the two of them to get to his next class. He hunched his shoulders and tried to minimize the sensory overload by breathing slowly through his mouth. He was afraid if he made contact with Harper—or Savannah, or, for that matter, with *any* one of these girls—if he touched her creamy skin, he might burst forth in a hairy, werewolfy frenzy and hump her right there in the hallway.

By 1:30 he was panting in frustration, trembling with pent-up energy. He left his books in the bottom of his locker and slipped off campus, walking quickly down the worn path into the woods behind the school. Well out of view of any possible watching students or teachers, Rex stopped at a large moss-covered boulder not far off the trail. He was breathing heavily as he sat down to remove his running shoes, socks and tee shirt. He hesitated, looking around again. There was no one to see. The heavy foliage obscured him from casual passersby. Nevertheless, he could not shake his mortification over what he was about to do. He had that hair-on-the-back of-the-neck feeling of being watched.

A chattering erupted above. A squirrel looked down at him from the canopy of the oak overshadowing the boulder. It flicked its tail and chattered again.

"Yeah, yeah, yeah." Rex shook his finger at it. "Laugh it up, fuzzball." He stepped primly behind the stone to remove his jeans, folding them neatly on top of his shoes. He wasn't quite sure what to do next. He braced his feet and concentrated, imagining the hairs rising from the back of his hands, from his thighs as it had the day before. He tried to think of his bones stretching in some directions, shrinking in others, morphing into the unfamiliar anatomy of the dog-shape. He grunted and strained without result.

The squirrel snickered at him once more.

"You're not helping," Rex snarled.

He tried again. And again. And again. He succeeded only in releasing a prodigious fart.

This wasn't working. He needed a new tactic. He brushed the sticks and debris aside and settled himself onto his haunches. He decided if exertion wasn't working, he would try to relax.

He breathed through his nose, noting the earthy smell rising from the forest loam, the decaying leaves and the moist undergrowth. He smelled the squirrel and some other small creatures living nearby. He heard them rustling in the foliage. He heard a tiny buzzing sound nearby and looked around. Maybe it was just his imagination? No. He saw an enormous fat bee exit a small hole in the oak tree and take off on its bumbling flight. He heard the buzzing increase and three more bees followed their sister out of the hole.

Wow. His hearing must be really good.

Rex felt overloaded. He could feel his thoughts swirling through his brain, beating randomly against the sides of his skull like birds caught in a cage. *Relax*, he thought. *Calm down*. Everything was too much. He tried to slow down, but the adrenaline would not let go.

Sometimes, when he had trouble sleeping he would try to direct all his attention to one minute place on his body. The way his heel touched the threads of the sheets. The touch of his little finger on his chest. It almost always relaxed him into slumber. *Might work,* he thought. He began to focus on what was happening in his own body. The wash of air in and out of his lungs. He thought about slowing his heart's agitated beating. He thought about slackening each tightened muscle and finally felt his limbs begin to loosen. He wasn't sure how long it took, but he felt tranquil and comfortable. He felt like he was calmer and… slower somehow. *Languorous*. He'd had that as a vocabulary word once, but that wasn't quite right. He felt more refreshed than tired. He remained very alive to his senses and the feel of his body and limbs. The sensations just didn't beat against him anymore.

Now he could begin to think about the dog he had become the day before. The fur, the shape of limbs and bones and how the muscles fit and connected differently. He felt the exhilarating pain as the change began. He howled once, twice, in concert with the waves of crushing pain as his bones seemed to dissolve and reform, shifting as his body rearranged itself. Then the pain stopped. Just stopped and bled away. He looked down at his paws and back toward his tail waving like a flag. He felt vigorous at a core level. He leaped into the air and twisted in joy. *I did it! I did it!* The squirrel began to shriek in alarm. Rex whipped his head around. *Squirrel!* He put his feet on the oak's trunk and snapped at the damned critter. "Back! Back! Back!" he barked. *You're nothing but a bite-sized, fluffy snack. Laugh at me! Come down here and I'll bite you in half.*

The squirrel declined.

When that game lost its interest, Rex took off at a run, racing through the trees, chasing small forest creatures and delighting in the feel of his long fur blowing in a wind of his own creation. It was glorious to think only about this moment, to turn off his responsibilities to his grandmother, his schoolwork. He could just be.

His senses were crowding him again, overloading his mind. The wind rushing past, filling his nose with every scent on the wind. It brought him to a level of awareness he had never reached in his human self.

He knew what Mrs. Anderson was cooking for dinner that night from the distance of several city blocks. Roast beef, slow cooked with carrots, potatoes, onions and celery. Light on the garlic, heavy with pepper. The Patels were cooking something exotic with spices imported from their Indian homeland. Mr. Miller, a few streets south, was passing fish sticks and raw broccoli around to his three boys.

Rex's hearing was better than it had been when he was fully human, too. He was able to identify conversations from behind the closed doors of the houses as he loped past, and a housewife calling her kids in for lunch three blocks over.

Even his visual acuity and focus were off the charts. The colors were different, but he could make out the individual hairs on the backs of those bees, and see the ants crawling among the leaves on the path he followed.

He slowed as he reached Victory Park where he installed himself on the hill overlooking the reflecting pool. He allowed his senses to wash over him as he tracked the confluence of people, squirrels, ducks. Those little brown birds that stayed all winter. He surveyed them all as if it was his life's purpose.

Though it was early afternoon on a weekday, the park was full of people, mostly young parents with children playing on the slides and swings and hanging bars. A handful of workers were finishing their bag lunches on the park benches along the paved walkways. Two turkey sandwiches, a peanut butter and jelly with carrot sticks and a salad with… ranch dressing. Wait. Lite ranch.

Ahead of him, a little girl—maybe three—wandered away from her mother who sat oblivious, chatting up a shirtless Don Juan who shared her seat. Rex stood, transfixed. A tingle of unease pricked the hairs on his ruff. The child toddled over to the low concrete wall that enclosed the pool and peered over the top. She rose up on her toes several times, before climbing onto the ledge. *Uh, oh. Not good.* She tottered momentarily then reached toward the paddling ducks. Rex rose to his four paws. *The girl,* Rex thought. *Lady. Your girl!* She couldn't hear him. And even if she could, he could not seem the necessary human words from his entirely canine throat.

That little girl was going to fall into the lake and no one was trying to save her! Almost of its own volition, his body launched into action. Rex lowered himself to a crouch and raced in an abbreviated arc, curving around to get behind the girl. He sped towards her and leaped on the ledge behind her. Carefully, gently, he nipped at her side driving her back off the ledge and away from the lake. The startled girl shrieked and ran into her mother's arms. *There. Mission accomplished,* he thought. *Now stay with your mom, kid.*

As Rex approached, wagging proudly, Don Juan rose and took a defensive posture in front of the pair. Rex skidded to a stop, panting with his ears pricked and his mouth wide open. The man wasn't at all thankful for Rex's help. In fact, he didn't even seem chagrined at having distracted the mom so much that she lost track of the child. "Watch out," the man warned the woman behind him. "He might be rabid."

*Rabid? What?* He clearly had misunderstood Rex's intentions. He was helping the girl. Saving her.

The man picked up a large stick and swung it like a baseball bat. Rex retreated a few paces and the man advanced, stomping, darting forward and brandishing the limb. "Call the police. Call the dog catcher. Get somebody out here with a gun. Right now."

*Wait. What?! A gun! This jerk thinks I'm really a dog. A Bad Dog.* The idea surprised him. When he had accepted the reality of his new condition, he thought of it more as a lark. An adventure. He never really considered how the world would react to him as a dog. Turns out, it was not so great. Rex had no way to explain, of course, and anyway, who would believe him if he could? And now he could end up in the pound... or worse. He could change back into his man-shape, maybe. He hoped he could anyway. But his clothes were still stashed in the woods next to that tree. He'd be butt-naked in front of the whole world. It would be far less mortifying to go animal control. *Crap. This is bad. What will happen to Grandma if I'm taken? She's too frail to get by without me. I need to get out of here right now.*

Rex looked again at the man. His face was florid and he was screaming about the police and shooting, and he was waving his makeshift weapon like some sort of cut-rate fencer.

The man advanced until the branch stabbed within inches of Rex's right eye. He felt his ears lie flat against his skull and his upper lip curl. *Great. That's gonna help calm things down,* he thought. Rex turned, tucked tail and ran. As he darted towards the woods and cover, the limb struck him in the hindquarters. Hard. He rolled and kept running, limping now.

The shouts faded as he reached the woods. He found a thorny thicket and crawled under to wait out the uproar. His breathing was rapid and panting. How could that man have misunderstood Rex so badly? No one had ever treated him that way. He didn't know how to react. *Guess I'll have to be a lot more careful about who and how I get involved in the future. Some people just don't deserve helping.*

Crunching on the gravel path and jingling. One of Kyleighburn's finest, Officer Tim Granger, jogged up the trail, his head swiveling right and left. The tools on his belt clinked with each heavy footstep, all except the handgun which was held silent by his hand on the butt. Rex had always thought Officer Granger's presence was a little intimidating. Now it was more than little. Just what he needed. This afternoon was certainly not going as he had expected. Rex's mouth pulled back in a rictus of fear. Every muscle seemed tight as a guitar string. He needed to calm down.

Rex tried the relaxation techniques he had employed earlier in the day. Breathe in. Breathe out. Breathe in. Breathe out. He lay there attempting invisibility, for hours it seemed, as the dusk drew close around the little stand of trees.

Time to get home. Grandma must be wondering where he was, and what about her dinner. Rex crept from under the bushes and worked his way back through the woods. Where he could, he avoided contact with any people who may be searching for a potentially rabid border collie. When he was forced to cross trails frequented by the joggers and mountain bikers, he did so quickly, slinking from undergrowth on one side of the path to the cover on the other side. Eventually he made his way to the part of the park where he had left the moss-covered boulder and his neatly folded clothes.

He crouched low, ready to spring up at the first hint of any intruder larger than that squirrel-with-a-death-wish who had taunted him what seemed like days ago. Again he followed his relaxation technique. He seemed to be improving, as he was soon rewarded with a noticeable slackening of the muscles in his back and legs.

His change was slower though. As he attempted to force the metamorphosis, his stress-exhausted mind refused to comply. He could feel the bones of his long face and snout melting back into the rounded shape of the human skull. He could watch the lengthening of his paws as the short toes stretched into the longer, slender bones of human hands and feet. But his legs and torso refused to budge. His pelvis and rear legs maintained the dog proportions, better for crouching and springing. Not so good for standing. It left the weight of his chest pressing entirely on his fingers. The stress on his newly restored hands was heavy. His mind flashed to a picture of a gorilla walking, long arms supporting the massive animal on fingers curled into fists. He tried that. It helped a bit.

What if he was stuck this way? He'd have to get a job as the Dog-Boy in a freak show. His heart began to race again as he imagined having to go to school with black and white dog hair sprouting all over his body. He could shave probably. But how fast would it grow back? He'd probably have a five o'clock shadow. All over his body. By noon! The annual cost of razor blades would be astronomical. He'd have to get an after-school job.

He howled. He thought he was a monster before. That guy in the park certainly thought so. But life in this half-state would hardly be worth living.

*Stop panicking. Relax.* He tried the calming breathing again. He focused on his chin resting on his front paw/hands. He put all his attention there.

When he woke, it was cool and the evening shadows had lengthened. He was naked, but fully human. He put on his jeans and shirt, his shoes and socks. Never had he been so grateful for shoelaces.

When he reached his home, he hurried to brush the leaves and sticks from his hair and clean himself up, then rushed to the kitchen to get dinner ready. A book sat on the table at his place. *The What's Happening to My Body Book for Boys.* As he sautéed several chickens, he leafed through the book and found nothing about dogs. Great. Completely useless. As if he couldn't check that piece of junk out of the library himself.

The incident in the park proved one thing to Rex: he needed to have better control. He began going to the park regularly to practice what he thought of as The Change. His speed increased in inverse proportion to the pain as his bones shifted under his muscles. He didn't have to concentrate as much anymore. It left more mental capacity to consider the information that now flooded his senses, to resist the pull of his instincts to herd the children who ran around the playground or to chase those damned squirrels that were literally everywhere.

Eventually his canine form became second nature. He found exhilaration in the flood of sensory experiences and the smooth functioning of muscle and bone. Even the wind blowing through the silky hair of his ears and his ruff was a thrill. It became his regular routine to effect a quick change and head to the park for an afternoon of joyous exuberance.

One sunny Thursday afternoon, when school had let out early for a teacher work day, Rex decided the day was perfect for a run. Rex trotted down the path away from the oak where he had taken to changing during the three years since he had begun his adventures in dog Skin. He headed towards his favorite hill in the park where he often sat to watch the people.

Ahead, he heard voices raised. Rex crouched and crept up to the bushes that separated him from the disturbance. Two people stopped along a path in a quiet part of the landscaped garden. Rex peered through the branches and recognized Harper and Jake.

Jake was a senior on the Varsity football team. He was a better than average quarterback, but he was a 100% first-class jerk. He had dated and spectacularly dumped nearly every girl on the cheerleading team, and now it seemed it was Harper's turn. Rex knew he slept with every girl he dated, or at least he'd told all his friends he had while he was changing in the locker room after gym. Why did girls always fall for jerks like that? Sure, he drove last year's Porsche. Sure, he was tall and had wavy dark hair and the plastic good looks that seemed to be the birthright of the offspring of the well-to-do. But show a girl respect? He wasn't capable. Yet Jake had a date every Saturday night while Rex sat home cooking dinner for his grandmother and watching reality shows on TV. It just wasn't fair

Rex had admired Harper from afar all through middle and high school When he passed her in the hallways, he could not help but inhale deeply, pulling her scent in through his nose and deep into his lungs. Then he would hold that breath as he wished he could hold her. Once, in his sophomore year, he had finally worked up his courage to speak to her. After much planning and practice he approached her after English class, opening his mouth to utter a studied "Hi," as casual as he could muster. But at just that moment his mouth grew dry and the sound that emitted from his parched vocal chords was nothing more than a croak. Like a toad with a mouthful of sawdust. It was pathetic. Harper looked up at him for the briefest moment, startled by the offending noise, then returned to her conversation with her friend Savannah. He could never bring himself to actually talk to her again after that.

Of course, Jake didn't have that problem.

There was no justice.

Jake loomed over petite Harper. He was standing too close to her and had begun screaming into her face.

"Why were you talking to him?"

"I wasn't!" Harper tried to step back but Jake grabbed her arms. He shook her and even at this distance Rex thought he could hear her teeth clattering.

Rex growled. Every muscle in his body tightened as his brain fought for control of his impulses. He wanted to intervene. He needed to. But what if the same thing happened as had when he tried to help the little girl at the pond? What if the dog catcher was called. Or the police? What if Jake had a weapon? Who would take care of Grandma Bailey then?

"You are my girl. MINE! You don't talk to him. You don't look at him." He shook her again and her head snapped back and forth.

"I don't. I love *you*."

"Don't give me that. I saw what you did."

Rex imagined sinking his teeth into the back of Jake' thigh and pulling him off Harper. He could almost taste the sour taste of Jake's blood as he broke the skin. No. Stop. He dare not take the chance. He had a responsibility at home. Maybe Jake would stop before—

"Jake, stop it. I love you! I've never even looked at anyone else."

"LIAR!" His fist crashed into her temple. Her head snapped back and she fell limp to the sidewalk like a marionette cut from its strings.

Jake stood over Harper for a moment, a look of disgust on his face. Then he stalked briskly away without another backward glance.

Rex raced to her side. He snuffled at her neck and licked the blood from her face. He could smell her breath, colored with a recent blast of peppermint breath spray. She was alive but unconscious. He should have run to her. He should have come teeth bared and ears back, ready to rip that Jake apart. Now look.

Rex whined at her. He tried barking, three crisp woofs.

She didn't wake. He howled, long and plaintively. Nothing.

He ran to the parking area at the head of the trail, barking frantically. A man turned and looked at him, eyes wide. He didn't come help though, only quickly packed his belongings in the back of a Jeep. *Have you never seen a single episode of Lassie, dude?* Maybe he needed a less subtle hint. Rex ran closer barking and reaching for the hem of the man's pants. The man made a feint towards Rex as if to kick him. Then he leaped into his car and pulled out, nearly striking Rex with the rear quarter panel.

*Hey! Dude!* Rex watched him go. The parking lot was empty. Even Jake had left. Rex put his nose to the ground and inhaled in a series of short huffs. He could smell where Jake had gotten into a car and the direction the rubber tires took as he drove away.

Rex went back to Harper. *What should I do? What* can *I do?* he thought. His clothes were off in the woods half a mile away. He couldn't change back to his human form without them and he couldn't leave her alone to go back for them. Not while she was still insensible and unprotected. What good was a superpower when you couldn't use it to help people?

He lay down beside Harper, licking her hand and her face. He wasn't whether sure the licking would help revive her, but Rex kept at it anyway. The salt of her skin, mingled with a rose scented lotion, tasted exquisite on his tongue. Even better, after he had washed all the lotion away, he was left with just the Harper-taste. Finally after what seemed like hours, forever, Harper moaned and began to move her arms and feet.

Rex whined, and her eyes opened, focused on his face. "What? Who are you? Do I know you?" She touched his ruff, the side of his face. He licked her again and she opened her eyes. "I'm OK." she said. Her voice was weak. "Timmy didn't fall down the well." She sat up holding her head gently in both hands. "At least not this time. Come here, boy." She twined her hands in Rex's fur and pulled. Rex planted his feet to give her leverage to help her stand. When she stopped swaying, he began walking down the trail back towards the parking lot. She followed slowly, placing each foot carefully, and holding her head as if afraid it would fall off and roll away.

"What now?" she said as she exited the trail head into the gravel parking lot. "My purse is in Jake's car along with my cell." She ground out a groan. Frustration mixed with pain. "I guess I have to walk."

Rex couldn't let her do that. She could barely stand as it was. He took Harper's hand gently in his mouth and pulled her towards the emergency call box next to the wooden bulletin board where the trail map and city announcements were posted. He barked twice.

Harper looked down at Rex. "Wow," she said. "Really? Aren't you the smart one." She patted him on the head. "Good boy." She lifted the phone and dialed, speaking briefly to the operator on the other end. Then she sat on the ground at the base of the sign to wait for the police. Rex sat at her side and offered her the comfort of his fur. She stroked him until the black and white cruiser pulled up.

The officer stepped out of the car and adjusted his belt. Something about the way he paused when he made eye contact made Rex wary. A nervous man with a gun was something to take care with. He'd done what he could to help Harper. Time to leave it to the police officer. Of course he would probably get all the thanks. She wouldn't even know Rex had been there in her moment of need.

Rex moved a few steps away and sat as the cop pulled out his notebook and a Bic pen out of his pocket. "What happened here?" the man asked. "Someone hit you?"

"No," she said. "I just… fell."

Rex cocked his head to the side. *Fell? Why would she say that?*

The officer gently checked the goose egg on her temple. He seemed not to believe her statement either. She was protecting Jake. The guy who hit her. He asked her several more questions. Different versions of the same thing.

As he watched her lie to the officer Rex realized that he didn't admire Harper nearly as much as he used to.

He turned and left her in dismay. He'd done all he could do.

Rex walked slowly, head down, following a little deer trail that angled deep into the woods. He didn't really care where he went as long as it was away from people. He was disappointed, with people in general and with Harper Gentry in particular.

No. Not disappointed. He was angry and confused.

He would have helped her against Jake. He would have stood up for her, championed her. But she wouldn't even stand up for herself. She preferred to have *him*—his lip curled at the thought of that utter…ass—as a boyfriend than someone who would truly love her. Did she not understand how wonderful she was? How any man would be lucky to have her? Yet she *lied for him!* Why would she do that?

And how could Rex love a girl who valued herself so little?

She was beautiful but weak at the core. A rose with a center that was eaten away by bugs. She wasn't worth saving. She would just throw his love away like it was trash.

Rex walked for miles, feeling the angst of lost love. Feeling the utter betrayal of a young man who innocently believed that when you offered aid and comfort the recipient would be grateful. That there was some justice in the world. He was a fool.

The sky was darkening to a dusky blue when Rex came upon the river. The Tottie flowed brightly over the boulders in the middle of the river, frothing and foaming through the rocks and stones along the bank. The soft smell of the water underlay the tannic acidity of the fallen leaves trapped among the branches of the trees overhanging the water. It was peaceful in a brooding sort of way. Perfect for Rex's mood.

There was a large flat-topped granite boulder half buried in the sand on the bank. Rex lay down on it and soaked in the residual warmth from the afternoon sun. He hung his head over the edge and stared at the water below, watching the minnows and a late season damselfly buzzing the surface.

Bark! Bark! Bark!

The sound came from behind him, startling him from his moping.

Bark! Bark! Bark!

Rex turned to find The Mayor standing stiff-legged and waving his thick tail.

The Mayor was a stub-legged, scruffy terrier that had lived in Kyleighburn longer than Rex himself had. Everyone called him The Mayor. He usually hung out on Main Street, accepting petting from passers-by and plates of food from area businesses. When new families moved to town, he usually popped round to the house to slip inside and approve the new residents. The remainder of his time was spent greeting tourists and having his picture taken with them. In fact he seemed to love having his picture taken, and photobombed nearly every newsworthy event from the groundbreaking of the new Walgreens (first major drugstore to come to Kyleighburn), to the burning of the old grange hall. Rex could still recall laughing at the scandalous photo of the induction ceremony of Marino Esposito as the elected mayor (lowercase) of Kyleighburn. In the front-page photo, The Mayor (always written in uppercase) was captured raising his leg on the podium as Esposito raised his hand to take the oath. Rumor had it that Esposito still hadn't forgiven the dog and that his recent push for a city-wide leash law was the result.

The Mayor barked again.

*Fine.* Rex stood and barked back. With every dogly gesture, he tried to convey "Leave me alone."

The Mayor bounced a couple of times and made a play-bow. Three more barks, a tight spin, and The Mayor dashed a couple of yards down the path Rex had followed in.

Rex turned back towards the river.

More barking. Rex wagged his tail in half-hearted acknowledgement.

He heard The Mayor's approaching steps mere moments before he felt a hard tug on his tail.

*Hey!* He yipped in startlement.

The Mayor did the spin-and-dash-down-the-path thing again. Rex turned his head away.

The Mayor was not giving up. Nip. Spin, race, return.

A tickle of a thought rose past Rex's funk until it became an easily understandable thought. *Timmy's down the well.* Great. Someone needed him. Hopefully this person will appreciate his efforts.

Rex sighed. *Alright. Mr. Mayor. Lead the way.*

Once The Mayor was sure Rex followed, he picked up speed and began to sprint along the riverside. Rex followed the grizzled dog, using his stiff tail as a rudder to manage the hard turns on the river trail. It didn't take long to reach the other dog's apparent destination, the bridge over the Tottie River. He skidded to a stop at the base of the narrow shoulder spanning the structure.

At the highest point in the arc, where the drop to water was at its dizzying farthest, a beat-up Ford pickup was stopped, its emergency lights flashing. There didn't seem to be any activity from the truck, but Rex could see a man sitting sideways in the driver's seat, the door open. His feet were planted firmly on the pavement. Just sitting, not doing anything. He didn't seem to be concerned about his vehicle being broken down. The tires were all standing, so he hadn't had a flat. He just sat there like he couldn't decide whether to get out or to step back in and drive away.

The Mayor looked at Rex, barked again and pointed his nose towards the truck.

At the second repeat, Rex got it. *Go check it out. Right.*

He approached the ancient Ford. The driver's front quarter panel had been inexpertly painted—with a brush, it appeared—in a color that succeed in not quite matching the dull blue of the rest of the vehicle. The curve along the rear tire was rusted through and had been sanded prior to the brushwork.

The driver was dressed in a pair of comfortably distressed jeans, ragged around the hem. Not the fashionable, purposely ripped jeans. These were the kind of jeans a man had worn for years and wouldn't let his woman toss out. Over this he had on a long-sleeved red-and-blue plaid flannel shirt, buttoned up at the sleeves and neck. Flannel notwithstanding, the wearer seemed to be some species of sasquatch. His long black hair was uncombed, sticking up as if it he had run his long fingers through it repeatedly. The hair sort of lost its independence as it entangled itself in the man's equally unkempt beard. There were a couple of thin braids mixed in there, but they too were scraggly, and one had come partially undone, standing at right angles to the rest of the pelt.

Rex sat at the tips of the man's square-toed boots and looked up at his face. A stranger. Rex had never seen him in Kyleighburn before. Not like he knew everyone. But this guy smelled of a nomadic lifestyle, open roads and diesel fuel and places faraway. And overlaying all of that was the more immediate scent of lots and lots of alcohol.

Under the shoulder-length hair he wore a nose ring and a silver stud peeped through his hairy lower lip. Heavy brows gave him a rough, intimidating appearance, but, from what Rex could see, his blue eyes were glassy and puffy. Rex guessed he'd been crying for quite some time.

Rex sat patiently, waiting for the man to acknowledge him. Clearly distraught, the man did not raise his head or move in any way. His arms were wrapped tightly around his chest. He barely breathed.

Rex wished there was something he could do. There weren't many options.

After several minutes Rex moved closer, sitting down directly beside the man to lean his warm body against the stranger's leg and lay his chin on the man's knee. He sighed gently.

A tattooed hand reached down to stroke Rex's silky fur. DRV4 it said. Whatever that meant.

The stroking continued for what seemed like forever. Barely making contact. Just silently gliding over the hair on the back of Rex's neck and shoulders. Softly, absently, as the man breathed in and out.

Then suddenly there was a hitch and a sharp sob. The hand clenched in Rex's ruff. "Mary!' he screamed. "Mary! Why?" The man shuddered and doubled over, falling to his knees.

*What should I do?* In his dog Skin, there wasn't much he could do to console the guy. Just be there, that was all. He couldn't shift back to human. It would be even harder to console the man after magically changing into a naked teenaged boy right in front of him. It would probably drive him out of what's left of his mind. On the other hand, after all the screaming and terror, he probably wouldn't be feeling sorry for himself anymore.

Now the man began rocking and cursing. "Why did you take her from me?" he implored. "What did I do to deserve this? I can't live without her." The tears ran down his cheeks and were lost in his beard.

Rex felt sure that man could use a hug, but that wasn't really an activity dogs performed well. The best he could do was to shove his long nose under the man's arm so that it draped around Rex's neck. Sure enough, the man turned toward him, pressed his face into Rex's fur and squeezed.

Soon the wracking sobs slowed to sniffles. "Thanks," he said, then the man began to talk. "I loved her." The yelling and swearing had modulated to a whisper. "She was my everything. She was going to have a baby in a few months and I wanted to do it right, you know?" He rubbed his eyes on his sleeve. "Now look. If only I hadn't insisted on going out to dinner that night. If only…" He stifled another sob and tried to recover with a weak smile. "We took the long way 'round, so we could drive along the river. I wanted it to be all romantic. I was going to propose over dinner."

Here was a long silence. He pulled a ring out of his pocket and turned it over and over in his fingers. "This was the ring I got her. Had it engraved and everything. 'Joe & Mary. Forever.' See? She didn't want it, though. 'No, Joe. Save the money for the baby,' she said. But I wanted to do it right."

There was another long break of silence. When he started talking again his voice broke. "I didn't listen and that's how I killed her. She didn't want a ring or a fancy dinner. But I had to do it the right way. And as we drove by the river to this fancy dinner she didn't want, with a ring in my pocket that she didn't want, I reached out to take her hand. And I musta looked at her. I can remember her smiling at me. She was so beautiful… All I could think about was how our baby would be beautiful just like her momma…." His voice trailed off and he smiled a bit to himself then. "And as we go 'round this little curve…. there was this truck… coming. A big ass truck, taking up the whole road like it was playing god damn chicken. And I had her hand so I couldn't steer well. And…

It was several minutes before he spoke again.

"And we ended up in the ditch. I woke up and I was still holding her hand. But she was gone. Her eyes were open and there was blood. So much blood!!

And her looking at me all wide and pleading. Asking why I killed her." He wiped his nose.

*You didn't kill her*! Rex wanted to shout. *You didn't! It was an accident.* But his dog Skin prevented him from communicating.

"She was everything." He whispered it. "And now I'm nothing."

*No. Not nothing, Joe. You have something worth living for. I'm sure of it.*

The man seemed to have taken on a preternatural calm. He stood. He brushed the gravel off the knees of his jeans. He patted Rex on the head. Thump. Thump. Thump. "Thanks for listening, man."

Joe walked casually toward to the railing as if he was striding across a room to meet an old friend. He stood on his toes and peered over at the roaring Tottie River thirty feet below.

*No! No!* Bark-bark-bark! Rex bit down on the hem of the man's jeans and pulled with everything he had.

The man climbed back down and stooped to take Rex's face in his hands. "No. It's OK, man. I know what you're trying to do. And it's OK. Don't worry 'bout me."

Rex sat down relieved. Joe began to rub Rex's cheeks, to smooth the fur over his eyes and forehead. Kindly. Gently.

"I'm fine. Really." He stood up and met Rex's worried gaze. "Alright?" he asked. Rex woofed softly.

"Alright then. Seriously. Thanks. You're a good boy." And without a backward glance, he stepped on the lower rail of the barrier and vaulted over the side.

*Wait! Wait! But—*. He had said he was fine. Rex ran to the railing and pushed his head through the bars. There was no sign of the man. No bobbing head. No plaid shirt floating downstream. But at least he didn't see Joe's broken body on the rocks below. *Where is he? Where did he go?*

*Shoot.*

Rex raced across the bridge to the embankment below sniffing the air for clues. Had the man come up for air? He might have done that while Rex was making his way to the shore. But there was nothing. Footprints on the shoreline? No. Where was he? He ran along the bank searching, stopping every so often to peer at the bank on the other side. It was a long way off. Rex was pretty sure if the man had made it to the other bank, between the distance and the rocky, shrub-lined shore, he wouldn't be able to see him from this side.

The pounding of his feet matched the panicked thumping of his heart as he ran downstream for what seemed like forever. Probably more like three or four minutes. No smell, no tracks. Nothing. Should he swim across? It would be a long and dangerous swim. And what if Joe wasn't washed that direction? Rex would be wasting critical time. Maybe run back across the bridge?

He looked up and down the length of the river, indecisive. *Go back upstream?*

*Keep looking downriver? What should I do?*

*Wait. What's that?* There was a bit of red snagged among the branches of a deadfall trapped in the swirling eddies among the boulders. Could be some sort of berries. No. The shape of the scrap of color was too regular to be natural. It could be the red-and-blue plaid shirt. Maybe. Rex whined and shifted nervously from foot to foot.

He'd never be able to extract the man—or the man's body—from the twisted branches. Not in his dog Skin.

There was no hope for it.

He looked around. Was there anyone nearby? If there was, this could get embarrassing fast. There were no voices. No crunch of gravel underfoot. Only the leaves rattled in the trees—a storm was blowing in this evening—but no people. The coast was clear.

Slowly he began. Changing was still a new process and he couldn't take the chance he might do it wrong. Step by step. Part by part. That was the way to go. Anatomy was not his strong suit. If he didn't pay attention he might come out of the change with his pancreas where his liver should be. He guessed that could be bad but he wasn't really sure.

*The knee bone's connected to the thigh bone. The thigh bone's connected to the... whatever that is.* So it went as the bones melted and realigned. Finally.

He was altogether—in his altogether. He hoped no one came along to see him wading naked into the river. The breeze sent a shiver up his naked backside.

But there was no time for delay or modesty. He waded into the froth, his feet slipping over the slimy rocks as he worked his way to the deadfall. The water was cold, frigid, having worked its way down from the mountains covered with early snow. It made Rex hold his breath as his body acclimated to the wintry chill. When the bank suddenly dropped off and dunked Rex under the surface the shock of it forced him to inhale. He came up spluttering and spitting out a mouthful of the stuff.

But he must not drown. He had a mission.

As he reached the mass of sticks and twigs, he saw the man. Mercifully, his head was above water, held aloft by his left arm woven over, under and through a snarl of limbs. The hand seemed twisted funny. He'd be lucky if that arm wasn't broken in at least three places. But then again it might not be an issue. The man wasn't moving.

Rex swam over and quickly learned how impossible it is to tread water while attempting to lift a 200-pound man off a bunch of driftwood. With no floor for leverage, all he succeeded in doing was shoving his own head under water repeatedly. He finally managed to work one leg over the largest limb so that he was semi-astride the mass, but he cursed aloud as his weight forced the limb to sink, carrying with it Joe's head. Rex grabbed his long hair in one hand and yanked his head above water while he broke off the sticks and twigs that trapped him there.

One by one the impediments fell away. It was exhausting. If he hadn't been cold and wet, Rex would have been soaked with sweat.

*This is taking too long,* he thought. *If it's possible to save him I need to be getting this finished.* "Ugh. I hate to do this," he said to the corpse-cold body. "Sorry, dude." He grabbed the twisted arm and felt the unnatural grinding and popping under the muscles as he bent the limb to free it from the deadfall. Plop! The arm fell free into the water and Joe's limp body began floating down stream again, arrested only by Rex's death grip on his hair.

Rex untangled himself and began kicking hard towards shore. The current fought him and carried them farther down river. Rex struggled against the flow until he could feel his feet touch the algae-covered riverbed again.

He dragged Joe onto the bank, rolled him over and thumped him hard on the back several times. He wasn't sure if this was the right thing to do for a lungful of river water. Maybe it wasn't because it didn't seem to do any good.

Rex had had a CPR class in Mr. Johnson's health class two years ago. It had been pretty much of a joke at the time. Rex and the other kids in his class made all the requisite schoolboy jests about French kissing the dummies. They asked the pretty girls to allow them to practice the two quick breaths part on them. Now he wished he had paid better attention in the class.

*Step 1. Shake and wake.* He grabbed Joe by the collar of his plaid shirt. "Wake up, Joe. Come on. Wake up, dammit!" The man's head lolled back like he was dead.

*Step 2. Call 911.* Well, there was no phone around. Nobody to help him. Alright, seemed unlikely, but, "Help! Help! Somebody help me."

*Step 3. Check for pulse.* No breathing. Nope. No pulse. Damn.

*Oh shit, oh damn.* Rex thought. He was really going to have to do this. How many times was he supposed to do the compressions? Twenty? Twenty-five? No. Thirty seemed right. He knelt by Joe's side and lined his clasped hands over the man's breast bone. Was that the right placement? One, two, three, four… he counted in his head. He'd have to do the breathing part next. *I wish it could be Harper I have to give mouth-to-mouth to,* he thought. *But no. Instead here's this hairy man I only just met. God apparently didn't love either of them. Figures. Oh no.*

He'd lost count. If Joe wasn't dead already Rex was likely to kill him because he couldn't keep his mind off a girl. A girl that earlier he had decided he didn't even respect.

He picked a random, reasonable-sounding number and started counting again—out loud this time. Twenty-three. It was something like that. Twenty-four, twenty-five, twenty-six, twenty-seven.

"Alright, dude. Twenty-eight." He said between exertions. "You seem a nice enough fellow. Twenty-nine. But don't get any ideas. Thirty. This means nothing."

He stopped counting. Deep inhale. He pinched Joe's nose closed and sealed his mouth over the prone man's lips. The bristles of his beard and moustache pricked Rex's lips unpleasantly as he blew twice into his lungs. *Yuck. Did women like this? Surely not.* As he resumed doing the chest compressions, he could still feel the tingling from the scratchy hair against his lips. It bothered him enough that he briefly rubbed his lips with the back of one hand between compressions. His own youthful facial hair was still pretty thin and patchy yet, but he made a mental note to shave regularly anyway.

Twenty-eight, twenty-nine, thirty. He readied himself. Deep inhale. He bent over Joe and began blowing.

"EWWW!"

Rex nearly swallowed his exhale. *Dammit!*

"Rex! What are you doing, you perv?" It was Savannah, Harper's friend. She stood frozen beside her bicycle. Her brows were pulled down at a disapproving angle, a look of distaste on her face. Her free hand clutched at her throat.

Rex went back to compressions. "One. Call. An. Ambulance. Seven. Drowning. Victim. Twelve. Male. Fourteen, fifteen, sixteen, seventeen."

"But why are you *nekkid*?"

Rex shouted with all the authority a bare-assed boy could muster. "Savannah, Move! Twenty-one. NOW!"

That seemed to activate her. She jumped onto the bike and pedaled down the path like her life depended on it. It didn't, but Joe's might.

His count having reached thirty, Rex blew the two prescribed breaths before starting the cycle over again. And again. And again. It seemed to go on forever. Where is that ambulance? Surely Savannah called them. She wouldn't just leave him like this. Would she?

*This is hard work,* he thought. *So exhausting.* It surprised him a little how strenuous the compressions were. Despite the chill from the icy swim, he was perspiring. Stinging sweat flowed down his forehead in rivulets into his eyes. He could feel it running down his back and see it on his arms. The clammy moisture cooled him a bit, but did little to energize him. *How much longer can I keep this up?*

*As long as I have to,* he resolved, but even as he thought it, he knew he was coming to the end of what he could do. "Come on, Joe. Help me out here."

He'd lost track of how many reps he'd done. Enough so his lips were raw from the scratchy beard and moustache. He wanted desperately to pause for just a minute, but he was afraid of losing momentum. If he stopped, if he gave in to exhaustion, he may not be able to start again.

He could feel each stroke of the compression coming slower and slower. *Don't do this Joe. You do have something to live for. I know it. Come back. Do. Not. Go.*

Rex was struggling to get in a few more strokes. Joe had given up. It looked like Savannah had abandoned him. What was the point? He was done. He had nothing left. *Dammit, Joe. If you can't be bothered to breathe, don't expect me to do it for you.* Twenty-eight… Twenty-nine…

"Ef you, Joe." Thirty. With the last of his energy he rose up onto his knees lifting his clenched hands above his head. With everything he had left he slammed his hands down onto Joe's sternum. *Pow!*

A giant gurgle of fetid water erupted from the man's mouth and nose. He convulsed and made horrible gagging noises.

Rex rolled him onto his side, thumping him hard on the back to try to expel any remaining water. *Oh, God. Oh, thank God.* "Are you OK, Mister? Joe? Can you hear me?" He'd been out for a long time. Rex had no idea how long, but minutes. Bunches of minutes. How long before brain damage sets in?

"Can you hear me, Joe?" he asked again.

Joe spluttered, horrible racking coughs and gasps as he tried to inhale past the remaining water in his lungs. It was almost physically painful for Rex to hear, but it made him joyful, nonetheless.

Finally, after what an interminable wait, Joe nodded past the wheezes.

"Thanks," he managed after several more stress-filled moments.

"You scared me." Rex could feel a big cheesy grin rise past his exhaustion. He'd never been so relieved in his life. He sat back on his heels, arms hanging limply from his weary shoulders. "I thought you were gonna die."

"What happened? Ahhh. My head hurts." He lifted his hand to the gash on his temple. It had begun to bleed again.

"You have a nasty bump there. It's probably gonna leave a wicked scar. You must have hit your head on the rocks when you jumped."

"Jumped? I jumped?"

"Off the bridge." Rex cocked his head to the side. "Don't you remember?"

Joe shook his head and moaned. "No,"

"You were talking about Mary and you were really sad. And then…. I couldn't stop you."

"Mary?"

"Your fiancée. You don't remember?"

"Uhnn."

Rex caught the edge of a sound heading their way. Was that—? He thought he heard—yes!—the ambulance siren. *Yeah. Now you come. Great timing, guys.* At least Savannah had come through. He'd have to thank her when he saw her in school the next day. And, of course, he would have to have a story to explain why he was "nekkid" beside the river with his lips on a strange man.

"Well, listen," Rex said quickly. "I gotta go. I don't think I can help you anymore, and I gotta get home to take care of my grandma. The ambulance is on its way, OK? Just wait here. OK? Joe?"

Joe nodded. He seemed to be still out of it. Good. Then maybe he wouldn't see Rex as he made his change. "And Joe, remember something. You got lots of reasons to live."

Joe looked at Rex as if he'd never seen a completely nude youth standing in the middle of a forest before. "I'm glad you were here. I think you risked your life to save mine."

"Well, I had to." Rex shrugged. "I just can't stand by and do nothin' when someone needs help."

"I did need it. Thanks, man." Joe stuck his right hand out to shake. As Rex took his hand, he saw the tattoo on the knuckles. LIFE it read.

"Alright then," Rex stood. "I'll make sure the paramedics find you. I hope things are better for you." He stepped a few paces away, behind a jumble of boulders and brush.

Moments later a smiling border collie rushed past the still coughing Joe towards the oncoming ambulance.

# Suspicion

Susan Turley

I THINK THEY'RE TRYING TO KILL ME. At least five of them, all over my dwelling, looking innocent and normal.

I can't prove anything, not yet, at least. I don't want to make them aware that I'm suspicious. You may think I'm hysterical, paranoid, foolish.

I walk into a room and find them lurking, just waiting for me to come close enough for their attack.

But listen, Hope. You have to believe me! They have their places, one in the kitchen, two in the bathroom. The one in the living room is the least dangerous—it's caged but could still manage to trip me. The Persian in my bedroom, though, that's the real killer. There are others but they aren't quite as menacing. I so rarely enter the other two bedrooms, the half bath or the dining room, so those five don't get much of a chance to try anything.

You're still not listening. I know you think I'm crazy. Follow me, then, and I'll show you.

Walk across the kitchen and stand at the sink. Do you feel that? Try turning to your left, as if you're ready to chop something. Didn't you almost trip just then? No?

Fine, let's move on to the bathroom. Right there beside the tub. I know you felt your foot slide just a little. Can't you see the danger I'm in? Stand in front of the lavatory now as if you were washing your hands. See what happens as you turn to dry them. Almost got you then.

As I said, the little Persian in the bedroom is the most dangerous. It's sneakier than the others. It slithers and slides across the floor.

I knew you'd take their side. Everyone does, since The Mind. For 40 years, people have said I was crazy; even those who heard the voice in their head then pretend it never happened to them, but they try to say I'm crazy. You want to make me look crazy; you want to let them win. I should take them all out and burn them. The blue one in the kitchen and its twin at the lavatory. The black one by the tub. The big cream one trapped by the coffee table.

And the most dangerous one of all. The silky little gray and brown Persian by my bed, a different color from all the rest but willing to slide and slither and menace. And one day, one of them will kill me.

**June 17**

# Potter and Psychiatrist to Host Charity Bash

Peter Kilpatrick, art teacher at Esther S. Potts Middle School, and Dr. Carl Younger of Maxwell-Younger Psychiatric Services, invite members of the Kyleighburn community to the first ever Therapeutic Pottery Bash on Saturday July 24.

"My students and I have crafted a lot of mistakes over the last 15 years," Kilpatrick said. I thought it would be a good way to put them to use, since people might have some pent up emotions after the catastrophe in the mobile home park. I contacted Doctor Younger with my idea."

Kilpatrick offered his "dud pile" to be used for a charity fundraiser to assist in relocating homes and to help fund the investigation into the collapse.

"We plan to sell ten broken pots for $25," Dr Younger explained. Then people can smash, bash or otherwise spectacularly destroy their purchases. The release of anxiety and anger will be quite therapeutic."

"And thrilling." Kilpatrick added.

"It's relaxing in a safe way," the psychiatrist said. "And I'll be on site to offer free private counseling sessions to those who need a little extra help with their troubles."

**Continued on page B7**

# The Tea Set

Mackenzie Minnick

THE CUP WITH THE FLAT, SQUARE BOTTOM should have been the easiest piece to make. The design itself was a simple flower, painted in black outlines with red and white filling in the tessellations. Yet Tara's hands, "claws" as she called them now, refused to pinch the clay closely enough to make the thin walls she remembered. Her hands cramped up too quickly and she had started this project far too late.

Tara thought retirement meant she would have more time to herself. More time for travel, more time to learn, more time to appreciate the world around her. But instead it became more time for doctor's visits, medical appointments, and pills. More time to realize she was too old to travel, more time for boredom, more time for regretting her life.

Tara picked up the asymmetrical cup and smashed it into a ball. The clay oozed out, staining her veiny-blue hands with its off-gray color. It was more satisfying to her this way, though she wouldn't dare admit it to anyone else. She was bringing chaos under her control. She could stop squeezing whenever she needed to or continue on until it plopped out of her hand. The small blobs of clay fell from her clenched fist, splashing onto the wheel like raindrops made of jelly.

She released her foot off the pedal powering the wheel. It was an old electric one, owned by the middle school art teacher. Mr. Kilpatrick was his name. It was his classroom Tara was in now. The room was of medium size, with eight round tables and a sink in the corner. Each table had four plastic chairs around it. Three of the walls proudly displayed artwork from the various students. The fourth wall had a whiteboard, with art-related posters held in place with magnets. One was about clay consistency and simple motions to get basic shapes. Tara had spent some time looking at it before she got started today, hoping to glean something that would unlock the mysteries of "throwing clay".

"Mrs. Windell," Peter Kilpatrick's baritone voice pulled her back into the room. "How did it go today?"

Tara turned to the art teacher. He was wearing a purple and green sweater, sleeves rolled up to his elbows, with maroon pants and shoes. For an art teacher, she thought he had an awful sense of style. His balding brown hair was haphazardly combed over, and his glasses had thick rims that created a heavy brow when he stood under a light. This was the thirty-year-old man allowing her the opportunity to try and correct her life. She didn't know how he persuaded the school to let her use their classroom. Tara had made the phone call a little over a year ago, following up on a tip that he had a pottery wheel she could use. He was incredibly delighted to help someone out in the community.

"Fantastic, Peter. Look at the tea cup I made." Tara said, gesturing to the spattered wheel spinning slowly in the back.

"You'll get there."

"Oh yes, with all the time left in my life, I'm sure I can fit in the ten thousand years I need to get it right."

Peter frowned. He looked ready to chide her, but instead grabbed a rag from a small cart of cleaning supplies left near the classroom door.

"How about I clean up tonight? You can wash up and get home," he suggested, turning on the faucet. He wet the rag under the water. When he stepped away, Tara took over the large sink. The water was painfully cold. She grabbed a nearby sponge and began to scrub harshly at the clay on her hands. The water carried it off down the paint-stained drain.

"One day, the school will give me a budget large enough to accommodate a new wheel," Peter said. "Until then, this thing will have to do. The kids love to watch it spin, but I don't trust them yet to treat it right." He carefully splashed more water onto the wheel and scrubbed. For a few moments, just the sound of the running water and brushing filled the room. Tara always appreciated Peter's ability to include silence in a conversation. Too many people always tried to fill the air, jumping in and over each other in an effort to spout out whatever was on their minds. Peter's way of idly speaking flowed in and out of the ear in a pleasing tone, rendering his words soothing if meaningless. Tara wondered if his students paid any attention in class.

She turned off the water and began to dry her hands with the paper towels nearby.

"I've ordered more clay-related books for you at the library," Peter finished wiping the pottery wheel. "They'll be arriving over the next couple of weeks, so check in with Delilah."

"Thank you."

"Will you need a ride home?"

"No, I'll walk," Tara rejected his offer. "Besides, what would the neighbors say?"

"Of course, Mrs. Windell, I didn't mean to offend."

"Then stop offering."

They finished cleaning in silence.

In the evening, just before bedtime, Tara sat in a cushy armchair in her living room, intensely staring at a photograph in her hands. The edges of the wooden frame were worn and contoured into her palms and fingers. The picture itself was an old black and white image of two women sitting at a table. They wore bright-colored dresses and big beaming faces. One woman poured tea from a large teapot into a cup with a square bottom and a flower on the side.

Tara knew the image was more reliable than her memory, but she couldn't help feeling that the picture was wrong. It didn't capture the light brown stain the cup had developed from not being properly cleaned from a black tea. It didn't hold the memories of her mother and grandmother sitting together and laughing a Sunday afternoon away. It was devoid of all the lessons her mother taught; instructions such as dealing with both kind and unsavory men, handling money and debt, keeping house. Politics, education, family history, all were passed down alongside a cup of tea and a sweet biscuit on the side.

It was the greatest comfort she could bring to her mother in the hospital, that last afternoon. Tara was seventeen at the time, and though it was ages ago, she could distinctly remember the contrast between her young arm and her mother's thin and wrinkly hand.

"The tea set. It goes to your daughter," her mother had whispered.

Tara looked at another photograph, one on her mantle. It was another old shot, but in color. One of herself, in her late-thirties, and her daughter, Catherine, when she was eight. They were sitting with their backs to the camera, turned around so you could see their fronts. She couldn't remember where it was taken, not because it was fifty years old, but because she and Catherine were so devoid of any joy and emotion that they could have been an interpretation of *American Gothic*. If she had only realized how sad her daughter looked and done more….

*Wistful thinking gets you nowhere,* Tara chided herself. She set the frame down and stood from her chair. Getting old is awful and painful. She turned out the lights and shuffled to bed.

By the time the sun was up, Tara was already washing the dishes from her breakfast and putting them aside to dry. Wednesdays are grocery days and getting there early meant short lines and first picks on the farm-fresh vegetables and meats. When half the town was just now rolling out of bed, Tara was at the store, checking avocadoes' firmness. When they were eating breakfast, she was checking out with a barely-awake grocery-clerk. And by the time the whole town was out and about, practically prowling for an opportunity to go "Hey, how are you? Do you need help getting across the street? Do you want someone to carry your bags? I can give you a ride!", Tara was happily home, stashing the perishables away into the fridge. Tara wasn't misanthropic, just found that most people were insufferable around the elderly.

Like now, at the library.

"Mrs. Windell, I'm so glad you came in!" Delilah's cheery voice echoed throughout the building.

"Delilah," Tara said, digging in her purse for a small notepad and pen. "Could you lower your voice? You only need to speak to me, not the dead."

"I'm so sorry!" Delilah's volume didn't change. "I'm just so excited to see you. You remind me of my mama, except she's a bit taller. I can't wait to see her when I visit over Christmas, you should see the gift I got her. It's a brooch about this big, with a giant blue opal in the middle—"

"Could you show me the numbers of the books that came in?" Tara interrupted.

"Of course! Anyway, the opal is set with this gorgeous silver filigree. I found this silversmith, he's only a couple of towns over…"

Tara wrote down the book locations, ignoring Delilah's retelling of her adventures in finding a gift for her mother. Business as usual, really. When she had finished, Tara put away her notebook.

"Thank you, Delilah, I have everything here," she interrupted again.

"Oh, yes, you're welcome." Delilah smiled brilliantly. Tara turned away. "Oh wait, Tara. There's one that hasn't been added to the system, I'll show you where it is."

The ladies walked through the stacks, Delilah still going on about the brooch she had gotten her mother. After she had thoroughly exhausted the subject, she moved on to discussing the presents for her father, brother, and all of the other members of the Chanda family. Tara bore this assault grimly. Any attempt to get her to stop talking would be pointless. Delilah stepped over the words of others without a care.

"I just cannot wait for Christmas!" Delilah sighed. They had reached the back of the library, near the area where the walls joined up with the attached museum. The E.P.P. Scott Library's interesting exterior, shaped a bit like an axe head without the stick, was emphasized by the large open spaces that served as the display for both sections. The offices took residence in the square portion, carefully constructed on top of each other. A big EMPLOYEES ONLY sign hung on the door, but Delilah propped it open so Tara could watch as she walked in, took a book called *Great Pot! The Doc's Guide to Pottery* off a stack, and walked out.

"Now, it's technically on loan to me, so please return it as soon as you can, but no later than a month," Delilah closed the door. "Of course, I trust you, Mrs. Windell, I don't make this deal for everyone."

She winked. Tara didn't.

"Thank you, *Miss* Chanda," Tara said, emphasizing the one thing she knew to drive the librarian away quickly. "I will find the rest of the books on my own."

Delilah quickly scurried away, presumably to bother another patron or to sit at her computer. Either way, it meant uninterrupted hours of studying in the library. Tara went to the stack that contained all of the art books, and sorted the numbers to volumes. The library had formed an impressive collection of pottery-related books due to her obsession, and Tara noted that some of the ones she had looked at before were currently checked out. She pulled three more tomes from the shelves, then went to the nearest table. From her purse, she pulled out her notepad, a pen, and a pencil. She also took out a small sketchpad. Her workstation established, she sat down and began to read.

*Visualize your project in your mind, mold it in your hands. If it isn't right, that's okay. You always have the time to get it right. Just keep your hands steady and the wheel turning.*

A smashed crater of clay was the result of that advice. The way lumps of it flew off as the wheel turned at a high speed was the most satisfying part of the evening, and Tara wished that she could keep the crater and serve tea out of that instead. It made more sense than most of the art books she read today.

Tara hated the self-help nature that dominated the pottery books. *Great Pot!* had been written by a doctor-turned-artist after he quit years of surgery. Despite it seeming like it had been aimed at geriatrics, Tara recognized the signs of the middle-aged man trying to remind himself that he wasn't anywhere near his expiration date. But what was most annoying was the constant reiteration from book to book: mistakes happen, just keep your hands steady.

"Keep my hands steady," Tara muttered. She extended hers now, grunting with the effort and pain it took to point her index finger. They shook and shivered. "Oh thanks, Doc. That was the one thing I wasn't trying to do." She stopped the wheel and then scraped the clay off for another chance. Peter came into the room.

"We could work on this together, Mrs. Windell." Peter offered.

"Then you'd do the work for me. Are you that tired of me?" Tara snapped back.

"No, Tara, of course not. I just thought if you had help, you'd get where you want to faster."

"I have plenty of time to get this right. The books say so."

"Of course you do."

Tara gritted her teeth and mushed at the clay. She splashed some water onto it and her hands.

"Stop saying that."

"Saying what?" Peter asked.

"'Of course'. You're already on my bad side. Saying a platitude won't magically fix it."

Tara wasn't looking at him, but knew he was currently biting down on the inside of his cheek to keep from smiling. It was his go-to trick to avoid smiling when a child did something wrong, but funny.

"I'll try to avoid it in the future," Peter said.

"And miss another sarcastic remark from me?"

"I'll undergo my suffering quietly."

"That's all I ask." Tara smiled. Peter was far too kind of a man to stay angry with for long. "I suppose I could use your help."

Peter smiled and put down a chair. Tara pointed at some sketches on the table, and spoke as Peter looked them over.

"I think I could draw it with my eyes closed now. I used stencils to keep the lines straight. I can see it all in my head, I can almost put it on paper. But the moment I try and throw it on the table, it"—Tara picked up some clay and dropped it—"splats."

Peter looked pensively between the clay on the table and the sketches. He rolled up his sleeves and wet his hands, then sat on the opposite side of the throwing table from Tara.

"Show me how you're making the cup."

Tara quietly spun the wheel and took a lump of clay. She took one hand and carved out the interior of the clay, using her other hand to support the appearing wall. Once she had a semblance of a bowl, she took her fingers and tried to pinch the top to make the edge narrower. The clay began to split and crack, and then collided with her hand, breaking the wall. The rest of the clay soon followed after as she mashed it in frustration.

"Okay," Peter remarked after a moment. "Let's try a different technique."

He took some clay, wet it, and began to roll it into strips.

Tara hadn't realized before how much Peter was like the man who had brought her to the state of North Carolina. Mr. Hurst was some political big-shot, looking for bright young people to work his campaign for the state senate. Tara had just acquired her Associate's degree from a community college that was notorious for denying women. She remembered marching in with her father and demanding to be let in on merit and with scholarships. She came back every two days on her own, asking about the status of her acceptance. By her first day of class, she already had the reputation for being an uncompromising force of willpower. Day after day, she pestered her professors about due dates and lessons. She attended every lecture, every set of office hours. When she received her degree in political science, the professors cheered the loudest at her departure from the school. The insane motivation and drive was what called her to the attention of the handsome, charismatic Mr. Hurst. In vague terms, he promised Tara safety and security in exchange for her help in getting him elected. He was gentle and non-confrontational. Tara accepted the job without hesitation.

Even now, as Peter spun the wheel in silence, his hands carefully massaging the clay into its shape, Tara could see some of the similarities between him and Hurst. There was that same aura of concentration, the focus and warmth their eyes emanated. Yet Tara also knew that Peter was not Mr. Hurst. Peter didn't ask anything of Tara and he was always clear in his communications.

In the countless hours Tara spent working on the campaign in her youth, typing and handwriting letters, contacting print-shops, scrimping, and saving, Mr. Hurst never once admitted he wasn't going to pay her. It took a month of him warding her off with promises and IOUs before she finally wore him down. She quit that day and searched for any position to cover her bills. After losing a month in Raleigh to Hurst's lies, her finances were in dire straits.

"Here," Peter said, as he handed the completed cup to Tara. It was beautiful, even unfired. It had a square bottom and top, but a round interior. There was a small clay flower ready for her to paint.

Tara held the square tea cup in her hands as securely as if it were a child. Peter opened up a kiln and offered his hand to take the cup from Tara, but Tara clutched it protectively for a brief moment. Realizing he was intending to fire it for her, she handed it over.

"I won't be able to fire it for a couple of days or so," Peter said as he closed the lid. "But I can leave it out during the day where the kids won't be able to destroy it until it's dry enough to go in the kiln."

"Thank you, Peter."

"Of co— You're welcome, Tara." He smiled. "Do you want a ride home?"

Tara bristled at first, ready to berate him for once again thinking she needed help. She relaxed when she realized he was merely offering a convenience.

"Okay, Peter," she said. "You helped me with the cup, I'll take a ride home."

They cleaned up the classroom and put the wheel and chairs away. Peter locked the door after they exited, and they went through the halls of the school and out the doors into the parking lot. It was evening, not quite sunset, but the sun wasn't high enough to be seen over the trees. The air was still humid and warm. Tara could hear some kids playing a game and yelling back and forth at each other. Peter unlocked his car, a dark blue Hyundai, and slid inside. He pushed open the passenger door.

"Sorry, the handle is broken," Peter apologized as Tara climbed inside. She handed him a slip of paper with her address on it, which he put into his phone. He started the car, and slowly backed out of the space. Tara watched the little arrow on his screen slowly orient itself to the road. ETA: 5 MIN, it read.

"Why teach?" Tara asked.

"I love working with kids, I guess," Peter responded, checking his mirrors. "They usually have no judgment and are surprisingly opinionated."

"But you're talented. You should be in New York or LA, surrounded by other artists, talking and making art every day, going to galleries and events."

"I could, but I like small town life. I can drive anywhere I want to go, I don't have to be constantly punctual or prolific, and I don't have to compete with my peers for a scrap of a chance."

Tara watched the mailboxes go by.

"No," she conceded. "You deserve better than here though."

"Maybe. But I choose to be here."

Peter slowed down, watching the house numbers as he looked carefully for Tara's home. He set the car into park and turned the engine off.

"Why are you here?" He asked.

"I'm too old to move."

"Then why did you choose Kyleighburn of all places to settle?"

"I always thought I was going to leave. Then one day, I realized it was too late to do so." Tara opened her door. "Good night, Peter."

"Good night, Mrs. Windell."

Tara shut the door with a loud thud. She ambled up the sidewalk to her front door, fumbling for her keys. Finding them, she turned and waved at Peter. Peter waved back, then started the car and drove off. Tara unlocked the door to her home and stepped inside. She breathed in the still air, appreciating the familiar scent of her perfume and house cleaner. She closed the door and locked it carefully behind her, twisting the handle roughly a couple of times to make sure it was secure. *Home.*

Home was always safe. Even in those early days, when Tara would go home each day without finding work, she would remind herself *I'm luckier than most.* At home, that almost appeared true, despite the fact she'd worn out every pair of shoes, or exhausted all of the nearby restaurants and offices in her job hunt. Yet home had the tea set, and when she poured herself a new cup, she could feel the comfort of her mother telling her to keep pushing on, keep going.

So she would read the classifieds and circle more potential opportunities and visit them the next day. She persevered in spite of the numerous employers who dismissed her for the slightest fault: she wasn't pretty enough, she had a mouth on her, she appeared too desperate. Although now she didn't have the tea set anymore, she had the pride of owning the house in Kyleighburn, a far more stable housing situation than the apartment in Raleigh. No aggressive landlords knocking daily for the rent. No fear of being out on the street. No having to slowly bring things to the pawn shop, parting with memories and sentiment. She stilled remember the broker looking through the pictures as he removed them from the album she was selling, pointing to the tea set and telling her he had a buyer looking for something similar. Tara spent far too many evenings staring at the set after that day. But that was the past.

The anxiety over the cup was starting to develop into an obsession again. Tara chided her childish desire to rush over to the school and check on its progress. Instead, she marched up and down the main street of Kyleighburn until her calves started to burn. She ordered a sweet tea and bagel at Corey cafe before heading to the library where Delilah had a small stack of books already set aside for her.

"Afternoon, Mrs. Windell! I already collected some of the books together for you so you don't have to track them all down." Delilah beamed.

"Thank you, but today I'm here for something a little different."

"Oh, what are you looking for? I can try and recommend something good if you don't have—"

"Do you have any cozies?" Tara interrupted.

"Of course! We have all types depending on what you want. Just the other day, we got our hands on a book series about antique boats and cold cases." Delilah jotted down several codes and handed them off to Tara.

Tara left the library with three novels in her bag and went home. She put up her feet and cracked open a book, pausing every once in a while to drink some of the tea and take a bite from the bagel. The heat of the sun and the occasional breeze winding into the room started to lull her into a soft sleep. Tara, eyes half-shut, lost track of what part of the manly love interest was sinewy this time and settled on just closing the book entirely and letting it fall to her stomach. She had almost drifted off when the phone started to ring.

It took Tara a couple of seconds to push off the waves of sleeping overwhelming her. She reached out and picked up the beige receiver and put it to her ear.

"Hello?" she said.

"Hi Tara." A voice like a bell responded. Suddenly, the breeze that had cooled Tara before felt like a stinging wall of ice. The sun that had warmed the room was gone.

"Catherine, is everything okay?" She asked, struggling to stand out of her chair.

The voice sighed. "Yes, everything is okay. I just wanted to know your Christmas plans."

"I don't have any as of yet." She reached the window and cushioned the phone between her shoulder and head. She managed to squeak the window shut.

"Okay, well, great. We might be coming your way this year. Penny is staying with some college friends of hers, so it'll just be myself and Bart. Is that fine?"

Tara paused at closing the curtains to the window. She knew Catherine was asking merely out of politeness to her mother, and while Tara did appreciate that courtesy, she also knew that for once, this year, she'd have a reason for family to be over.

"Actually, Catherine, I'd love for you and Bart to visit this year."

"Okay, we'll see if Bart's mother is—oh! Wait, are you serious?"

"Yes, I have the perfect gift for you as well."

"Um, okay. I'll have to get back to you with our plans then. Goodbye." Tara thought the click at the end of the conversation was almost hesitant.

She chuckled to herself. Catherine had inherited some of Tara's mannerisms. Tara was happy to have caught her off-guard.

Tara waited on a bench near the entrance of the school, tapping her foot vigorously. She couldn't keep herself from fidgeting. She flitted her eyes like a hummingbird—first to the pavement, then the sky, then the door, then back. Pavement, sky, door. She could feel her heart beating faster and faster. To quell its racing, she left the bench and scurried towards the door. She peered through the glass, attempting to see into the building. No one was in sight. With a sigh and her heart still pounding, she took to pacing up and down one of the long lines in the sidewalk, placing one purple-flowered shoe in front of the other. *One, two, three...* She hadn't done this in years, but she felt her heartbeat settle along as her counting rose higher. *Thirty-seven, thirty-eight...* She stopped staring at her shoes and looked out across the school lot, watching the shimmering dance created by the haze from the heat. Ethereal dancers on ephemeral floors.

There was a metallic clang from behind her. Peter stood in the door, holding it open.

"What took you so long?" The cold air of the school was already bothering Tara's joints. Peter didn't answer, keeping his eyes straight down the hallway. Tara noticed that she was beginning to outpace him.

"Was there any trouble from the kids today?" she probed.

"The kids were fine."

"Did your boss say something to you?"

"No, I haven't seen him."

"Were you stuck grading projects?"

"No."

They arrived at the classroom. Tara couldn't puzzle out why Peter was behaving oddly. He was normally the engine powering their conversations, yet he was avoiding any sentences longer than five words. She watched him carefully as he opened the door to the kiln. When he turned around, she felt her heart fall. The tea cup was in a pile of pieces in his hands, cracks and splits in each shard.

"This happens sometimes," Peter almost whispered, as if he were talking to a child about why the dog wouldn't wake up. "There's nothing we can do to prevent it, we can only just try again."

"It's not fair," Tara grit her teeth. Her eyes traced the outline of each shard, looking at their fiber splits. "It's not fair." The large pieces teased the semblance of a cup, the shards like the fine leaves of a tender tea. "It's not fair!"

Peter set down the cup. The pieces clinked together in discordant tones. Tara's vision blurred, the shards blending together in a puddle of gray. They were almost whole again, like when she had cradled it just two days earlier.

She blinked, and the breaks and cracks came into sharp focus again.

"Breathe, Tara," Peter touched her shoulder.

She hadn't even realized that she had stopped. With a shudder that shook her small frame, she drew in the air, the scent of cleaner filling her nostrils. When the smell hit her throat, she coughed. That was all it took to let a couple of tears escape from the bubble that was forming on her eyes. She swatted them away like a horse's tail after flies.

"Where's the clay?"

"It still has to be kneaded—"

"I'll do it."

She took the gray block and mashed it onto the table. She heaved it up, folded it over, kneaded into it like a cat kneads a wool blanket. Slight twinges of pain in her joints fired up in a strobing pattern. *This sucks.*

Heaved the clay again. *This sucks.*

Pressed it into the table surface. *I have to call Catherine and tell her not to come.*

Folded it over. *Again.* She paused to wipe her eyes on her sleeve again.

Tara sighed, then looked at the gray mass in front of her. She punched her fist into it. The clay absorbed the blow, then sucked in her fist. She wrestled it free.

A clunk, followed by a gentle brushing signaled to her that Peter had brought the wheel out and set a chair for her. Tara looked at him in time to see him glance away from her eyes. He straightened out the plastic seat and then, like a child trying to avoid chores, left the room. With a grunt of effort, Tara took the clay she had been kneading and set it onto the wheel. The pressure on her ankles disappeared when she sat down. She hadn't even noticed it. She didn't have the time to care. *I need to finish this.* She pushed the pedal and started the machine up.

From the moment she put her hand to the lump spinning around, she could tell she hadn't spent enough time softening it. It grated against her hand, pushed and fought every attempt to guide and gouge it into a shape. Tara felt a dark fog descend on her head as her hands dropped to the sides. *Catherine won't even want to speak to me.*

The clay spun around in front of her. *I have to do this.*

Tara shook her head. She reached out and caught most of the clay as it spun around into her hands. It dragged at her arm like a heavy current. She struggled her arm free, clenching her muscles. They were sore already.

*I have to do this. But I can't.*

She pushed and pulled the clay in her hands. She closed her eyes. *I can't do this. It's too late.*

She could see her younger self back again at the pawn shop, holding the box with the tea set, nervously approaching the counter.

*If I just had held on for a little while longer.*

The broker's soft smile as he counted out the bills for the two hundred dollars that would stave off the landlord and get her food. It was enough money for her to look through the classifieds for a week, find and interview for a dozen jobs, and get hired as a teller at a bank.

*I wouldn't have lost it in the first place.*

Going back to the pawn shop to buy the set back, and it was already gone. The arguments she had with the shopkeeper, sleepless nights and crying. It all reappeared with its full force, like clearing the leaves off of a well-trod path. A path that she had tried time and time again to destroy. She felt a heat rise in her. A tornado of fire spinning up to burn all this embarrassment to ash.

*You kept yourself back*, it raged.

*What else could I do?* Tara begged.

*Be rid of the past*, it rampaged.

It consumed her.

*Be rid of the past.* Tara repeated.

*To hell with it all. Make the damn cup!*

Tara opened her eyes and threw the clay down, ready to knead it once more at the counter. She realized a half-second too late that she was still at the wheel, and it was spinning. The clay hit the edge of the wheel, and Tara watched as the wheel wobbled and tilted, coming free with a loud CLANG. The wheel collided with the edge of the bowl and it took off. It spun across the room, splattering clay everywhere and slamming into tables and the wall. Tara shielded her face with her arms, yelping.

Peter opened the door as the wheel came to a stop, spinning in a circle. He rushed to Tara's side.

"Are you okay?" he asked, gently taking her arms down.

Tara stared at the wheel, now resting on the floor.

"I—I don't know," Tara finally answered. It was true. She couldn't feel the rest of her body, and her mind whirled like it had spun off with the wheel. She felt Peter carefully exam for any bruises or cuts on her arms and back.

"Do you want me to call an ambulance?" He said, pushing in various spots.

"No… no, I'm fine." Tara felt fear drain away, only to be replaced by shame. She had broken the one wheel in Kyleighburn, and Peter couldn't afford to replace it. "I'm sorry."

"It's okay. You're not hurt, that's all that matters." Peter soothed. He went to the sink, dampened a paper towel, and came back. He wiped the clay off of Tara's cheek. She didn't know clay had gotten on there. "It's not your fault."

"Yes, it is. I wasn't paying attention." Tara jerked her head away from Peter's hands. He paused, then pointed at the pan the wheel had escaped from.

"Look at that." He said. "The metal around the grommet was rusting. The rubber must have torn."

Tara saw the small amount of brown on the metal pipe leading off the motor.

"Even if it was your fault, that doesn't matter. What matters is that you are okay." Peter continued, then handed her the paper towel. "Go on home, I'll clean up."

"No, let me help," Tara slowly stood up. Peter shook his head.

"Your clothes."

She looked down. Her shirt was covered in gray spatters. "Oh."

"Looks like the clay threw itself, instead of you throwing it." Peter smiled.

Tara hadn't been back to the school for a few days. Peter had called twice, but she recognized the number and let the answering machine take it. She deleted the messages without listening. The house had been cleaned thoroughly, even behind the fridge and under the bed, though she loathed those parts for the aches they gave her back. Now there was the issue of the wheel.

Tara sat her kitchen table, staring at her television. A sitcom was on, but the volume turned down low. The actors were gesticulating wildly in reaction to some over-crazed plot. She fiddled with a black pen in her hands, sheets of paper on the table in front of her. An apology was in order. Probably some money too. The check was already signed, just needed an amount. She could probably ask Delilah to help her look up some prices. But before she could even think to make the trip down to the library, she needed to write this apology.

She pretended she was Peter, receiving the note at his desk. She opened it up, revealing a blank check and three words: *I'm sorry—Tara.* It seemed cowardly.

*I'm sorry for what?* She thought. *For forgetting where I was? Having a 'senior moment'?* Or was it for bringing her entire being, with years of regret, mistakes, and rage into his life unnecessarily? She had sought him out, like a predator, no, a parasite. She took advantage of his kindness and generosity until he was just as deprived as she was. "I'm sorry" barely disturbed the dirt, but they were the only words that came to mind.

Tara tucked the card back into its holder, then carried it to the front door. *Tomorrow*, she thought as she put the unsealed envelope on top of the stack of library books she had borrowed.

The next day, after a small stint at the library, Tara made her way to the school. It was just after hours, when most of the students had left to go home, but before many of the teachers had left for the day. Tara considered going in and leaving the envelope at the front desk, but the thought of having to explain why she was leaving a note made her stomach turn over. So instead she was walking through the parking lot, looking for Peter's dark blue car. With any luck, she could stick the card under his wiper and go home without any awkward conversations. She saw the bumper to the Hyundai two spaces away from a disability ramp. As she approached, she saw the driver side door open and Peter was looking through a bag. Tara immediately turned to her right and walked behind a car, but the grind of her heel on asphalt caused Peter to look up.

"Tara?" Peter said, standing and placing his arms on the roof of his car.

"Hi Peter."

"You've been avoiding me." Peter shut the car door.

"Absolutely." Tara looked at the pale blue envelope in her hands.

"What's that?"

"My apology. It's not very good." Tara proffered the card.

"What are you apologizing for?" Peter inquired. "The wheel? You did nothing wrong."

"But it happened because of—"

"Because of nothing," Peter's tone was reassuring. "Accidents happen all the time and this time you were the victim. Remember, I examined the wheel? It could have broken at any moment."

"Well, there's a check in there for a new one. I didn't know how much it cost."

"Thank you, but honestly, Tara, I'm glad you're okay." Peter smiled. "I hope you can see that for yourself."

Tara pinched her lips between her teeth, and squinted at Peter.

"What are you doing?" she asked.

"I… what?"

"Nothing. You have the apology and the check, I don't care what you do with them." Tara turned on her heel and quickly walked off the lot. She tried to ignore the spinning sensation around her brain.

*He's supposed to be mad*, she thought. *Maybe he's trying to seem graceful.* But Peter was graceful by nature. A kind and gentle soul. If something upset him, it would be immediately visible, and she doubted he was capable of the subterfuge necessary to appear graceful while angry.

"Tara!" Peter's voice derailed her train of thought. She turned again. Peter was striding towards her, envelope fluttering in the wind.

"Self-pity is toxic," he said, stopping short and holding up the envelope. "It's a poison that you mix and take yourself. And this, this check and apology, it's a cry for help and punishment."

"Peter, what—"

"I'm not done," Peter interrupted. "If you really, truly feel sorry, then I have one condition before I can accept this." Tara stared over Peter's shoulder, watching the clouds laze across the sky. She resisted an urge to ignore him, say something caustic to shove him away, just so she could go home and be miserable in peace. Peter deserved better than that.

"I only buy the wheel if you promise to come back and finish the tea set."

"Finish?" Tara snapped back. "I haven't even started! I haven't made a single piece yet!"

"You made one that broke. That's fine. It's a setback—"

"Setbacks aren't inconveniences anymore, they're… giant piles of God-knows-what that say 'this is where you stop forever'. You have time, Peter, I don't."

Peter stood quietly, eyebrows slowly furrowing until they nearly joined into one hefty brown caterpillar. The sun cast it into a long dark bar over his eyes. Tara could see his frustration rising, boiling inwardly until, like a steam whistle, he sighed.

"You're being ridiculous," He said. "You're assuming the end without even trying. It's like you're getting ready to watch a movie at the theater, and you can't figure out if you have time to pee before the film starts. Just go! If you miss the first five minutes, well, you were expecting to anyway. But you could miss nothing. And either result is better than getting your pants wet."

"You're comparing death to having to go urinate."

"It's what I got." Peter crossed his arms. "And it's better than what you're doing. Now, it's either a new wheel that you come in for or the kids don't have any pottery class until the school replaces the old one."

Tara gritted her teeth. *Damn it.*

"Fine!" She turned away again. She couldn't deprive the kids. Even if it meant failing. She walked faster to push the thoughts out of her head.

"Tara? Where are you going?" Peter called after her.

"The library. I need to get those books back."

Tara received a call from Peter the day he picked up the wheel. He told her to arrive a couple of hours earlier than usual, before school let out, and to bring along any books she had checked out from the E.P.P. Scott Library as well as a picture of the tea set. When she arrived at the school building, a female administrator in a navy pantsuit opened the door.

"Mrs. Windell?" she asked.

"Yes?"

"Ah, good. My name is Amber Timms. Follow me to the front desk; we'll sign you in. Then you can go to Mr. Kilpatrick's class."

Tara followed the middle-aged woman to the front desk. Two boys sat in small chairs nearby, one holding an ice pack to his forehead, the other with a torn shirt. They both took care to avoid eye contact with Amber and Tara. Amber went behind the massive wooden divide that sectioned the room into two uneven parts. She pulled a pen from a cup and tapped the clipboard in front of Tara.

"The usual: name, date, and time." Amber said, before sitting down into a wooden chair with a plush cushion on top. As she began to tap away at the computer, Tara wrote her details out carefully onto the clipboard. When she finished, she passed the pen back to Amber, then waited. Amber kept her eyes locked onto her computer screen, scrolling leisurely through some website.

"Excuse me, so what do I—" Tara began.

"Go on ahead. You're all set. Just come back this way when you're done."

Tara left the main office. It was odd walking through the school. She was used to silence and the sound of her feet echoing through the emptiness. Now she could hear children talking to each other, teachers giving quizzes or having the children count up as a class. The light was wrong, beaming in through the large windows instead of softly illuminating the halls. She even noticed bits of trash everywhere, scraps of torn paper and wrappers that caught on the bumps of the walls, or daringly flew across the floor, caught by some current of air. The floor itself felt like it was sticking to her shoes, probably some juice or other sugary beverage that had been errantly spilled. Tara briefly debated if the janitors were paid enough for the care they provided to the school.

Soon, however, she reached the door of Peter's classroom. Tara could hear the children laughing and yelling long before she arrived, and when she pressed her ear to the smooth wood door, she could just make out Peter's voice, though not what he was saying.

She knocked. The children immediately quit their noise, and there was a faint rustling like the sound of a multitude of chairs being pulled out. A couple of seconds later, and Peter opened the door. He had a streak of green paint down his cheek and a smock that was smeared in a variety of paints, clay, and colors galore.

"Ah, Tara!" exclaimed the walking Picasso painting.

"Hi Peter, you appear to be living art."

"The kids get overeager," Peter smiled as he waved Tara in. She stepped inside. There were about twenty fifth-graders inside, all seated at the round Formica tables. They stared at her like paparazzi, watching and waiting for her to make a move or sound. "Class, this is Mrs. Windell."

"Good afternoon, Mrs. Windell." They droned with the sound of a rehearsed greeting. Tara couldn't help but smile at the sound of how canned it was. *They're all going to be little jerks when they're teenagers*, she thought. Yet none of them gave a clue as to why she was there so early. None of them had anything out on their desks either, although an offending green spill at an empty seat gave a clue as to how Peter earned his stripe.

"Now, Mrs. Windell, I have told the class about your donation of a pottery wheel to my class, and they wanted you to come in to thank you in person." Peter's smile grew into a grin. "Alyssa, if you will."

A girl with braids and a denim jumper stood up and went to the closet where Peter kept most of his supplies in. She pulled out a giant piece of paper and held it up. It was a giant thank you card, covered in drawings and signatures. Alyssa handed it to Tara.

"Thank you, Mrs. Windell." The class droned again with the same rehearsed voice. Tara barely caught Peter rolling his eyes. She looked at the card and tried to speak, but the words caught at the back of her throat, and instead she clammed her mouth shut into a tight smile. If she tried anything else, she might have cried.

"Tara, if you could have a seat here," Peter gestured to an empty, non-greened seat. Tara took the chair and set her tote bag by her feet. "Okay, kids, I'm going to fetch something from the back. How about those of you who volunteered show off some of your work?"

A boy with a dragon on his shirt stood up and grabbed a sheet of paper from the counter. He held it up.

"I'm Ben, and this is my de-picture of what it would be like if robots made dinosaurs and had them invade Kyleighburn," he stated proudly. "Here's a stegosaurus with a laser gun on its back, and it's shooting at the lighthouse, and there's the mayor fighting off a T-Rex with a sword, and—"

The drawing was indeed incredibly detailed, Tara noted, even if it was a bit silly and simplistic. The seven children after Ben had tamer ideas with more care put into their pictures, and there were some very gifted students. Tara had a difficult time keeping track of Peter, who seemed to reappear and disappear silently. Erika, the seventh child, had just finished showing off her lovely color pencil irises when Peter interrupted.

"Thank you, Erika, those came out fantastic with their colors, and your shading has improved by ten-fold. Now, Tara, I know you have an important project that you have been working on for quite a while." Peter went to the front of the classroom, near the whiteboard. "May I see the photo?"

Tara reached into her tote and removed the picture of her mother and grandmother at Sunday tea. She passed it over to Peter.

"Now, I know most of you remember our unit on famous artists." Peter walked over to the whiteboard and grabbed a magnet. "Artists like Jackson Pollock and Andy Warhol made a lot of money from their work. But sometimes, a piece of art can be priceless just to the person who made or owns it. A homemade piece of jewelry won't fetch too much at a market, but is a great Christmas or birthday gift." Peter stuck the magnet on a corner of the photo, and let it hang there. Tara felt a knowing suspicion, and instinctively clutched the handle of her tote and pulled it closer to her feet.

"So, in addition to everyone learning how to work with clay, we're going to make something that will be valuable because we made it together. Something with what is called sentimental value."

Tara felt her tears well up.

"We're going to make a tea set with Mrs. Windell."

The rest of the day was spent with the kids playing and using the clay for the first time. Some caught on very quickly and others needed more heavy guidance from Tara and Peter. Tara was impressed at how deftly some of them maneuvered the clay into shapes of snakes and flower petals, then mashed them up again to make something else. Ben kept trying to make dinosaurs and have them "eat" other clay dinosaurs until Peter told him to share the clay.

After the class was finished, Tara cleaned up as Peter looked at the books she had checked out, writing down ISBN and titles so that he could fill out his own collection. When Tara went home that night, instead of feeling like a prison for her anger, her home was filled with a promise of tomorrow, a promise she hadn't felt since she first moved to Raleigh.

The first week passed by quickly. Since there were only so many hours in the school day, Peter requested permission for an after-school arts club, which was passed without much fuss. The kids, with the added time, were making simple bowls and cups soon enough. Tara found herself overwhelmed with assistance, as some of the children had gone home to watch YouTube tutorials so they could make cooler things. She couldn't help but laugh and smile as the kids talked, bickered, and told stories about their days, and she loved the fact that most stayed quiet to listen to her as she spoke. They viewed her as an adult, but not as old, and it was okay if she didn't keep up with them.

By the second week, several viable bowls and cups had survived the kiln and were in good enough shape to be painted. The day they were pulled, Tara had held each one and felt all over the slightly porous and rough texture of the ceramic. She laughed when she saw that Ben's self-styled "Dino-cup" had also survived the process, although several of the spikes along the handle had fallen off or smoothed out. She suspected that Peter decided that safety was more important than staying true to dino-style.

When Tara arrived on Monday afternoon for the art club, she was delighted to see that many of the pieces had started to be painted. She took a cup for herself, a square one she had made on which Erika had imprinted a flower, and sat down with Alyssa and Peter to gab and paint.

"I can't believe I'm saying this, Peter," Tara beamed. "I'm happy you made me do this."

Peter set down his brush.

"Then you'll love this," he said as he stood up and went into the back. Tara looked at Alyssa, who only shrugged and dabbed more blue paint on to the bowl she was holding. Tara turned her attention back to her cup, which she was painting white, and brushed on a few more strokes when Peter reappeared in the doorway. He was holding something covered by a cloth in his hands. It was fairly large and round. Tara set down her cup and brush.

"I've been working on this during my off hours. It was tricky to get right, but I think you'll like it." He set down the object in the center of the table and pulled off the cloth. It was a teal tea pot, about ten inches tall set with a smooth mosaic of glass that depicted a sea floor. Nearer to the top, the pot had more striking and vibrant colors, like a sunset. The spout had several kelp painted around it. Tara gasped. It was massive, and it appeared heavy.

"I might have gone a bit overboard," Peter said.

"You did, but I love it."

The entire set was done on Friday. It was set up when Tara walked into the room, and the class cheered and clapped as she went around exclaiming at how lovely it was. Peter found another teacher who was free to take a picture of everyone, and printed off a copy for Tara to keep next to the one she had of her mother and grandmother. That evening, Peter loaded the set into his car, and Tara got into the passenger seat. For the first time in a while, the pain in her joints didn't bother her as much.

"So, what will you do your new set? Have a cup of chai on Sunday afternoon? Sip some green tea while staring wistfully at the rain?" Peter asked, chuckling at his own joke.

"Actually, Peter, I plan to give the set to my daughter."

Peter stopped trying to clip his seatbelt in.

"You have a daughter?"

"Mmhmm. Catherine. She's older than you."

"Does she live in town, or…?"

"No, she's out of state. She calls once a year or so. I was not a good mother to her."

"That can't be true."

"Maybe. But I was obsessed with trying to leave something for her to remember me by. A perfect thing that she could share with any kids of her own. I was so concerned that my own failings would be passed down to her that I never really tried to connect with her. I missed out on my own daughter growing up. Now she has her own children. She grew up fine in spite of me."

Peter took the natural pause to start the car and pull out onto the road. Tara looked at her wrinkly hands, wondering at what point they started to look like branches with walnut knuckles. At a red light, Peter sighed and shifted in his seat.

"I can't say for sure," he began. "I wasn't there. Yet I think you did the best you could with whatever baggage you had. Sure, you made mistakes, but as long as you're still alive, you have time to correct them."

"That's why I'm giving her the tea set."

Peter rubbed his chin.

"I think that's a nice gesture, but I'm… unsure if it's the correct one."

It was Tara's turn to shift in her seat. She was confused over what he meant. *The tea set is all I have,* she thought.

"Why?" She asked.

"The set was meant for you. You built it, with the children at the school. If anything, it means more to you and them than it could ever mean to

Catherine."

"Okay, Eight-ball, what do I do?"

Peter pulled into Tara's driveway and shut off the car. He got out and pulled the set from the back.

"Simple acts of care, I suppose. You're not going to be able to insert yourself back into Catherine's life, especially if she has willingly shut you out, and a tea set isn't going to magically restore however many years that chasm has divided you. No grand gesture will work. But a bunch of little ones, slowly added up over time, now that could work."

Tara got out as well and pulled out her keys. She proceeded up her walk and unlocked her door, pushing it open for Peter to walk through. As he grunted with the box, she reflected on his advice. She had planned to give Catherine the set for Christmas, to make up for the years of mistreatment.

Peter set the box containing the set onto the kitchen table, and unpacked the newspaper wrapped pieces from it. He unwrapped the cups and pot first, putting them to the side and tossing the paper back into the box.

The more she thought about it, the more Tara realized that she didn't even have a semi-accurate picture of how Catherine would respond. *What if she hated Ben's dino-cup or the pot? Then all that time would have been wasted.* Even worse, the tea set could go in some forgotten box for years on end. She didn't want that. It was meant to be used.

"You're right," she announced, startling Peter. "The set should stay with me, at least until I pass."

"What about after?"

"If she still doesn't want it, then you can have it. Or the kids. It should go to someone who can appreciate it."

A couple of days later, Catherine called again to confirm their Christmas plans with Tara. Tara hesitated initially. Since she wasn't giving the tea set after all, Catherine and Bart would be visiting needlessly. But Peter's advice about small gestures pushed her into telling Catherine and Bart to arrive in Kyleighburn about a week before Christmas.

Tara had a lot of assistance when it came to decorating her house and yard with strings of little white lights. The art club's affection had been growing since its inception. Two students almost didn't need prompting when it came to climbing to the roof of Tara's house to install the icicle lights on her gutters. Tara had the most fun unpacking her cardboard boxes of decorations. She hadn't pulled them out in years, so each package was its own surprise to see what was inside.

The caroling party idea came from a fortunate mixing of events. The art club listened to the radio as they cleaned the room at the end of the day, and once Halloween had passed, it was constantly streaming Christmas carols, to the point of nearly sprouting a fir tree. Yet none of the students seemed to mind, and some sang along with the music. Tara herself was still puzzling on an appropriate way to show her appreciation for everything the club had done for her. She settled on throwing the party for Peter, his class, and their respective parents.

The day of the party, Tara pulled together some furniture to make a long table and covered it with a holiday cloth. In the center, on a silver tray, she displayed the tea set, trying to get each piece enough space for everyone to view. Pulling back from it, she felt like she had climbed Everest. Something in her heart had been conquered, something that had seemed insurmountable for far too long.

Peter arrived first, followed soon by Ben and his family. Before Ben's father had a chance to set down the lasagna he was carrying, Ben had rushed forward and grabbed his cup to show it off. The Gallaghers, the Duncans, the Twiddys, and more came as well, bringing more food for the potluck. The whole house was filled soon with students and parents, all laughing and playing and talking.

Tara herself felt a bit overwhelmed, trying to play hostess, but thankfully Peter took over when he saw her tiring out. There was nearly enough noise to drown out Catherine and Bart's knock at the door.

Tara almost didn't recognize her daughter. Sure, she had received a card every year with a new photo, but it had been nearly twenty years since she last saw Catherine in person. The deepening laugh lines through the normally cherubic face, a bit more weight, and a new hairstyle would have been enough to completely confuse Tara, but she saw the same sharp, almost hawkish eyes that pierced through metal. Tara's same eyes, some would say. Bart, however, looked roughly the same as he did when they got married. A balding, mildly confused, bumbling turnip.

"Tara," Catherine said, look over her mother's shoulder into the house. The guests hadn't noticed the door yet. "I thought for a moment we had the wrong house."

"Hi!" Tara exclaimed as she ushered them in. "I know, it's a bit unusual for me too to have the place so lively. But I wanted to show you what I've been doing. Just set your stuff on the inside there."

She turned to face the soft glow of the party and cleared her throat. The room quieted.

"Everyone, this is my daughter Catherine and her husband Bart," Tara said. "This is their first time in Kyleighburn, so please help me make them feel welcome."

Most of the parents smiled warmly or offered a hearty wave. Tara took Catherine and Bart around to meet everyone individually, before ending up at the banquet table. Catherine took one look at the teapot and furrowed her brow.

"Is that...?" she started, reaching out and taking the handle.

"No. Peter Kilpatrick made that with his students." Tara said. "What do you think?"

"It's interesting… kinda ugly, but interesting."

The sound of laughter caused them to look up. Mr. Duncan and Peter were standing a couple of feet off, and had clearly overheard the comment. Catherine didn't give them the pleasure of a blush.

"So it's not the one you sold." She directed to Tara.

"The kids sculpted and painted the whole set," Peter preened.

Catherine leaned in a bit closer to Tara.

"Is this why you wanted Bart and me to come down?" she murmured.

"No, of course not." Tara answered quickly, but Catherine leaned away quickly before she could continue. Catherine walked around the table, carefully examining the tea set like a polar bear circling around a camp site. Tara watched her, wondering what could be on her mind. It might have been a mistake for Catherine and Bart to arrive the evening of the party, as they might be too tired to deal with such an enormous amount of people. On the other hand, Tara wasn't sure she could handle them by herself. The prowling was getting to her. She shook her head and moved to Peter.

"Did I do something wrong?" Tara muttered to him.

Peter glanced at Catherine, still examining the set. "I don't know. Go mingle. If she's anything like you, she'll say something when she wants to."

Tara decided to occupy herself by handing out song lyric books to the guests to prep them for the caroling. She tried to seem jovial, but Catherine's attitude filled the back of her mind with gloom. When her basket of books was empty, she parceled out small bells and bright flashlights for the carolers to keep them safe.

"Are you coming along?" Peter asked.

"No, someone needs to watch the house and have something ready for when you all come back." Tara responded.

Bart, surprisingly, volunteered to go along, having found a couple of friends amongst the dads. Catherine, as well as some of the older parents in the group, chose to stay behind. Tara was clearing up the table when Catherine took up a plate.

"So," Catherine began, fiddling with the teal dish. "It's not the set, or the caroling party. Are you dying?"

"Excuse me?"

"The reason you wanted Bart and me to visit."

"No!"

"Then why? It's been thirty years since we last had a holiday together, and twenty years since we even saw each other in person. If you're not dying, then what could you possibly want? Is it the set? Am I supposed to accept that as what, some fantastical gift? It's hideous!"

*Christ,* Tara thought, as she looked at Catherine's indignant expression. *Is there anything I can say or do at all? Is it even worth trying at this point?* A thought of Peter, working with her over the last few weeks flashed in her mind, and she took a deep breath.

"I know I have always been self-absorbed as a mother. And that has been awful of me. I am proud of the woman you have become in spite of my worst tendencies, and I wanted you to come here because I am getting older. I'm not dying immediately. But one day I will go and I'd at least like to know the person I bore into this hell of a world. So I invited you here because that's the first step to achieving that, and if you think that's selfish of me then fine, dammit, I'll take a tiara too."

Tara swept the rest of the dishes up into her arms and carried them into the kitchen. She resisted the urge to smash them down onto the countertop, opting to instead take out her frustration out on a bottle of soap, squeezing the blue goo into running water of the sink. She grabbed a sponge and plate and angrily set herself to task, scrubbing each plate.

*Useless. The whole thing is useless. She's going to leave tonight and I'll have made a fool of myself. Everyone will*—A clatter next to her derailed her train of thought. Tara stopped washing the dishes. Catherine had found a towel decorated with embroidered flowers and was drying a cup.

"Bart and I had a decent drive," Catherine said quietly, looking at the cup in her hands. "Honestly, despite the fact he looks like a vegetable, he's a fun guy for road trips."

"You could have chosen a lot worse," Tara responded. Catherine smiled and wicked away more moisture with the towel.

"Yeah, but you gotta work with what you get in life. Even if it takes a long time to get it to what you want."

"I don't have much more patience for anything to take a long time," Tara said. She could hear the carolers singing somewhere out in the neighborhood. "But I've found out that a lot of people are happy to help make a long time shorter." She could feel tears starting to well up again.

"So," Tara cleared her throat. "What makes Bart such a wonderful road tripper?"

Tuesday, June 14

# Mystery Lights Baffle Police

Kyleighburn police received four reports over the weekend about lights in the old Jacobson Department Store building, which sits next to City Hall in downtown Kyleighburn.

The building has been empty since 2005, when owner Carl Jacobson retired and moved to Cape Coral, Fla. Jacobson has tried to sell the 80-year-old biuilding, but admits the two-story structure needs a lot of work.

"I get these calls every few months," Jacobson said in a phone call. "The police tell me they never find anything damaged or vandalized, or any sign that anyone's been in the building."

Jacobson said he has let the building alone in the past two years and understands that it is covered with honeysuckle vines.

"I'm going to have to decide what to do with it, he said. "I hate to tear it down; I'd love to find someone who would buy it and restore it. It might make a good office building or apartments if someone was willing to invest in it."

# Soul Mate

Barbara Kirk

# 79 A.D.

"I'm not going to make it! I'm not going to make it!" His labored breathing made his lungs ache, and his heart pounded like a drum. He bent over, hands on his knees, while he tried to slow his breathing. The pain in the back of his calves was excruciating from the miles and miles he'd run during the night and into the morning hours, searching for safety.

Dominic Camilius straightened, looked over his shoulder to make sure he wasn't being followed. Perhaps all was well now. But he trudged on. With each step he felt himself weakening. If he died, who would miss him? His family was gone, killed by King Demus's ruthless soldiers in a surprise night raid in their small village outside of Rome. Men, women, and children had lost their lives. Dom was lucky to have escaped.

The evil king wanted all the land he could acquire, and he cared not who he sacrificed. It was a means to an end. He'd won. Next, he'd overtake Rome where it bordered his land and kill Titus, the Emperor. And then Demus would be ruler over all the land. Woe to the Roman citizens.

Dom stopped suddenly. Was that a tree he saw in the distance? How could anything that size survive in a barren, desolate wasteland?

He pushed himself to keep walking. His body swayed to the left, then to the right. The closer he got to the tree, the weaker he felt. His strength was waning. The heat from the sun was blurring his vision. Sweat rained down his forehead into his eyes. He wiped away the moisture with his forearm and winced. The sunburn on his face, arms, and back of his neck made him feel like he was being stung by hundreds of bees.

The closer he got to the tree the bigger it looked. Only fifty more paces and he'd be able to sit in the shade and rest. He'd sleep for a while, just until he gained enough strength to continue walking. He was so thirsty; his stomach clenched from hunger. He felt ready to pass out as dizziness crept up on him.

*Keep going, keep going,* he encouraged himself. A few more paces and rest would come.

Finally, he stood under the majestic tree and thanked the gods for the shade.

Dom dropped to the ground and leaned upon the tree trunk. Rest was all he needed. He closed his eyes. As he let his body relax, his heartbeat slowed. His breathing evened out. He tried to clear his mind of all the devastation he'd witnessed since last night.

The night raid had taken the village by surprise. King Demus's men had shown no mercy. They'd laughed as men, women, even children, were cut down with swords and arrows. They watched their quarry crumple to the ground in death. They'd tossed burning torches onto the thatched roofs of huts, burning families alive in their homes. They'd even slaughtered innocent animals with their swords. It sickened him.

He counted himself fortunate that he'd gotten away. He felt like a coward, but his family was dead; he had to save himself. When he realized that escape was futile unless he acted quickly, he grabbed the ring he'd created the night before and slipped it on the little finger of his right hand. The silver ring with a beautiful red ruby at its center was worth a fortune. He'd been paid in advance for the work by a Roman citizen. Dom's work was well-known throughout the countryside. People came from miles around to have expensive jewelry made by the silversmith, Dominic Camilius. His money bag was full of handsome payments. He was the wealthiest man in their small village, but one of the most humble. When a weary traveler came through needing food and lodging, Dom was always willing to help them.

There'd been much talk throughout the land over the years about a prophet named Jesus who'd died on a cross more than forty years ago. Rumor was that He'd been raised from the dead. Incredible! The man had claimed to be the Son of God, and He'd had twelve disciples who followed him. He'd taught masses of people. In one of his sermons he'd preached about caring for the needy. To treat others as you would have them treat you. He preached that the God in Heaven was the One True God, who had created the earth and sky and all that was in them.

Dom had been taught that there were many gods. So he didn't hesitate to pray to Zeus and Mother Earth. Except that they'd never answered his prayers. He'd never been able to get the words of the prophet from his mind after he heard the story. It seemed that the more Dom did for others, the more his business grew and the richer he became. Maybe there was something to Jesus's teachings. Perhaps Dom was being rewarded for helping others. By Zeus or by the Christians' God, he didn't know. For whatever reason his business prospered, he wouldn't stop being kind to others. It was the right thing to do.

But Dom wasn't about to leave his valuables behind to be pillaged by the soldiers who thought nothing of stealing from the dead. So he'd put the ruby ring on his finger and grabbed his money sack full of coins and secured it to his belt.

Now that he was lost out in this barren wasteland, he didn't know if he'd even survive. He had only one regret in his life; he'd never married. He wanted a wife and a family. Sons and daughters to fill their home with laughter. He'd even had half of a small heart tattooed on his left bicep. Had it dyed red. The missing side belonged to his soul mate.

In all his five and thirty years he'd searched for his soul mate but never found the woman he'd spend the rest of his life with. He'd go to his grave without having his dream fulfilled. The gods had not seen fit to bless him with the love of a good woman and an heir.

Perhaps if he prayed to Aphrodite and asked the goddess of love and beauty to bestow her favor on him, she would *send* his soul mate to him. He'd pray loud enough to get her attention, and she would listen to his supplication. Or should he pray to this God in Heaven that Jesus talked so much about? Whether he prayed to the Christian God or to Aphrodite, if he died here under this massive tree, his prayer would be in vain. And he lacked the energy to even speak in a whisper.

His shoulders slumped, and his head lolled against his chest. Slumber beckoned him. He'd rest for just an hour. Then he'd be on his way.

His mind drifted. Darkness consumed him as he felt himself falling, plummeting downward as if he were a heavy boulder. His arms grappled to reach for something to stop the fall, but there was nothing but air. His arms and legs flailed. His body spun. When would he hit bottom? Would his body shatter into a thousand pieces? Would anyone find his broken body or recognize what was left of him? Would the animals and buzzards find him and feast on his flesh and bones?

Even as he fell into this nothingness, he was aware that his backside was still in contact with solid ground. He could hear the birds chirping in the tree above. A slight breeze had begun to blow, cooling his hot skin. But why did he still feel like he was falling? The spinning was out of control. He tried and tried to force his eyes open, but they felt so heavy. They remained closed as he searched the darkness within his mind, finding nothing.

He tried to open his mouth to speak, but the desperate scream caught in his throat; he couldn't release it no matter how hard he tried.

The ground began to shake beneath him. What was that smell? Was that sulphur permeating his nostrils? Mount Vesuvius? The ground shook harder. Then the loud explosion coming from the distance rent the air. His body shifted. But his mind was still spinning and falling into nothingness. It didn't make any sense. Then he felt the ground split open beneath him, and his body fell into a pit. As it hit bottom, the spinning in his mind finally stopped. Then dirt fell upon him. He couldn't move. The earth continued to tremble and shake uncontrollably as more dirt rained down upon him. Sheer panic overtook him but he was trapped.

He felt the branches of the tree he'd been sitting under wrapping around him, weaving their way through the dirt, surrounding him, as if protecting him. Around his arms and chest, his legs and feet, and covering his head and face. Except for his eyes. Why not his eyes? If the dirt didn't smother him, the branches would. But yet, somehow, he could still breathe. Then little by little, his body became as one solid mass of rock.

The longer he lay in that pit, the heavier the dirt weighed down upon him. He was being crushed. He would soon succumb to death. The ruby ring he wore and the sack of coins hanging on his belt would not be enough to buy his entrance into the afterlife.

**1979 A.D.**

Leon Dodson was a land developer who'd had his eyes on a piece of property outside of Pompeii for years. It had never been a victim of the lava that had spewed out of Mt. Vesuvius twice in history, first in 79 A.D. and then in 1944. He'd had the land checked by a geologist and it was found sound. This would be the last housing development he'd build. Then he could retire. Breaking ground had begun in March, 1979. Considering the area of land he needed to build on, he rented several Caterpillars from a local equipment company outside of Rome. Just digging the ground apart to put in the foundations could take months. The ground was full of large boulders that would have to be removed and hauled away.

Leon stood by his construction trailer watching the work progress. They'd been digging for four days. Mountains of dirt waited to be hauled away. A Caterpillar scooped up a load of dirt from a deep hole, the operator dumping it on a rising mound. Something rolled down the side of the dirt.

"Stop! Stop!" Leon yelled, running toward the huge machine.

The machine operator cut the engine and hopped out of the cab and down onto the broken ground.

"What's up, Boss?" the burly man asked.

"Look."

Both men walked over to where Leon pointed. At the bottom of the pile of dirt lay the most amazing statue they'd ever seen. It looked like a peasant man from the days of Roman kings, expertly carved out of a large tree trunk, then covered with some kind of transparent rust-colored resin. They'd never seen anything like it before. Was it even a statue? As they looked closer, they noticed a silver ring with a red gem at its center on the pinky finger of his right hand. How could a peasant afford an expensive looking ring like that? There was a bulging money bag tied to a woven belt. Maybe this peasant was a thief. Then they noticed, on his left upper arm was a red tattoo that looked like half of a heart. Did they even draw hearts in ancient days like the ones children drew on Valentine's Day in school?

"What're we gonna do with it?" the machine operator asked.

Leon took his ball cap off and scratched his head, then returned the cap to his head.

"Well, I guess I have to report this. But I'm not sure to whom."

"Should I keep digging?"

"No. We'll have to stop temporarily. It's hard to tell what else might show up."

Leon called to his other operators using his walkie-talkie and told them to stop digging. They were all to gather at the office for a meeting.

Although the men were unhappy to find out they'd be out of work until this matter was cleared up, they understood the stoppage. There'd have to be an investigation, and who knew how long that would take.

The local historical society in Rome came to retrieve the statue. It was loaded into a long wooden box filled with Styrofoam peanuts for protection. The lid was nailed in place and, because of its weight, it took several men to lift it into a huge truck. It was taken to the Kicherian Museum to be studied. Kicherian was one of four museums that made up the National Roman Museum in Rome, Italy.

Several archaeologists and a geologist were called in to inspect the land that was being dug up. By the end of two weeks, nothing else had been discovered, so the digging resumed.

It took several days of study and research to come to any conclusions concerning the beautiful statue. It was believed to be made of petrified wood. Beneath the transparent coating, it had been carved intricately, making it look life-like. The man was dressed in a tunic that went down to his thighs. He wore a belt woven out of thin braids. A small money pouch, seemingly filled with coins, hung from the belt. His feet were shod in simple sandals. He was tall and looked to be a handsome man.

Two archaeologists worked side by side in the workroom in the underground rooms of the Kicherian Museum to clean the dirt out of all the crevices on the statue and then hose it down. They chipped away at the solid rock on the bottom of his sandals to study the resin. Why had someone felt it necessary to cover the statue? Fortunately, the resin had preserved the work of art. The only odd thing was, the eyes of the statue hadn't been covered, yet they were still intact. It was difficult to validate the age of the statue because it was impossible to get to the statue itself. But after testing the resin for its age, they dated the statue to be from about 100 A.D. It would make an exhibit that would draw millions of people to the museum.

One thought ran through their minds. What if this statue had actually been a *real* man who had fallen into a pit, was covered up with dirt and over the years had become petrified? How long would that take to happen, anyway? There was no way they could prove their suspicions. It was all speculation. So they kept their thoughts to themselves.

The statue was given to the Kicherian Museum by the Historical Society and was put on display outside the building. This particular museum displayed archaeological collections and ancient sculpture. There it stood for the next thirty years.

For the following eight years, the statue was included as part of a world-wide tour of Roman artifacts. It was always placed at the entrance to the museums. Tourists were fascinated by it. People touched it, even though the signs warned against it. Extra security was added just to protect the statue. Of all the Roman artifacts that were on display in the various museums, the statue of the petrified man always drew the most attention.

**2017 A.D.**

The small town of Kyleighburn, North Carolina, has been struggling economically. In order to get the town on the map, so to speak, they decided to renovate the lighthouse located on the island. To promote the project, the town council encouraged shopkeepers and residents to create their own lighthouse and put it on display. Before long, small lighthouses began popping up all over town.

The town council also met with Mayor Esposito and discussed commissioning the National Roman Museum to come to Kyleighburn with their display of Roman artifacts and the mysterious statue carved of petrified wood. The statue had been the topic of discussion on talk shows for years. Surely a display at their local museum would draw in residents from the surrounding counties, as well as tourists willing to travel from parts unknown. They pitched their request, pointing out that it could help their economy.

"Look, Mayor, don't you see? After visiting the museum to see the Roman artifacts," the president of the town council argued, "people would stay in town and shop the local stores."

The mayor gave the request a moment's consideration. "It'll be expensive but I think it might work. Go ahead and get the plans put together."

A couple of months later the museum in Kyleighburn proper received the shipment of Roman artifacts, and set up the display along the east wall of the building. Guards were stationed at both ends of the display. The curator also enlisted the help of several volunteers as additional backup security.

Newspapers throughout the state reported that the tour of Roman artifacts would be on display for four weeks at the local museum in Kyleighburn. The much-talked-about statue thought to be made of petrified wood and sealed in a hard resin warranted special mention. Everyone was invited to come.

The statue had always stood at the front entrance to museums and had to have a security guard placed outside just to protect it. So the curator thought, why not put it on display in the beautiful courtyard? That might not deter people from touching it, but they would put up a sign warning people not to touch the ancient relic.

The tall statue of the Roman peasant was placed on the tile near the lovely concrete water fountain in the courtyard. He appeared to stand sentinel as people walked through the courtyard admiring the lovely flowers and the fountain. Dom became the main attraction. Numerous people stopped to look him over and admire him. His long hair and tunic of ancient times, even the sandals on his feet, captivated the people. He wore a silver ring with a red gem on his right pinky finger. It was amazing to people that anyone could have carved this giant man and placed a valuable ring on his finger that couldn't be removed. A money bag hung from his braided belt. Many speculated if anything was actually in that bag, but it had probably just been carved to look that way. Half of a red heart tattoo was visible on his upper left arm.

Yet, what was most unquestionably the most fascinating feature of this statue was that his eyes looked real. They stared straight ahead but the pupils narrowed in the sun and dilated as the sun went down. As lifelike as they seemed, they never blinked.

Dom was alive, but was he really living? It seemed more than ten life-times ago he'd sat under that tree. He'd smelled sulphur, then the ground shook, and split open. Mount Vesuvius had erupted. He'd fallen into the pit and was covered up with dirt raining down on him. But hadn't died. How was that possible? That tree he'd been leaning against had something to do with it, he was sure. It had been uprooted and fallen into the pit on top of him. He'd felt the branches winding their way around him, except for his eyes. Then a sticky substance had coated his body, turning hard, and he couldn't move.

How long he'd been in that pit he didn't know. The spinning and spiral fall that he'd taken into the darkness had stopped abruptly. His mind was always thinking. About his job as a silversmith. About his family. About the surprise attack on their village. The same thoughts kept running through his mind, year after year after year.

Then the ground began to shake again. Had Vesuvius erupted again? As the earth trembled, he wondered if the pit would open up so he could climb out. But his body couldn't move because of the hard substance covering him. Eventually the earth stopped trembling and nothing happened. Once again, the years passed.

For the third time the earth trembled. It didn't seem possible that Vesuvius could erupt for the third time. He was just about out of patience.

But something was different this time. The earth on top of him became lighter. There was less pressure on his person. Unexpectedly, he was scooped up out of the ground and dumped on a huge mound of dirt. His body rolled over and over until he landed at the bottom. Freedom!

Men were shouting but their voices were muffled because his ears were covered with a hard shell, and their language was unfamiliar to him. They knelt beside him. They examined the ring on his finger, his tunic, his bag of coins on his belt and the heart tattoo on his arm.

He was put in a carriage that moved without horses. It had been a really bumpy ride. They took him to a room in the lower caverns of a building, and laid him on a slab.

Two men wearing thin white coats brushed dirt from the hard shell that imprisoned him. He couldn't move. He couldn't blink his eyes. And he didn't understand what they were saying. The men inspected him from head to toe and even scraped something from under his sandals. Then he was stood upright and sprayed down with water from a long flexible tube of some kind.

A couple of days later, he was placed at the front of what had once been a government building in Rome in 79 A.D., the time in which he had lived. Only a shell of the building existed now. There he stood for many years. During that time he learned different languages from all the tourists that came through seeking to learn the history of the city.

The tour guides explained many times over the years, in many different languages, that Mount Vesuvius had erupted in the year 79 A.D., destroying the city and inhabitants of Pompeii and then blew again in 1944. That was why the ground had shaken when he'd first sat under that huge tree to rest. And his body had been trapped in a deep pit for almost two millennia. How could that be?

Yet it should be no surprise. Standing at the entrance during all these years he learned much about current daily life. The style of clothing had changed. It was scandalous to see women who wore only scraps of clothing, their arms and legs exposed. Men looked at those scantily-clad women with lust in their eyes. Women batted their eyelashes in return, and men and women embraced and kissed in public. It was more than he could endure. What had happened to humanity over all these years?

One day, several men came up to him and looked him over. Then they tipped him back, picked him up, and laid him in a box filled with something one of the men called Styrofoam peanuts, whatever that was. A lid was put over him and nailed in place. The box was lifted and he felt himself being placed in a noisy carriage and carted off to who knew where. Then the box was moved again and put into another carriage that made an *extremely* loud noise as it started to move. He felt himself tilting back, then leveling. Suddenly his ride became smoother. He felt like he was floating on air.

It was dark inside the box, but it didn't bother him. He'd survived being buried alive for more years than he could count. Even though he'd been freed from his grave long ago, he wondered when the outer shell he was stuck in would break away so he could *truly* be free.

Suddenly he felt himself shift inside the box. He was tilting again in the opposite direction. A short time later, the carriage seemed to bounce and then stop. The box he was in was removed from the carriage, then put into another carriage. The ride was rough and rushed. Finally it slowed and stopped. It was then that he realized that he'd never heard the clip-clop of horses' hooves as he was transported from one carriage to another. What means of transportation had he been placed in?

The box he was in was removed from the carriage and taken into a large building. He could hear the screech of the nails as they were pulled from the lid. His body was removed from the box and stood in a corner of a large room. He heard someone say he was part of a Roman museum tour.

He stood there, silently observing. Out of the corner of his eye, he saw tables being set up and things put out on display. Items that he knew were from his time. But to everyone else, they were referred to as ancient tools and artifacts. To him they were garden tools, tools to fix chariot wheels, and clay pots.

It seemed that every couple of months he went through the same process. He was put in a box and taken in a truck and then in a plane, he'd heard someone say. His ride always began and ended in confusion with a smooth peaceful ride in between. Then he'd be placed in another museum in another city where the same items were put on display.

People came from far and wide to marvel over the artifacts, as they called them. They would "ooh" and "ahh" and get all excited. To them, everything they saw was old or ancient. To him, they were normal household items used for daily living or everyday work.

When someone passed by him standing in his corner, they'd study him from head to toe. Some people would grunt in disbelief, comment that someone had wasted their time carving a man out of petrified wood, and then move on. What was petrified wood? He didn't know. But maybe it had something to do with the hard covering he was encased in.

He had no trouble seeing straight ahead and he was able to move his eyes, but for some reason, he was unable to blink. Women would walk up to him and bat their eyes at him and giggle. Even in his present state, he knew when a woman was flirting with him.

"You're beautiful," they'd say. "I wish you were real." Well, he *was* real. He just couldn't move or speak.

The women always found the half-heart tattoo on his left arm. They'd trace it with their index finger and coo at him. "I'll be the other half of your heart," they teased. But not one woman appealed to him. And he never felt their touch.

Maybe someday the gods would find favor with him. Surely they'd seen what he'd endured over the years. Surely he was worthy of being made whole again. Maybe then he would find his one true love—his soul mate. But after all these years, he'd begun to doubt the existence of the gods. Maybe there *was* only one true God. Maybe that's why Dom hadn't died when the ground had swallowed him up almost two thousand years ago. Maybe this Christian God in Heaven was looking out for him and would give him back his life. He could only hope. Maybe that's why his body had been found. He made a decision. He was going to pray only to the One True God. If God answered his prayers, then he'd know that Jesus had the right of it—He *was* the Son of God and there was only *one* true God.

Year after year Dom was moved and he went through the same process every time. Set in a corner; watched the people come in to a room full of old things; then at closing time, the lights went out and the people went home. The quiet hours gave him time to let his mind rest until daylight when people would come back to the room he was in and ogle him all over again.

He grew bored over the years. How many had it been? Thirty? Forty? He didn't know. Would this never end? People came to the museum to see the old artifacts. But they were always anxious to see the man made out of petrified wood. He was something different.

One day, a teenager, as tall as Dom, walked up to him and looked him in the eye. The boy scrutinized him. He scratched his cheek in thought; scratched his head; hummed a couple of times. The boy chuckled.

"What're those eyes made of, Buddy? Are they real or glass?" Then the boy did the unthinkable. He took two fingers and poked the statue in the eyes.

The statue groaned as loudly as it could, scaring the boy. He jumped back in fear just as two security guards came and grabbed him by both arms and dragged him out of the museum.

*If only I could speak. If only I could blink,* Dom thought. *Will I never be released from my prison?*

Being in Kyleighburn, North Carolina, was like a breath of fresh air. He stood in a beautiful courtyard near a water fountain. He basked in the sound of the happy water as it splashed into the small circular pond. It was a glorious sound. With the sun shining and the flowers and shrubs growing about him, it was a haven. Maybe he could stay here for the rest of his life. All this traveling was getting on his nerves. He harrumphed to himself. It was just wishful thinking. Someone always came back and took him away, moving him to another location. When would this all end?

He'd survived almost two thousand years. Was he immortal? Had the gods blessed him with unnumbered years? It was a lonely life he lived. But he wasn't really living. He couldn't even eat. All he did was stand in one place for people to gawk at him. Women swooned over him. Men admired him. But what kind of life was that?

Dom knew he was trapped for eternity. After all these years, he was doomed to boredom and a life of unhappiness. He'd prayed for years to be able to close his eyes and just sleep. But sleep never came.

He heard workers setting up the display inside the museum building. Since he was facing in that direction, he could see them carefully remove small packages from boxes, unwrap the items and set them on tables. They worked for hours getting everything set up just as the curator demanded.

Attached to the museum was the local library. He'd love to visit it and choose a tome to read to while away the hours. It was one more thing he could not do. Trapped as he was he could only stand there and be warmed by the sun.

Maybe Ceres, Mother Earth, would restore his life. Perhaps that was why he was standing outside. Perhaps, after all these years, she finally saw him worthy of being restored back into a living human being again. But how could he prove himself worthy? He couldn't move, walk, or speak. So if Mother Earth didn't see fit to restore his life back to him, who could?

His thoughts returned to the One True God. Perhaps He could do what the other gods could not do. After all this time, he was pretty sure that the other gods did not exist. He'd seen no evidence of their works over the years. No matter how much he'd prayed to them.

*Well,* he thought. *This is my life now. But how much longer can I exist?* He spent his days standing in one place, listening to people talk about their visit to the museum and rave about the man carved out of petrified wood. He snorted to himself. He still couldn't figure out what petrified wood was. He didn't think he'd want anything made from any kind of wood unless it was something useful; like a table or a chair.

Mercy Grace Romano was a much sought-after geologist. She was on staff at UNC—University of North Carolina—in Chapel Hill, North Carolina, in the Department of Geological Sciences. Her Master's and Doctorate degrees hung proudly on her office wall behind her desk. She was thirty years old, stood five feet six inches, and had light brown hair and deep brown eyes. She was single, but not by choice. All she seemed to do was work, so there was no time for a man in her life. But her secret dream was to find her soul mate.

She taught throughout the school year, then during the summer months she traveled all over the world heading up geological digs with a group of students who loved the earth almost as much as she did.

Her classes were always full each semester before the end of the registration deadline, and every semester, there was a waiting list of students hoping that someone would drop the course so they could step into that slot.

When the school year concluded, Mercy Grace would be spirited away by plane to parts unknown, hired by corporations and land developers who needed her expertise to inspect the ground they were intending to buy or build on. Her knowledge of the earth surpassed any information gained from a textbook. Students signed up to go with her, at their own expense. They wanted to learn from the master. There wasn't anything she didn't know about dirt.

But the time had come for Mercy Grace to make a decision—take a break from teaching and get some much-needed rest or keep going at the pace she was going and end up burned out. Giving up the career she loved with a passion was not an option.

Before the current spring semester ended, she'd turned down several offers for all-expense paid trips to Europe and Asia throughout the summer months. But she'd decided to go to Myrtle Beach and spend two weeks on the beach doing nothing but relaxing and swimming in the ocean.

She had two choices; drive from Chapel Hill where she lived to Myrtle Beach, South Carolina, or fly and then rent a car. She checked her search engine on the computer comparing the time it would take to fly as opposed to driving. One flight left from Charlotte and another left from Raleigh. It would take time to drive to either airport plus flight time. One flight even had a stop-over. She didn't feel up to driving. Her body begged for rest. *Let someone else do the driving,* she thought. She could always use a rental car to drive back home. After some much-needed rest, she'd be able to handle it. With that decision made, she booked the shortest flight from Charlotte and called it done. The flight would land at the Myrtle Beach International Airport and she'd rent a car.

The other day she'd read an article in the paper about a Roman artifacts display, along with a statue made of petrified wood, that was being brought to a small town, Kyleighburn, in southern North Carolina. It had been unearthed by a land developer digging near Pompeii back in 1979 where he was going to build a new housing district.

Being in the dirt business, as her colleagues liked to joke about, it piqued her interest. Perhaps she would drive home from Myrtle Beach in a rental car, after all. After two weeks of rest, she could enjoy the drive. She'd be driving through Kyleighburn, so she'd take the opportunity to stop and see the statue.

So on Thursday, after graduation in May, Mercy Grace packed her bags, tossed them in the trunk, and left for the airport. She parked her car in the parking garage, checked in, and waited for her flight to be called. Her flight left on schedule. They'd been in the air for about an hour-and-a-half when the captain made an announcement.

"Ladies and gentlemen," he began. "May I have your attention, please? This is Captain Rivers. We're going to have to make an emergency landing in a field near the small town of Kyleighburn. We've run into some mechanical difficulties that will make it unsafe to continue on to Myrtle Beach. I apologize for the delay."

"Great," she said to no one in particular.

Well, if they were landing near Kyleighburn, she'd probably have time to go to the museum where the Roman artifacts were on display and see this unusual statue. Being a geologist, it would be exciting to see something that large made of petrified wood. But if the statue was dated back to 100 A.D., it likely wouldn't be in very good shape.

Then, instead of driving back home after her two weeks in Myrtle Beach, she'd fly back since she was already stopping in Kyleighburn.

The plane landed in a large field outside of Kyleighburn around nine o'clock. Three school buses pulled up alongside the plane. As passengers disembarked, they were guided to the buses. It was a short drive into the center of town where everyone was let out in front of city hall. The local government building was beautiful. It had a very Romanesque look, which made the display from the National Roman Museum seem like it had finally come home.

Mayor Esposito met the buses and greeted the people as they stepped out onto the sidewalk.

"Ladies and gentlemen, welcome to our fair city." The mayor stood tall, his shoulders back, his head held high, looking over his nose as he spoke. "It's unfortunate for you that your plane had this unexpected landing. But we welcome you here in Kyleighburn. Please, feel free to shop and mill about town. Just tell the shopkeepers that you were on the plane that made the emergency landing and that Mayor Esposito said you could have a ten percent discount on your purchases." It was a nice gesture but hardly fair to the shop owners without the *official* word from the mayor. Could the shop owners take a loss in profit? Just because there was an emergency landing, did that justify shoppers taking advantage of a discount? Maybe the mayor had an agreement with the shop owners to make the offer when the occasion arose. If Mercy Grace was going to buy anything, she wouldn't mention the discount; she'd pay full price. It was the right thing to do.

The mayor seemed cordial enough, but Mercy Grace got the feeling that the man thought pretty highly of himself because of his position in the small town. He never stopped talking, even when someone tried to ask him a question. Finally, when there was a break in his long speech, the people dispersed.

Mercy Grace stood along the edge of the sidewalk and looked left and right to see where all these places were that the mayor had talked about in his long speech. The center of town looked clean and well-taken care of.

"Mayor Esposito," Mercy Grace said. "Could you tell me where the museum is located?" Of all the places he'd talked about, why hadn't he mentioned the museum? And that's where the Roman artifacts display was. It would be a big money-maker for the town. What kind of mayor was he, anyways?

"It's down the street, that way," he told Mercy Grace, pointing to the left. "Just a couple of blocks away, within walking distance. The library's right beside it. And if you go down here to the right, it's just a few blocks to the Tottie River. If you go further down the road from the museum, you can visit Magnolia Park. It's a lovely park. And don't miss all the little lakes around town. They're nice places to sit and just take it easy. And you'll have to check out all of the decorative lighthouses around town."

Once the mayor finally shut up, Mercy Grace made a run for it. He was just trying to be helpful, so she hadn't wanted to interrupt him. But she wasn't interested in seeing all the other landmarks he'd told her about. All she'd asked about was the library. She figured the mayor just liked to hear himself talk.

As she walked, she checked store windows, noting some cute outfits. Pretty current for a small town, too, she thought. Maybe she'd do some shopping after she left the museum.

The museum shared a building with the E.P.P. Scott Library. Neither side of the building looked very big. But looks could be deceiving.

Mercy Grace walked up the stone steps and entered the museum through the electronic doors as they swooshed open. She paid the admission price at the reception desk and then took her time walking around. It was bigger than it looked. Most of the museum displayed memorabilia of by-gone days in Kyleighburn. She studied old photos of founding families on the walls and a crude map of the original layout of the town.

While it was all interesting, she wanted to see what artifacts the archaeologists had unearthed in Rome. The whole east wall was set up with tables full of Roman tools, household utensils, cooking pots, clay plates and serving dishes, along with jewelry, and several articles of clothing. Mercy Grace could just imagine how excited the archaeological team had been when they'd unearthed these items.

For just a moment she regretted her decision to take a vacation. Mercy Grace missed her job and she missed being out on a dig. Maybe she'd call one of her contacts and ask if they were planning to do any excavating within the U.S. There was always something interesting to find. She'd nixed her opportunity to travel this summer. But there were a lot of places in the mid-west where she could 'play in the dirt'. It was her job but she enjoyed it so much that it didn't feel like work.

After spending the better part of an hour inside the museum looking at all the displays, including the Roman artifacts, she made her way through the back door into the courtyard.

When she spotted the huge statue standing by the water fountain, her legs felt weak and the blood rushed to her head. The statue of the man was so lifelike she thought he might start talking to her, welcoming her into the beautiful courtyard. She took small steps toward him. The statue had to be about six feet, two inches to her five feet, six inches. Looking down at his sandal-clad feet, she saw he wasn't mounted on a pedestal or base of any kind. His hair was pulled back into a ponytail, held with a thong and hung between his shoulder blades. He was wearing a simple tunic so he obviously was a peasant. What puzzled Mercy Grace was the fact that the statue wore a silver ring with a red ruby in the center of it on his pinky finger. How could a peasant afford a ring that valuable? Perhaps he'd been a thief and stolen the ring from a Roman citizen. But she reminded herself that he was just a statue. Whoever had carved him hadn't thought about the peasant's station in life.

She walked around him and gasped when she saw his left arm. Under the layer of translucent resin, was a tattoo of a half-heart etched in red on his upper arm. The other half of the heart was missing, just as it was on *her* left bicep.

Mercy Grace walked back to the front of the statue to face it. She quickly looked around the courtyard to see if anyone was watching her. She was alone. Except for *him*.

She tilted her head back to look up at him. He was gorgeous. He looked more like a Roman god than a peasant.

An awareness came over her that she'd never felt before. Her life was going to change. And it had something to do with the statue.

"Sir," she said in a soft gentle voice, "my name is Dr. Mercy Grace Romano. I'm a professor of geology at the University of North Carolina in Chapel Hill. I hadn't planned on coming to Kyleighburn today, but my plane had mechanical difficulties, and we had to make an emergency landing in a field not far from here. I'd heard that the display of Roman artifacts would be here. I was planning on stopping here on the way back from my vacation in Myrtle Beach, but, for some reason, I'm here now instead of later. I've heard about you, and I think you're the most fascinating part of the display. You look so real. If you *were* real, you'd think I was daft talking to a statue.

"I teach all year long and then during the summer I travel all over the world working for corporations and land developers. I won't bore you with what I do. It gets kind of complicated, anyway." She sighed. "My parents and grandparents have hounded me for years about getting married. I *want* to get married, but with my busy schedule, there just isn't time to meet anyone.

"Here's the funny part of my story. I had a tattoo of a red heart drawn on my left bicep years ago. One half of it is red but the other half is empty because it belongs to my soul mate. But I haven't found him yet." She turned sideways and showed him her arm, as if he could really see it. "Here's where the story gets even funnier." Her eyes filled with tears. "You have the other half of the heart on your arm. How can my soul mate be made of petrified wood?"

Mercy Grace put her hand on the statue's arm, covering the half heart. She felt warmth radiate from his arm. She jerked her hand away. How could his arm be that warm? She looked up at the sky. It was cloudless but the trees in the courtyard cast a shadow over the statue, blocking the sun. Even if the sun had been shining on the statue, it wouldn't have penetrated just one small area. She touched his hand, but it was only slightly warm. She cupped his left cheek with her hand. It was warm but not nearly as warm as his arm. She laid her hand on his chest, where his heart would beat if he was a real man. She squealed in surprise and jumped back. His heart *was* beating.

"What's going on here?" she asked the statue, her eyes wide as a saucer. "If you're carved of petrified wood, how can you radiate heat? And how can your heart beat? *You are not alive!*" she told the statue. "The archaeologists say you date back to the year 100 A.D. There's no way your heart can be beating."

She walked around him to see if there was a latch on the statue's back where a battery had been placed, making the statue a fake. But the back of the statue was solid. And besides, it had already been authenticated by archaeologists.

She walked back in front of him again and looked up at the statue's face. Was that a tear ready to fall from his left eye? She stepped closer. And then the tear fell down the statue's cheek.

Mercy Grace felt her head spin and her knees go out from under her. In the next instant, her world went black and she collapsed to the ground.

Dom saw the back door of the museum open and a young woman walk through, coming directly toward him. She was beautiful. She was of average height and petite. She was dressed like most modern women; in men's trousers and a pullover shirt. He wondered what she would look like in a proper tunic or a stola. Her earrings were made of small gems. She wore no other jewelry and her lips were natural. No red dye on this woman's lips.

When she got right in front of him, he could see she was even more beautiful than she was twenty paces away. A jolt went straight to his heart when she looked up into his eyes. When she spoke, her voice was smooth as silk as she told him about herself. She was educated. A teacher of Mother Earth. Perhaps she was Mother Earth herself, come to tell him she'd found favor with him. She could use her powers of love to release him from this spell he'd been under for years. The hard shell that held him prisoner could be broken. Then he could live out the rest of his life as he'd once hoped to.

Except that he was living in a different age and time now. Life would never be the same for him. People dressed differently, talked differently, worshipped differently, and lived a completely different societal life than he had when he'd lived outside of Rome.

The woman looked him over, from head to toe. She walked around him. When she walked to his left side and saw the tattoo of the half heart on his arm, he thought she would swoon. He thought *he'd* swoon when she turned and showed him the tattoo on *her* left arm. They were exactly the same.

She laid her hand right over the tattoo. Over the years, countless women had touched it. He'd never felt a thing. Until now. Then she touched his hand, his cheek, and then laid her hand over his heart. His heart was beating so wildly, he was just sure it would break the casing he was entombed in so he could be set free of this prison he'd been condemned to.

A tear ran down his cheek. Then the woman actually swooned and dropped to the ground. He moaned and tried to call for help. But it was impossible to get anyone's attention. Had she died of shock? Right here in front of him lay his soul mate, and he was helpless to aid her.

A man came rushing out of the building and into the courtyard. He went straight to the woman. Others from inside followed. Dom sighed in relief. Help had come just in time.

"Ma'am. Ma'am. Are you okay?" The worried security guard patted her cheek to rouse her.

"What? What?" she asked breathlessly, as she shook her head to clear the cobwebs from her brain.

The security guard put his arm behind her back and raised her up into a sitting position.

"Are you okay?" he asked again.

"What happened?" she asked.

"You must have had too much sun. You passed out."

Mercy Grace knew she hadn't passed out from the sun's heat. This statue had a living man inside of it. If the statue dated back to 100 A.D., he was a living miracle.

"Oh." She wasn't about to explain what had actually happened to her. They'd think she was crazy if she told them the statue on display was alive.

"Here. Let me help you up," the guard offered.

He took her by her hands and pulled her to her feet.

"Thank you," she told him.

His brows furrowed. "Can you stand on your own?"

"Yes, I think so. Thank you." She offered him a weak smile and he released her hands.

"Okay, then. I need to get back inside." He turned and walked back into the building followed by all the on-lookers.

When she was alone again with the statue, she looked up at him.

"I don't know what's going on here, sir, but it's very mysterious. I don't believe in magic but something happened to you a long time ago and you've been imprisoned in this…whatever it is." She motioned with her hands toward him as if he could look down and see what form of regalia he was encased in. "I'm gonna go over to the library next door and do a little research. Although I don't know exactly what to look up," she said softly, more to herself than to the statue. She looked up at him. "If there's anything I can do to help you, I will. But I can't imagine what. If you're almost two thousand years old and still alive, will you die if you're exposed to our air? Will you survive at all? You might die of culture shock." She laughed, then sobered. "I'm sorry. That wasn't funny."

What was the matter with her, talking to a statue as if it could really hear her? Could it? If there was blood pumping through his veins, since his heart was beating—or had she only imagined that?—she had to do something to help him. If he was released from his prison, what would that do to the display? And how would he survive in the present day?

She had to be out of her mind trying to rationalize her thinking. The petrified wood, or that hard resin over the petrified wood, would have to be chiseled at in order to break it apart if it could even be accomplished. She didn't have the means to attempt it and even if she did, she'd be arrested for damaging a relic from ancient times. The statue was irreplaceable.

She shook her head. Maybe she was insane, but she needed to do some research on Rome and Mount Vesuvius and petrified wood. She had plenty of time while they repaired the plane. Hopefully, she'd uncover the mystery surrounding this statue. If there really was a man inside the petrified wood, he'd be okay. He'd survived all these years, hadn't he? But how much longer would he have to be entombed as he was? Being gawked at and scrutinized by the public? This was all out of her area of expertise.

She asked herself if she really wanted to get back on that plane and fly to Myrtle Beach once it was repaired. Discovering the secret of this mysterious statue was much more important to her than a vacation. Especially if she would be saving a life! Something told her she couldn't leave.

She went back inside the building and walked up to the reception desk where people were paying their admission fee.

"Excuse me, ma'am," she said to the woman who was ready to pay her admission fee. "I just need to ask a quick question." She looked at the receptionist. "I need to go next door to the library to do some research. I'm a geologist and there're some things I need to look up concerning that statue out in the courtyard. When I'm done at the library, could I get back in and examine the statue again or do I need to pay the fee again?"

The woman thought for a moment. "You say you're a geologist?" Mercy Grace nodded. "Sure. You've already paid the admittance fee." She gave the young woman a pleasant smile.

"Thanks. Here's my business card to prove I really am a geologist."

She pulled a card out of her back jeans pocket and handed the card to the woman, then rushed out the door and over to the adjoining library. After getting directions to the historical section, Mercy Grace looked over the bindings of the books on the shelves. There was a book about ancient Rome, another of the architecture, civilization and culture, and mores during the reign of Titus. Then she found exactly what she needed; a book on Roman statues. She had enough food for thought so she sat down at a long table with her stack of books. Before she sat down, she went to the front desk and asked for some scrap paper to take notes on. The woman gave her a half-dozen sheets of paper and a pen.

Mercy Grace took her seat and got started. The library was open until eight o'clock, but she needed to gather as much information as she could so that she could get back to the museum. Once the plane was repaired, should couldn't hold up the departure. She'd just have to remain behind because she needed to re-examine the statue and see if she could figure out a way to break through the resin and release the man. Had anyone ever tried to break through the hard shell? Probably not. For all intents and purposes, he was a statue.

For the next hour, she read over the information the books offered.

History was fascinating. Rome and Pompeii were two places she'd never been before but would love to visit.

As she looked through the book on sculptures of ancient Rome, she thought about the talent it had taken to create the sculptures and busts that had graced Italy.

But what of the statue that was on display in the courtyard of the museum? Who had fashioned him? There was no record of the sculptor. He was a perfect work of art. And where had the resin come from that had become as hard as petrified wood? His body radiated heat and his heart beat in his chest. How could he have been alive all these years? Was it humanly possible? He'd been buried underground for almost two thousand years; no food, nothing to drink. Logic said no, it wasn't possible that he could have survived. But yet he did. How was she going to release him from his petrified state? And *should* she? What would happen to him once he was no longer in bondage? How was it possible that she could she feel his body heat and his heart beating through that hard, thick resin? It didn't make any sense.

Mercy Grace closed her eyes. *Lord,* she prayed silently. *I know nothing is too difficult for you. You know I've prayed for years for a man to come into my life. I've been looking for my soul mate. That's why I had only half of a heart tattooed on my arm. This statue has the other half of my tattooed heart. He's my soul mate, as ridiculous as that sounds. Now that I've found him, I feel like someone's playing a joke on me. The poor guy's living in a petrified prison.* She laughed softly to herself and then the tears began to fall down her cheeks. *I felt his heart beat, God. How can that be? Of all the men on this earth in my time, You chose someone for me from the year 100 A.D. Really? If this is supposed to be the man You want me to have as a husband, then please perform a miracle and release him from his petrified state. Please God. You're the only one who can help him. Thank you. Amen.*

Mercy Grace opened her eyes and closed the book she'd been looking at. She pushed it aside and stood up.

The building began to shake. She grabbed ahold of the edge of the table to keep from being tossed onto the floor. The table she was holding onto shook. The stack of books she'd been perusing slid off the table. Books fell off the shelves onto the floor. Then the building settled. She rushed outside to see people standing all along the sidewalk. Everyone was talking about what had happened.

Had it been an earthquake? The road on the street was intact. None of the windows on the stores were broken. All the trees seemed to still be standing. Then someone announced that the trailer park had collapsed. Perhaps there *had* been an earthquake.

Mercy Grace heard a loud buzzing sound off in the distance. Within moments the sound grew louder. Then she could see the swarm of bees that looked like a black cloud as it moved up the street. The high-pitched shrill was so loud it hurt her ears. She threw her hands over her ears, but it didn't help. So she ran into the museum for safety.

A woman ran in behind her.

"Don't go outside," she told everyone that could hear her. "There's a huge swarm of bees coming up the street. Nobody knows what kind of bees they are or where they came from."

Those standing about began to mumble their concerns.

Mercy Grace went to the back of the museum where the glass doors faced the courtyard. She had to check on the statue. She gasped. She couldn't believe what she saw.

At least a hundred bees were hovering over the statue's head. What were they up to? Why had the statue attracted their attention? She wanted to run out and shoo them away. And the longer she watched, the more concerned she became. She called the security guard over so he could be a witness to what she saw.

"Look," she told him, pointing to the statue. "Why would the bees be interested in that statue? Do you think it has something to do with that resin?"

The guard took off his hat, scratched his head, then put it back on his head. "Beats me. Never saw anything like it."

The pitch of the bees' fluttering wings increased in decibel. The resin covering the statue began to crack as if someone had struck it with a sledgehammer. Shards of resin began to fall to the ground. And the bees still hovered. Did the bees have a sixth sense to know that the statue needed help? How could that be?

Mercy Grace and the guard looked at each other, their mouths hanging open in awe.

"Maybe we should go out there and help him," the guard suggested.

Mercy Grace shook her head. "No. Not with all those bees out there. Once he's free of that hard shell, he's going to need some time to get his bearings. It's best to wait."

"But he's just a statue. He's not *real*," the guard informed her. The guard was called away but Mercy Grace just stood there and watched the miracle unfold.

Within minutes the man was free of his prison. He dropped to his knees and took in a deep cleansing breath. He closed his eyes, opened them, and blinked furiously. He looked around the beautiful courtyard. He smelled the lovely fragrance of the flowers and heard the tinkling of the water as it descended into the fountain. He pushed himself to a standing position. He swayed but righted himself, took several steps forward, then backward, making sure he could keep his balance.

Freedom, he thought. Sweet freedom. After all these years. The earth had trembled. Is that what had brought the swarm of bees? They'd surrounded his head but hadn't tried to attack him. As their wings fluttered, he heard a cracking sound and the hard shell encasing him began to break away. When he was completely free, the bees flew away, as if knowing their job was done.

It felt good to be alive. And a whole man.

Then he saw her. She stood behind large glass doorway. Just watching him, her eyes wide open, her mouth in the shape of an O. She was mesmerizing. Beautiful. And she was his soul mate.

He beckoned to her to come outside. She hesitated. Then she pushed the glass door open. With careful steps, she walked toward him. He stood rooted to his spot, waiting for her to get closer.

"Who are you?" she asked, her voice not much more than a whisper.

"My name is Dominic Camilius."

"It's a miracle you survived being trapped in that resin. But here you are. But are you real?"

"I am as real as you are," he told her. Then he reached his hands out and cupped her cheeks. A feeling of warmth and tingling went up his arms and straight to his heart. There was no doubt that he'd found his soul mate. He leaned down and kissed her.

She didn't know what to expect of the man after he'd been freed from his prison, but when he cupped her cheeks she thought she would pass out again. Her cheeks tingled and the feeling went straight to her heart. He was going to kiss her so she closed her eyes. She wanted to savor every moment his lips were on hers. Was this man really the one God had chosen for her?

As a geologist, she had a lot of questions for him. "What happened to you? Why were you in a petrified state all these years? How did you stay alive?" Those questions could wait.

She savored the kiss for as long as she could. His lips were firm but soft on hers. She'd been kissed before but not like this. Then he stepped away from her and she wanted to groan and complain that she wasn't done kissing him back.

He motioned for her to sit down with him on one of the concrete benches so they could talk.

"Do you go by Dominic?" Mercy Grace asked, leaning back against the back of the bench. She placed her hands on her lap.

He looked down at her hands on her lap. Her nails were rounded and smooth. But he could see small scars that convinced him she was a woman who worked hard and wasn't afraid to get her hands dirty. "My family called me Nicky but everyone else called me Dom."

"What do you wish me to call you?" she asked, her voice as smooth and sweet as honey.

He shook his head. "I care not. Whatever you choose is fine with me."

"I'll call you Dom. My name is Mercy Grace Romano. I go by Mercy Grace."

He smiled at her. "I like that."

"Thanks. Now, Dom, I'm really curious about you. Will you tell me about yourself?"

Her eyes widened as he told her his tale. But he had nothing to hide. He was a silversmith and made expensive jewelry mostly for the citizens in Rome and Pompeii. He made simple things, like candle holders, spoons and kitchen items for the local people.

Then there'd been a night raid, and his family had been brutally murdered and the village burned to the ground. She shed tears for the lives that had been lost. He told her about the earthquake and Mount Vesuvius erupting. The ground had opened up and swallowed him. The tree that he'd been leaning against had fallen on top of him, its branches wrapping around him. Then dirt had completely covered him and trapped him for years. Then he'd been dug up by some huge beast. At least he'd had a modicum of freedom. They'd taken him away to be examined by two men in white coats.

For years he'd been on display as a statue. Women were always touching him and flirting with him as if expecting him to respond to them. But he'd never felt their touch through the hard shell that covered him. Not until Mercy Grace had touched him.

His story seemed preposterous, but she knew no one could make up a story like that and sound so convincing.

"Wow! That's pretty incredible. There're pictures in the history books of you covered in that resin but no information about you. Just questions about who had carved you and why you were covered in that resin. How did you survive almost two thousand years?"

"I do not know. I spent a lot of time praying to Mother Earth to restore me but she either didn't hear me or felt me unworthy to be released from my prison."

Mercy Grace just stared at him. Then it occurred to her that he came from the first century. It was in 79 A.D. that Mt. Vesuvius erupted for the first time. People at that time worshiped Roman Gods. "Well, the truth is, Dom, there's only one God. He's the One True God in Heaven."

He nodded. "I heard that said many years ago. There was rumor of a man named Jesus that had claimed to be the Son of God. But I did not know which god they were talking about. Others who called themselves Christians said He was the Son of the Living God. I had many years to think about it. For all the prayers and supplication I had made to Mother Earth, she never answered my prayers." He shrugged his shoulders. "So I figured I was not worthy of her attention. Then I started praying to the Christians' God just in case there was any truth to His existence." He shrugged his shoulders again. "I do not know what to think about deities."

"Dom, I want you to know that what you heard about Jesus many years ago was not rumor. It was the *truth*." She went on to tell him stories from the Bible about Jesus—His birth, His ministry, His arrest, His death on the cross and His resurrection from the grave. "Jesus died on the cross for our salvation. If we believe in Him, he will forgive our sins and make a place for us in Heaven when we die."

"It is an amazing story. If Jesus died for all sinners, past and present, is it possible he would save a person like me? How can I get Jesus to become a part of my life?"

Mercy Grace smiled at him and took his hands in hers. "Dom, Jesus would love to become part of your life. Will you pray with me?"

He nodded and closed his eyes. When Mercy Grace finished leading him in the sinner's prayer, they both said "Amen" and opened their eyes. Tears streamed down her cheeks. She could just imagine the angels in Heaven rejoicing.

Dom reached up and dried her tears with the pads of his thumbs. "Thank you. I truly feel different in my heart."

"I'm so happy for you," she told him, placing both her hands over her heart.

"You have saved my soul, Mercy Grace. Without you I would not have learned the truth about Jesus. And I would not have been freed from my prison."

"I didn't save you, Dom. Jesus did. I'm just glad He used me to share the gospel with you. And God found a way to release you from the resin that has held you for so many years."

Dom nodded and was thoughtful for a moment. "What do we do now?" He looked at the shards of resin covering the tile where he'd been standing by the fountain. "I think the museum display is ruined since I am no longer a statue."

"We'd better go inside and let everyone know what happened. They won't believe it." She grabbed his hand and pulled him into the building.

They went inside the building to tell the curator and the people standing about what had happened when the bees had hovered over the statue. The resin had cracked and fallen away, releasing the man that had been encased inside for almost two thousand years. Several women passed out on the floor. Others ran out of the museum in fear. A man and woman walked up to him and touched him on his arms and chest to see if he was real.

The people's reaction didn't really surprise him. He felt bad for the women who had swooned. They lay on the floor in a heap. And he felt bad for those that had fled in fear for their lives. He was not going to hurt anyone.

The security guards rushed to the courtyard and saw the evidence of the broken resin the man had been trapped in. It was a miracle!

Dom's stomach made a loud noise. "I think perhaps I am hungry. I have not eaten in years."

Mercy Grace laughed. She took him by the hand and led him outside before they were detained and questioned any further. They followed their noses down the street toward a family-style restaurant where they could smell peppers and onions cooking.

When they walked into *The Kitchen Table*, all conversation ceased. Heads turned and everyone stared at them. She was in jeans and a tee shirt, and Dom was wearing a tunic and sandals. She could just imagine what the people were thinking.

Mercy Grace ignored everyone's stares. Yes, Dom was dressed differently and looked odd and out of place. The sooner they ate and left the better. Then she needed to take him shopping. Dom certainly could use some new clothes so he didn't attract so much attention. She led him to a booth near the back of the restaurant.

Dom looked at the menu but wasn't able to read it since it was in English. He could only read Greek and Latin. She read off the list of entrees but he had no idea what kind of food it was, so he asked her use to order for the both of them. Since she had smelled peppers and onions as they'd walked up the street, she ordered them each a Philly cheesesteak sandwich with fries, along with a chocolate milkshake.

When the food came, Mercy Grace offered to say the blessing.She took Dom's hand in hers and bowed her head

This was something new to Dom, but he let Mercy take the lead. He bowed his head as she gave thanks for their food.

Then they started eating.

Dom ate like he hadn't eaten in ages. And he hadn't. He thoroughly enjoyed the food. As they ate, he had her tell him exactly what everything was made of. And why the milkshake was so cold.

The waitress came with the check as they were finishing their food. Mercy Grace explained to Dom that the piece of paper she'd laid on the table was their bill. She also told him it was customary to leave a tip as a thank you for the waitress's kindness and help in caring for their needs while they ate.

He reached for his bag of coins on his belt. "Please. Allow me," he offered. He pulled out two coins and laid them on the table.

"Is that enough? Or should I give her more?"

Mercy Grace looked down at the coins Dom had laid on the table. One was gold. The other was silver. They were ancient coins with the face of King Titus on them.

"Dom!" she cried out in shock. "These coins are worth a fortune."

"No. They are only worth a few denarii."

"We've got to go to the bank. Maybe they can tell you how much they're worth. Put them back in your pouch." He complied.

Mercy Grace pulled a couple of bills out of her wallet and dropped them on the table. Then she stood up, and picked up her purse and the check. She took his hand, pulling him from the booth. She went to the register at the entrance of the restaurant and paid the bill with something she called "plastic." She grabbed his hand again and pulled him out the door, heading across the street to a men's clothing store.

She waited until a car went past before starting across the street. But Dom hadn't followed her. She turned and saw him still standing on the sidewalk. He looked white as a ghost.

"Dom?" she asked, walking back to the sidewalk. "What's wrong?"

He swallowed over the lump in his throat. "I fear all these events are moving too quickly."

"I'm sorry. But we've got to get you into some regular clothing. Clothing of *this* time. You're going to draw too much attention to yourself the way you're dressed."

He looked down at his tunic and sandals. "They look fine to me."

Mercy Grace laughed. "Sure they do. In your time. But not in 2017. Come on. I'll help you pick out some clothes."

"Will I have enough money to pay using my coins?" He wasn't going to have a woman paying for his wardrobe.

"Dom, your money is too valuable to spend on clothing. Just keep it in your money bag for now."

He gave her a curious look.

"Once we get you into some new clothes, we'll get to the bank and see what they can tell us about your coins' value."

"A bank?"

"A place to exchange money."

He was more confused than ever but he went across the street with her to the men's store. He'd never seen so many clothes to choose from, and in so many different sizes and colors.

An hour later, he came out dressed in a pair of blue jeans, a white polo shirt, socks, and a pair of sneakers. He also carried four plastic clothing bags and she carried two more. Now he looked like everybody else.

He had to practically run to keep up with Mercy Grace as she rushed down the street to the bank. They went inside and Dom stopped abruptly. This was a bank? There were cubicles along the left side where people sat at desks. On the right, people stood behind a wall but the top half of it was glass. It was a curious place. The furniture that people sat on in a waiting area was made of wood and some type of cloth he was unfamiliar with.

They sat down to wait their turn. A woman walked out of one of the offices and approached Mercy Grace.

The woman smiled at Mercy Grace and Dom. "How can we help you today?"

"We need to see the bank manager. He has some old coins and we need to see if the manager can tell us how much they're worth. Show her one of the coins," she told Dom.

He opened his pouch and removed a coin. He reached his hand out so the woman could see the coin on the palm of his hand., which he handed to the woman.

Her eyes grew wide. "Just one moment," she told them and then rushed away.

A moment later, the woman returned to the waiting area and gave the coin back to Dom. He placed it back in the coin bag.

A young man of medium height, thinning red hair and dark eyes, and an increasing middle, walked up to them. He smiled but it didn't reach his eyes.

He extended his hand to both of them. "Hello. You wanted to see the manager? That's me. I'm Gerald Winslow Franklin. I understand you have some old coins?"

"Yes," Mercy Grace told him. "We wondered if you could tell us how much they're worth?"

Dom held up his bag of coins.

The bank manager looked at the bag. "Come into my office." He turned and walked to his office, rounded his desk and sat down. He showed no concern whether they followed him or not.

Dom was a gentleman. He allowed Mercy Grace to enter the room before him. They sat down on the chairs in front of Mr. Franklin's desk.

"May I see your collection of coins?" He laid his arms on his desk, waiting to be given the pouch of money.

Dom untied the string on the pouch and dumped the gold and silver coins onto the man's desk. The man looked at the coins but seemed unimpressed.

"Who's the man on the coin?" Mr. Franklin asked.

"King Titus," Dom informed him.

"From what year?" He inspected the front of the coin, expecting to see the year. Finding none, he turned it over and found none on the opposite side.

"79 A.D."

Mr. Franklin's right eyebrow shot up into his forehead. "Really? Are you sure these aren't fake? How can you have something that old? These could be very valuable if they're real."

"They're not fakes. I've had them for a long time and was told they were of great value," Dom told the man.

"I'm not a numismatist. There's a coin shop next door. Take them over there. The owner can answer your questions."

"Thank you for your time," Mercy Grace told the banker. She wanted to get out of there. He was the most unfriendly banker she'd ever met. "Let's go, Dom." She stood up, ready to go. "Put the coins in the bag."

Dom felt like a child again, being told what to do. But he was in a new century and women apparently liked taking control. He liked Mercy Grace but she was rather bossy. Maybe it had something to do with her profession.

He scooped the coins back into the bag, picked up his shopping bags and followed her out of the office. He didn't give the bank manager another glance. The man was rude and unfriendly. He hadn't even stood up when they left his office. If Dom had treated his customers that way, he'd have been out of business in a day.

The coin shop beside the bank was small but full of merchandise. The owner stood behind the counter, sitting on a tall stool. He greeted Mercy Grace and Dom with a smile when they came in. He stood up and introduced himself as Sonny Shaw, owner/manager.

"I have some coins. I do not know how much they are worth," Dom told him. He dumped the coins onto the counter for the man to inspect them.

The man's eyes grew wide.

"We were just at the bank. The manager thought they were fakes," Mercy Grace told him. "But they're real. From the year 79 A.D. That face is Titus, Ruler of Rome."

"They certainly *are* real." Sonny's day just looked brighter. "Where did you get these?" Mr. Shaw looked up at Dom.

"I have had them for a long time."

"These are very valuable. I can probably give you a good idea how much they're worth. But what do you wanna do with them?"

Dom shrugged his shoulders and then looked at Mercy Grace. She was from this time and knew better how to direct the conversation.

"We'll probably sell them," she told the coin dealer.

"All right. I need to get my *Red Book*. It gives the going rate for coins." He turned to look at a row of coin books he had on the shelf behind him. He picked up a red book and brought it to the counter and began leafing through it.

He stopped on a page near the front of the book. Near the bottom he slid his index finger across the page and stopped. He kept his finger there, raised his head just far enough to look at the coins on his counter and then back at the book.

"Here you go." He turned the book around so the man and woman could see where he was pointing. There was a figure for gold coins and a different one for silver

Mercy Grace's eyes grew wide. Then she looked up at the man. "Really?"

"Yes, ma'am," he agreed with a smile.

"Who has that kind of money to buy coins?"

"You'd be surprised," he told her honestly.

"Can you buy any of these coins?" Dom asked.

The man scrunched up his face and scratched his head. "Well, I might be interested in several of them. I can't afford to buy them all. But if you can wait for a little while, I'll call some of my coin dealer friends that might want to take a look at these. Before I call them, you need to know that we can't offer you the price it says in this book. The *Red Book* gives you the retail value of the coin. Since we have to resell the coins we buy, we can only offer you about half that amount."

Mercy Grace chewed on her bottom lip, giving the man's words some thought. She looked at Dom. He shrugged. He didn't have a clue what they were talking about.

"Okay. We'll wait."

"Great." The man gave them a big smile. "You're welcome to look around the store. I'll be in the back making the calls."

"Okay," Mercy Grace told him.

They looked around the store. He sold coin books and coin magazines. There were small plastic bottles to hold coins of different sizes, plastic sheets to hold coins and others to hold paper bills. There were binders to put the plastic sheets in. There were two shelves of blue folders to put coins in. There were three showcases full of coins displayed in plastic frames and velvet cases, and another showcase of coins that had been made into jewelry. Mercy Grace came to the conclusion that coin collecting was a very diverse but expensive hobby.

Mr. Shaw returned a couple of minutes later with good news.

"There are four coin dealers that want to see these coins. I gave them the *Red Book* prices so they'll be prepared if they want to buy any from you. They'll be over in the next fifteen minutes."

"Okay," Mercy Grace acknowledged. "I think we'll wait out on the bench in front of the store until they come."

"All right."

"Let's go, Dom," she told him. They picked up the shopping bags from the floor in front of the showcases and went outside.

They sat on the bench in front of *Coins, Etc.* Mercy Grace needed to let Dom know exactly how valuable his coins were and that she'd do the haggling with the coin dealers. But she'd look at him to get his opinion when the dealers made comments or asked questions. Dom would need to agree with whatever she said. She tried to impress upon him that, if these men bought all of Dom's coins, he would be getting a lot of money by U.S. standards.

Money had never been a motivating factor for Dom when it came to creating beautiful jewelry for his customers. He valued his talent for creativity, but not more than he valued his family. Dom couldn't imagine how much Mercy Grace's coin and paper money was worth. He'd never seen paper money before. And what was the standard for wealth in this country and this century?

Five men showed up at *Coins, Etc.* to see the Roman coins that were for sale. One of the men had called another dealer he knew and the man could hardly wait to see the coins brought to the coin shop.

Dom and Mercy Grace went back into the shop, shopping bags in hand, when the men arrived. Dom dumped the coins out on the counter so they could examine them.

The men oohed and ahhed when they saw the great condition the gold and silver coins were in. There were eighteen coins. Among them they decided they'd buy three coins apiece but they wanted to haggle, trying to find fault with this coin and that coin. Mercy Grace pointed out that the coins were in excellent condition considering their age. Then consider the fact that the coins hadn't been lost in the destruction of Pompeii by Mt. Vesuvius, back in n79 A.D. And how many of these coins still existed? She wasn't going to let these men take advantage of her just because she was a woman trying to make a deal. If they wanted them, they'd have to pay a fair price. She was sure they'd make a hefty profit when they sold the coins.

She gave the men a final price, one for the silver, one for the gold.

"Take it or leave it, gentlemen." And she stared them down.

They looked at the coins greedily.

"Okay," they seemed to say in unison, opening their large checkbooks they carried. "Who do we make the checks out to?" one of the men asked.

"Mercy Grace Romano."

Each man wrote out their checks, tore them out of their business checkbooks, and handed them to Mercy Grace.

She looked at the check the store owner, Sonny Shaw, gave her. The amount was less than what the other men had paid.

"I don't understand, Mr. Shaw. Why is your check less than what the other men paid?"

"It's my commission for getting these other dealers to come in to see your coins."

Mercy Grace looked at the man like he'd lost his mind. Then she looked at Dom. He was bewildered. He had no idea what was wrong. Then she looked back at Sonny Shaw.

"Mr. Shaw. Might I remind you that had it not been for Mr. Franklin at the bank, we wouldn't have brought these ancient coins to you. If this is how you do business, perhaps we'll take these other three coins with us. We'll find someone else to sell them to."

"Now wait a minute," he demanded. "That's not fair. When I sell something that's on consignment, I get a percentage of the sale."

Mercy Grace looked at Dom. "Did we bring these in here on consignment?"

Dom knew by the tone of her voice the answer was to be no.

He shook his head. "No, we did not."

She looked back at the store owner. "You're going to get a hefty profit out of these coins once you sell them. You never said a word about a commission or had us sign any agreement prior to these gentlemen coming in that we owed you any fee. So, are you going to buy these coins at the same price these other men did, or do we leave? With three coins?"

"Hey, Sonny, I gotta go," one of the men said. The others joined in and said they had to go, too. They knew this wasn't their fight. They took three coins apiece and walked out of the store.

Sonny let out an exaggerated sigh of disapproval. "All right. I'll rewrite the check for the agreed amount."

"Very good. Thank you," she told him. She'd won. But she'd done it on principle and for Dom's bank account.

She accepted the new check, thanked the man again for his business, and walked out of the shop with six checks in her pocketbook with Dom following her.

"Now what?" he asked his soul mate.

"Do you think you could eat again?" She looked at her watch. "It's about dinner time."

"I have a lot of years of eating to catch up on. Yes. What did you have in mind?"

"Would you like to go back to the restaurant where we had lunch, *The Kitchen Table*? I don't know about you, but I like their cooking."

Dom's face lit up. "That would be wonderful. I liked that sandwich you ordered. What was it called?"

She laughed. "A Philly cheesesteak."

"I'll take another one of those."

"I think you need some variety. We'll see what else sounds good. Let's go."

They went back to *The Kitchen Table*. But this time when they went in, they looked like a normal couple, since Dom was dressed like any other twenty-first century man. They stuffed their shopping bags under the table.

When the waitress came to their booth, Mercy Grace ordered turkey and dressing with steamed broccoli for two. And two strawberry milkshakes.

While they waited for their food, Mercy Grace explained to Dom that she was going to take a picture of each check and deposit the money in her bank account for safe keeping. It could be done without even going into a bank. Later Mercy Grace would open up an account in Dom's name and then transfer the money from her account into his.

"I have no idea what you mean, but I trust you," he told her.

He watched as she used a thin gadget she called a cell phone and took something she called pictures. Then she said the money was in the bank. It boggled his mind, but he trusted what she said to be true.

Their food came and after the waitress walked away, they both bowed their heads and silently said grace over their meal.

After they finished their dinner, they went straight to the police station to see if they had any word about the repairs on the airplane she'd been on that morning.

The chief of police came out to the reception desk and spoke to Mercy Grace.

"Have you had any word about the plane repair?" she asked the police chief.

"No. You'll need to check with the airport in Myrtle Beach."

"What?"

"The pilot would have contacted them to let them know what happened. I can get you a number if you'd like."

"That's okay," she said, clearly exasperated. "I'll get it on my cell phone." With a few clicks, Mercy Grace pulled up the number for the airport in Myrtle Beach.

She was informed that repairs had been made and buses were being sent back into town to take the passengers back to the plane.

They left the police station and started walking back toward City Hall, shopping bags in hand, where people were already boarding the buses.

"Mercy Grace." Dom stopped abruptly on the sidewalk.

"What do I do? You are leaving. I have nowhere to go and no money."

Mercy Grace thought for a moment. "Just get on the bus and go along with me. I'll talk to the pilot and see what arrangements I can make to have you included as one of the passengers. You can go with me to Myrtle Beach and then we'll try to figure out what you should do."

"Very well." Dom had to trust Mercy Grace completely. She'd been doing an excellent job of helping him since he'd broken free of his prison. She'd get everything worked out. Because soul mates took care of each other.

They loaded the bus, stuffing their shopping bags at their feet, and ten minutes later the three buses pulled out and took the passengers back to the field where the plane sat, engines revved and ready to go. The passengers disembarked from the buses and walked over to the plane. Two flight attendants stood at the bottom of the stairs to help the passengers back into the plane.

Mercy Grace stepped up to one of the attendants.

"Excuse me. I need to talk to the captain."

"He's doing a final check of the plane to make sure everything's in order before we take off. Is there anything I can do to help?"

"Well, maybe. You see, my boyfriend arrived in Kyleighburn to spend a couple of days before he came to meet me in Myrtle Beach. But since I had this unexpected stop, we met up. Is it possible for him to go the rest of the way with us on the plane? I'll be glad to pay for his ticket. I know I saw a lot of empty seats."

The young attendant chewed on her bottom lip. "I'll go talk to the captain. Wait right here. I'll be right back."

She followed the other passengers onto the plane, making her way to the cockpit. Five minutes later she came down the flight of steps and walked over to where Mary Grace was waiting.

"Miss, the captain said it was okay if your boyfriend goes with us. It's not an emergency, but he said he'd do it as a Christian friend."

Mercy Grace gave her a big smile. "Oh, thank you. We really appreciate it. Will you please tell the captain we said thank you?"

"Of course. You two go ahead and board. We'll be leaving in just a few minutes."

Mercy Grace jerked her head in the direction of the stairway. He glanced at the attendant and thanked her for her help, then followed his soul mate up the steps and into the belly of an enormous… Chariot? It had so many seats he couldn't count them all.

Mercy Grace stuffed their bags in the compartment above their heads

As the plane's tires bounced on the bumpy ground, it reminded Dom of trips he'd been taken on in a sealed box. The plane tilted, then leveled off. It was no longer a bumpy ride, but nice and smooth. Was this how they'd gotten him from one city to another all those years he'd been part of the museum displays?

While they were in the air, Dom asked Mercy Grace a lot of questions about airplanes. What were they were made of? How could they stay in the air without falling from the sky? How could they fly above the clouds, and how could so many people fit in the plane without weighing it down?

It didn't take long to reach the Myrtle Beach International Airport in South Carolina. When they landed, Mercy Grace rented a car and went to get her suitcases at the luggage pickup. The things she'd bought for Dom were in plastic bags. She'd have to get him a suitcase.

She drove to the hotel, which wasn't far from the airport. Dom held onto the dashboard for dear life. This thing called a car had to be under a magic spell to go without the aid of horses. Mercy Grace laughed and tried to explain the mechanics of horsepower even though she didn't understand what happened under the hood of a car. Perhaps Dom had been taken, as a statue in a box, to museums in vehicles such as this. The sound of the tires on the road were familiar to him.

It was a simple matter to secure a room for Dom. The room next to hers was available. She paid for their rooms with a credit card, which puzzled Dom when she didn't use money. They rode in a box up to the floor where Mercy Grace found their rooms. She showed him how to use the key card. Then once inside, she showed him how to flush the toilet and turn the shower on to get hot water in the bathroom, use the TV remote control, and how to make a call on the telephone.

Dom's head was spinning. So much progress had taken place over 2,000 years.

Mercy Grace had promised Dom they'd go shopping the following day. His new clothes she'd bought him in Kyleighburn were still in plastic bags. She knew he'd also need some toiletries and a razor to shave his five-o'clock shadow. And she'd get him that much-needed suitcase.

When he climbed into the soft bed with bright white sheets, he closed his eyes. It was a euphoric feeling. He slept better than he ever had and woke feeling rested. They had breakfast in the hotel dining room and then went shopping. She even bought him a swim suit, which made him feel scandalous in just a small piece of cloth, and a beach towel.

Over the next couple of days, they swam in the ocean and talked about life and their interests as they sunbathed on the beach. Dom didn't know when he'd had such a relaxing time. And the more time he spent with Mercy Grace, the more he loved her. His parents would have loved Mercy Grace, too.

And for the first time in years, he was homesick for Rome.

"What's wrong? You're awful quiet," Mercy Grace said to him. She lay on her stomach and propped her chin on her stacked hands.

Dom lay on his back with his eyes closed. He sat up and turned sideways, folding his legs to sit Indian-style.

"We have to decide what to do after we leave here, Mercy Grace. You have a job to go back to, but I have nowhere to go."

Mercy Grace sat up and turned toward this man she'd fallen in love with at first sight. The kisses they'd been sharing lately had made her heart fill up to the brim with love. The way they'd met was unusual, but God had brought them together.

"Dom, we're soul mates. I can't explain why God had us meet the way He did, but we've found each other, and I don't want to lose you."

He reached over and took her hands in his.

"Mercy Grace, I never thought I would meet my soul mate. Once the ground swallowed me up all those years ago, I thought I would die. But I did not. I believe that God had me brought to Kyleighburn so I could find you. And your plane was to have difficulties so that you could land and find *me*. You have been so kind to care for me since my life was returned to me. You have fed me, clothed me, and brought me here so we could get to know each other better."

Mercy Grace was touched by Dom's admission. He recognized that God worked in mysterious ways.

Her whole body tingled as he held her hands. He was always gentle with her and their love for each other grew the more time they spent together.

"A lot of women used to try to attract my attention when they walked by my work stall. In my time," he clarified. "They would purr silly words to me and flutter their eyes' lashes. Such shame. But I knew in my heart that none of them were my soul mate. None of them could fill the empty heart on my arm. Then I met you. I love you, Mercy Grace Romano. I know we have only known each other such a short time, but I would be very honored if you would be my wife and the mother of my children."

"Yes!" she squealed, accepting his proposal without hesitation. "I'll marry you," she told him and then threw her arms around his neck, her heart overflowing with love for this unique man.

His kiss held a promise of eternal love. When they separated, Dom pulled the silver ring with the red ruby off his pinky finger and placed it on Mercy Grace's left ring finger. It was a perfect fit. He held her hand up to his lips and kissed the ring, pledging his undying love to his soul mate.

The following day they drove to Conway to the Government and Justice Center to apply for a marriage license. By what had to be divine intervention, they were able to get the license within twenty-four hours without Dom having any proof of identification.

Since they had to wait until the following day to come back and pick up the license, they went shopping again. Mercy Grace bought herself a white summer dress to get married in and she bought Dom a new suit in an exclusive men's store.

After they picked up the marriage license at the government office the next day, they were married by a minister in a small chapel they found online in Myrtle Beach.

They'd agreed to live in Chapel Hill. Dom would study to become a naturalized United States citizen. Mercy Grace would resume her teaching at the university, and Dom would start his own silversmith business and design rings to sell online. When she traveled to go on geological digs, Dom would travel with her so he could see the world as a man, not a statue.

Had their discovery of each other been a work of magic? Or had it been orchestrated by the hand of God? They believed it was the latter.

Over the years, their family grew. They never questioned how God had kept Dominic Camilius alive for almost two thousand years. Or that Mercy Grace's plane had had to make an emergency landing. Or if there was magic or an unknown entity in Kyleighburn, North Carolina, that had released thousands of bees. A swarm of those bees that had had a mission to see to it that Dom was released from the prison he'd been encased in. And most importantly of all, they'd been thrilled that after meeting each other, Mercy Grace had been able to lead Dom to the Lord.

Whether it was by fate or the hand of God, each event had been necessary for two soul mates to find each other.

Tuesday, June 14

# Bank Hosts Car Show

Kingman National Bank's Kyleighburn branch is sponsoring a car show at 1 p.m. Saturday on Main Street, across the street from the Jacobson's Department Store building. Classic cars from the NASCAR Hall of Fame in Charlotte will be featured as well as some local vehicles.

Bank manager Gerald Franklin said he worked with a number of NASCAR drivers and teams when he was working in the bank's Charlotte branches, giving him the opportunity to bring the museum's traveling cars to Kyleighburn.

"I've kept my relationship with the drivers and teams even while I'm so far away from the city during my stint here in Kyleighburn." Franklin said.

"I'm hoping I'll soon be back in Charlotte and can continue those associations."

Among the cars NASCAR is sending are the cars of Dale Jarrett and Richard Petty. Local cars being featured are a 1935 Nash owned by Kyleighburn mayor Marino Esposito and a 1965 Shelby Cobra.

**From the Office of Mayor Marino Esposito**
Kyleighburn, North Carolina
910-442-xxxx

Mayor Marino Esposito is pleased to announce that he has persuaded the North Carolina governor and the Federal Emergency Management Authority to declare an emergency and release state and federal funds to help with the cleanup of the Ky-Leigh Trailer Park after the recent disaster.

"I keep telling people that Kyleighburn doesn't need a town manager," Mayor Esposito said. "I know what's best for this town and I know how to get people to agree with me."

Mayor Esposito's hard work has paid off with the promise of $1 million in relief funds from the state and more than $2 million in federal funding.

"We can get houses built for these people who have lost their homes and everything they owned," said Mayor Esposito. "With the building supplies that were donated by my friends in New York, we will soon have everyting ready to make these lives better."

Town council members praised Mayor Esposito for his hard work at getting the funding the town so desperately needed.

"We are so impressed by what Mayor Esposito was able to accomplish," said council Chairman Danny Foster. "It is really wonderful how much he has done for the town in the nine years since he became our Mayor."

Mayor Esposito said he is working hard to help the people of Kyleighburn. "This is a harder job that people might think it is," he said. "But I am willing to slave late into the night if it will help improve the lives of everyone I'm responsible for."

Mayor Esposito was elected to the town Council in 2003, and as Mayor in 2004. He is in the first year of his fifth two-year term.

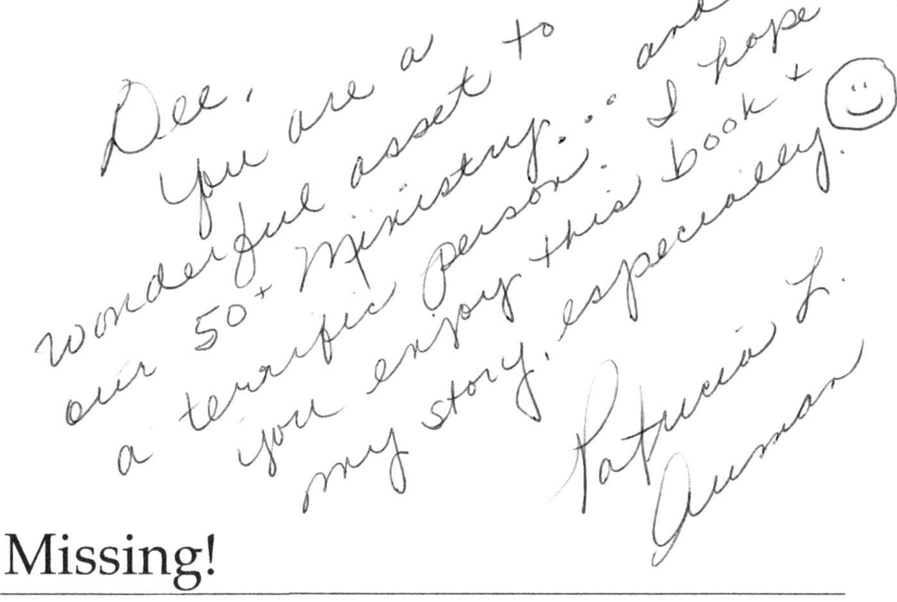

Dee,
You are a
wonderful asset to
our 50+ Ministry.. and
a terrific person. I hope
you enjoy this book +
my story, especially.
Patricia L.
Auman


# Missing!

Patricia L. Auman

SHE SAID NO. Ten-year-old Billy Gallagher was unable to hide his disappointment. He crossed his arms over his chest, pursed his lips and exhaled deeply through his nose.

"Humph."

"Billy, I want you to stick around the house. A bad storm is predicted sometime in the early evening. You and DaQuan can hang out tomorrow after school." said his mom, as she proceeded to untangle the cord attached to the vacuum. "Stuart said he'd be here around six-thirty to fix the leaky pipe under the kitchen sink. We need to clean up around here. I will not have him come into a dirty house.

*A dirty house?* "Geez, mom. It's only the plumber. Didn't you go to high school with him?"

"As a matter of fact, I did." she replied.

"Was he your boyfriend?"

"Gosh…no. Not a chance," she answered, but she was blushing nonetheless. "Son, there's a cloth in the drawer next to the sink in the kitchen. You can help by dusting the furniture."

Billy's eyes widened. *She wants ME to dust the furniture?* He was mortified—like the time he heard the preacher use a cuss word when the door to the church slammed on his hand. "Aw, mom. Really?"

"Go on," she said. "Dusting won't kill you." She plugged the cord into the outlet and pressed the "on" button.

Billy inched his way into the kitchen and found the cloth. He gripped it along one edge, holding it a foot away from his face, grimacing, as if it was dripping with pond scum.

After walking back into the living room, he tapped her on the arm. She cut off the vacuum and swung toward him.

"Do I have to dust, mom? I promised DaQuan I'd meet up with him after I did my homework. It's all done."

"Remember, tomorrow's Friday. You've got a spelling test. You got four wrong last week."

He rolled his eyes.

"I saw that, young man," she said, shaking her fist.

"It's four o'clock. It's still early. Can I please go to DaQuan's? He's waiting for me."

"Tomorrow," said his mother, firmly. "Get the dusting done." She pressed the "on" button again. The roar from the motor blocked out Billy's reply, which was probably a good thing.

Angrily, he flung the cloth onto the floor and plopped down on the bottom step of the staircase. His elbows rested on his knees and his lower lip jutted out, almost aligned with the tip of his nose. He sat there pouting…but only for a second.

Her back faced him as she moved the wand across the carpet.

*Now's my chance.*

He gripped the post, raised his body, and began to tiptoe across the tiny foyer toward the front door. With his eyes fixed on her, he crept silently, but realized she was oblivious to his presence, let alone his mischievous departure. After turning the knob, he nudged the door open—giving himself just enough space to slide through. Then he closed it very slowly. Free at last.

Leaning against the side of the little saltbox house that Billy called home, stood his red bicycle—secondhand, but reliable. On the back of the bike in a wire basket was a bag filled with tools and other items a boy needed for unpredictable emergencies. He hopped on and rode away, ignoring the consequences that would befall him when he returned home.

DaQuan's house came into view as he rounded the corner. When he rang the bell, no one answered.

*Where's DaQuan?*

They had been exploring the area by the river and had found some arrowheads. Not wanting to sit home when there were Indian artifacts to be found, the two boys had planned to meet that afternoon, but it appeared that Billy would be scouting around the site by himself. The adventure boggled his mind, and he found the excitement invigorating.

Billy pedaled through the neighborhood until he reached the downtown area that led near the river. Silas Baird sat on a wooden bench in front of the barber shop whittling with his pocket knife. He waved. Billy waved back. Old Miss Fullerton, gray-haired and robust—some of the boys at his school called her *Two Chin Fullerton*—was carrying a bag of groceries, which Billy assumed had been purchased from Foster's Grocery at the end of the street. She nodded her head at him as he rode by. He smiled and nodded as well. On the sidewalk in front of the Meat Market was The Mayor, looking lifeless, except for the twitch of his left ear, as if it were dancing to the rhythm of the music from the café next door. Billy pulled his bike alongside the curb and thrust his foot out onto the sidewalk to maintain his balance.

"Hey, Mayor, you want to go with me to the river?" he called out to the dog.

The Mayor looked up at him and yawned, unmoving from his spot.

"Really, you should come with me."

The dog's eyes stared up at Billy, totally uninterested.

"Suit yourself, Mayor. I'm leaving." He positioned his foot back on the pedal and took off.

A year had passed since Billy's dad left and never came back, but he didn't miss him one bit. He loved his dad, that is until he started hanging out at the bar down the street with his new friends—two guys who had been hired at the auto repair shop where his dad worked. In the wee hours of the morning he'd return home—drunk and mean. At nine-years old Billy learned firsthand how liquor could not only transform your body, but your soul, too. On a few of those bad nights his dad woke him up from a sound sleep and took a strap to his behind for no reason. Not only that, he called his mom bad names and made her cry. Billy loved his mom and wished he could do something to help her, but his dad was too strong and much too big. His mom would tell him to go to his room and shut the door, but he'd hide behind the bannister on the stairs and watch. It wasn't easy seeing your dad shove your mom into the wall or punch her in the face. She pleaded for him to stop, but he often laughed. One morning at breakfast Billy noticed that his mom was wearing sunglasses. She didn't go to work that day or the next day either.

His dad had grown tired of coming home to a lazy wife—so he said. Billy resented his dad's words. He knew that his mom wasn't lazy. For twelve years she had worked the day shift at the Hoffman Furniture Factory from seven in the morning till three in the afternoon. After work she'd tidy up the house, make the meals, do the laundry and take him to his baseball practices and games when his dad's work schedule made it impossible. Sometimes after a win, she would take him to Burger Buster where they'd enjoy a burger and fries. After his dad left, she told him they couldn't stop at Burger Buster anymore, since she had to pinch pennies. Billy didn't understand what pinching pennies meant, but he missed those fun times.

After his dad began drinking, he started calling Billy a stupid kid. Billy knew he wasn't—he was on the honor roll at school and was one heck of a ball player. When they played the Pirates, the team everyone said was the best, he'd hit two homeruns and caught a fly ball that would have allowed two more runs to score. Even though they lost by one run, the coach patted Billy on the back and told him how proud he was of him. Despite the loss, Billy felt like a superhero.

He planned to be a lawyer when he grew up—put bad guys like his dad in jail—kick their butts. But the future was the future. Billy was still a kid and he had disobeyed his mother. Maybe he was a bad seed like his dad, but he didn't think so.

Before those men came into the picture, his family would go to the beach together, play Putt-Putt and eat at The Taco Barn every Tuesday night. His dad taught him how to swing a bat and catch a football. They were a happy family, but it didn't last.

When Billy reached the site by the river, he checked his watch—almost five o'clock. His mom, more than likely, was stewing over the fact that he had wandered off. He hadn't done the dusting like she asked, either.

"I'm gonna be in big trouble," he muttered and kicked a few stones with his foot. "Sorry, mom, but we're doing something important here."

He grabbed the bag from the back of the bicycle and laid it on a grassy spot. After removing a small spade, he knelt on the ground and began to dig. His preoccupation with finding artifacts at the river was the fault of DaQuan's teacher. She had told the class that Indians had lived near Tottie River centuries ago, and when DaQuan told Billy, their curious nature won out. The boys found ways to sneak away after school and on weekends, hoping to find the remains of that village. How awesome would that be? If his dad ever showed up, he'd discover how wrong he was. Billy Gallagher was a name people were going to remember.

Within minutes the spade struck something hard. Billy bore down into the dirt with his fingers and unearthed what appeared to be a bowl—old and worn.

"Whoopee! Wait till I show DaQuan," Billy exclaimed, as he held the object high, scrutinizing the bottom and all around the sides.

Satisfied with his find, he carefully laid it upon the mound of dirt beside the excavated hole. A shadow suddenly hovered over him. Billy looked up and saw The Mayor.

"So you decided to join me after all." He pushed himself up from his kneeling position and pointed at the bowl. "See what I found, Mayor. Pretty cool, huh?"

The Mayor raised his snout and began to howl, loud and long. The hair on Billy's arms stood up, sending shivers from his head to his feet.

When The Mayor's frightening interlude ceased, Billy exclaimed, "What the hell did you do that for?"

The Mayor gazed upwards and then stared back at Billy.

"Are you trying to tell me something, ole boy?"

Within minutes the weather changed. Dozens of goosebumps dotted Billy's skin, as the temperature took a dive. His short-sleeved T-shirt hadn't prepared him for this sudden change. Instinctively, he hugged himself and began rubbing up and down his arms for warmth. The wind blew fiercely, thrusting its strength against his back, causing him to stumble forward. Dirt swirled around and up into the air—some got into Billy's eyes. Even though his mother said to never rub them, he did just that with the corner of his T-shirt. Then he blinked over and over until they felt better. In the distance trees bent sharply toward the ground, unable to maintain their vertical posture. Dark gray clouds blanketed the sky where few had lingered only moments before. A streak of lightning cracked in the distance and thunder resonated overhead.

"Coming here was not a good idea." He swallowed hard and felt a knot form in his stomach. He called out, "Mom, I need you."

A pair of bees, buzzing in unison, caught his attention as they encircled the perimeter around him.

"Go away," he shouted. His arms flailed wildly as he batted against the air to protect himself.

Two bees multiplied into six, and six became twelve, and although they maintained their distance from him, their presence made Billy uneasy. He sensed danger—and although he had no explanation for it—he knew the bees felt it too.

Billy crumpled to the ground. "I wanna go home. I wanna go home."

When he looked up, the bees were gone. Huge droplets of rain had begun pelting down upon his head and face, as the sky erupted into a fit of rage.

*Could it be that the gods are mad at me for digging here?* "Don't be mad," he yelled up to the heavens, "I didn't mean any harm."

He grabbed his bag, threw it into the basket and hopped onto the seat of his bike. Faster and faster he pedaled—the wheels seemed to have a mind of their own as he moved up and down the landscape that he could barely see. He squinted and stretched his neck forward, as rain dripped over his eyes.

"What's that over there?" he asked himself.

Billy coasted before pushing hard on the brakes. He spread his legs apart and straddled the bicycle.

"Hey, it's not raining on me anymore," he said, but the intense darkness made it impossible to determine where he was.

He twisted backwards and laid one hand on the seat for balance while the other fumbled inside the wet bag. "Got it!" he uttered. The silver flashlight had been one of only a few things his dad had left behind, tucked away in a small rusty toolbox inside the garage. After he slid the button forward, a bright light beamed throughout the space.

*What is this?*

As Billy took stock of his surroundings, The Mayor sat outside in the rain… and watched.

Maggie Gallagher was furious with her son, but she decided it was more important to take care of some business she had at the bank before confronting him at DaQuan's, quite certain that's where he was. Because the bank was always open 'til six o'clock on Thursdays, she had plenty of time to get ready. Three days earlier she had received a letter threatening to foreclose on her home, since she was two months in arrears. It stated that the mortgage payments were to be paid in full by May 25, a mere two weeks away. It was signed by no other than the overly ambitious Gerald Winslow Franklin, the thirty-year-old bank manager at the Kyleighburn National Bank. Ask anyone, they all would attest to the fact that he was probably the most hated person in town. Although, he had dazzled his wealthy clientele and those that ranked above him, hard-working citizens like herself were hard-pressed to find favor with the young banker's pompous attitude. He was all about making money—

nothing else mattered.

A one-week extension was all she needed—until June first—the day she'd receive her monthly check fattened up with over twenty hours of overtime. When the furniture company asked for volunteers to work extended hours, three days per week during the month of April at the usual salary plus time and a half, her hand flew up so fast she thought she had dislocated her arm in the process. She had arranged for Billy to stay at DaQuan's. His mom was so accommodating—thank the Lord.

Standing naked in the bedroom closet, she swished the hangars back and forth searching for something to wear that would sway Mr. Franklin. Being only five years older than he was and still attractive enough, she fancied using the assets God gave her, but within limits, of course.

*How about I don some alluring cologne and wear a dress with low cleavage?*

Then again—who was she kidding? Gerald Winslow Franklin would never give her that extension. He'd probably end up throwing her out of his bank on her derriere. But she knew she had to give it a try.

At five o'clock she leaned against the brick wall beside the main doors of the bank, nervously contemplating what to expect. She had dressed the part—a light pink cotton blouse that showed off a hint of cleavage, a black skirt that complimented her shapely legs and whopping four-inch heels. If the Tin Man, the Lion and the Scarecrow could summon up the courage to face the great and mighty Wizard of Oz, she could certainly face Gerry. Giving him a nickname made him less threatening. She even laughed.

*Oh, God. How can I laugh? That man possesses my future.*

Being a single parent was no easy task. She lived from paycheck to paycheck with no assistance from Billy's dad. He left, and she never saw him again—no child support, no drop-in visits to see his son, and no forwarding address. Stranger yet was the fact that the former love of her life had never contacted her regarding a divorce.

*I can do this.*

Although her stomach was turning somersaults, she thrust her shoulders back, held her head high, and entered the prominent establishment. In her usual spot behind the main desk sat Mrs. Fogarty, a middle-aged antithesis of the Mr. Gerald Winslow Franklin.

"Oh, Mrs. Gallagher, how nice to see you today." Her voice overflowed with sincerity. "Is that a new blouse you're wearing? I love the color on you."

"Thank you," she answered.

"How's that boy of yours? School's almost over for another year. Three more weeks and he'll be a fifth grader. Is that right?"

Maggie nodded.

"Where does the time go? Young 'uns these days…they grow up so fast."

"Yes, he's doing fine."

"So what can I do for you on this lovely May day?"

"I'm here to see Mr. Franklin. Is he available?"

"It's the first time he hasn't come to work since he was hired six months ago. No details. Just said he wouldn't be coming in. May I leave a message for him?"

"No, thank you. I'll stop back tomorrow."

With her high heels clicking, she made a swift escape and headed down the sidewalk to her car. Once inside, she sat back against the seat, closed her eyes and heaved a sigh of relief.

A horn honked. Startled by the noise, her eyes flew open. *Get a grip on yourself. It's time to retrieve your son at DaQuan's.*

She rang the doorbell, but no one answered. By leaning over the rail on the left side of the porch, she was able to peer into the living room window, but all she could see were two empty chairs and a couch.

*Maybe they're in the backyard.*

Down the driveway she walked, toward the garage at the far end. The side door was ajar—their car was gone.

She scratched at her cheek. "Humph, no one's home. Where's Billy?"

It was almost five-thirty, dark foreboding clouds had quickly replaced the sunshine and glimmer of the afternoon. By the time she buckled her seatbelt, the sky lit up like the fourth of July and rain began pouring down. She stepped on the gas and bounded for home.

"Wow! This is cool," Billy said, as he gazed around. "A cave. I found a cave." The boy possessed no fear, just a deep sense of curiosity. With the flashlight occupying his right hand, Billy grasped the handlebar with his left, guiding the bicycle along the path that led deeper into the belly of the rocky structure. *Maybe there's a bear in here or a fox or even a wolf.* He flashed the light up and around. *Maybe they're watching me right now, but I'm not scared.* He didn't see any, but it didn't mean they weren't there.

After a while, he encountered a fork in the path. While he pondered which direction to follow, he ripped open a bag of potato chips and ate ravenously. Then he stuffed the wrapper into his pocket.

"Eeny meeny miney moe…I'll go this way," he said, and veered left as if he were being led by an invisible string. The potato chip bag dropped from his pocket onto the ground. The back wheel of the bike rolled over it.

Up ahead he encountered a plethora of vines so dense it made the tunnel nearly impassable. Unable to maneuver the bike any further, he laid it down on its side and twisted his body through the thick foliage into a small clearing.

"Oh, geez. No…no…no!" Billy began to panic. He pushed up and down on the red button of the flashlight—off, on, off, on—again and again, but it was no use. *The batteries must be dead.* He was alone, trapped in darkness.

"Somebody help me. Anybody…somebody." His body slumped to the ground. He buried his face in his hands and cried.

"I'm here, Billy. I'll take care of you."

Billy opened his eyes. The cave was suddenly inundated with light, colors of the rainbow swirling and glistening with an alluring glow. As Billy stared, a human figure began to take shape and emerged from the brilliance, arms outstretched.

"Dad?" Billy gasped, a different kind of fear penetrating his gut.

"Yes, it's me, son."

"Please don't hurt me, Dad," Billy cried, as he scrunched down into a ball and shook uncontrollably.

"Oh, Billy. I'm not going to hurt you. Do you have any idea how sorry I am for the things I did to you and your mom?"

Silence.

"I got caught up in the free-spirited life style the guys at work had. Before I knew it, I was doing drugs and drinking like a fiend. I had turned into a monster. I am so, so sorry."

"You were a mean dad," Billy shouted, refusing to look up.

"People make mistakes. I trusted the wrong people. If I could only go back…I'd do things different…make you proud of me."

"You were a good dad 'til you met your, eh… friends," a tinge of bitterness salted Billy's voice.

"Some friends," replied his dad. "I let them ruin my life."

"How'd they do that?" Billy finally raised his head slowly and gazed up at the glowing figure.

"When I left you and your mom, I stayed with them in the trailer park. I did things I am not proud of. Lost my job, too. One night we all drank too much, and I got this crazy idea to go cruising down the highway on Slim's motorcycle. I hadn't gone far when I missed the turn, swerved off the road and slammed into a tree."

"Serves you right."

"I suppose so. I got hurt bad. In fact, I died."

"Huh? What do you mean, dad?"

"You can't see the wreck from the highway—too many overgrown bushes and trees, but it happened where the red sign points to Lochness Lake."

"Does Mom know you're dead?"

"No one knows, Son." The light was beginning to fade. "Don't worry. I'm here to protect you. Remember that."

Then he was gone. Darkness enveloped the space once again.

Had he been dreaming? *I'm awake. I know I am.*

In his lap was the flashlight. "Please work, you dumb flashlight."

He pushed the button upwards. Light illuminated the path. "O my," he exclaimed. "How'd that happen?" But he was glad it did.

The little adventurer forged ahead, tearing at the vines that blocked his way. Deeper and deeper, penetrating the labyrinth like an enthusiastic spelunker on his first exploration. By the time he emerged from the foliage, he had grown weary—his feet plodded along, his energy depleted. He bent down and inhaled deeply. When he lifted his head, a flickering light in the distance caught his eye and the sound of someone crying echoed throughout the chamber.

Maggie Gallagher's frustration was mounting. Not only was she at a loss as to where Billy was, but six-thirty came and went without any sign of Stuart. Her phone call to him went directly to voicemail.

She had called DaQuan's house several times since returning home, but there was no answer. She had called the parents of her son's other two friends. Nothing. It was seven o'clock. She decided to try again.

"Hello." The man on the other end was DaQuan's dad, who went by Doctor Bob—named after his African grandfather, Bomani.

"Bob, this is Maggie Gallagher. Is Billy with you?"

"No. He's not here."

"He was anxious to meet up with DaQuan after school—rode off on his bike and hasn't come back. I don't know what to do."

"Our whole family went over to my mother's for dinner. We just returned home. Let me check with DaQuan."

She could hear the two of them conversing in the background.

"Was Billy supposed to come by after school?"

"Yes, sir."

"He left the house and hasn't returned home. His mom is worried. Do you have any idea where he might have gone?"

"No…no, sir."

Doctor Bob spoke into the phone. "Sorry, Maggie. He doesn't seem to know anything much. Would you like me to drive around and look for him?"

"Would you? I'm going to do that right now, too. Keep in touch. Thanks."

Maggie walked out to the porch and gazed up the street. She had expected Billy to come riding up any minute, soaked to the bone, but so far, he hadn't. In the distance she spotted a vehicle approaching. "Surely that's Stuart."

The car forged past with no signs of stopping.

"Stuart must have had something better to do. All that really matters is that I find my son!"

She pulled out of the driveway and sped off. The streets were deserted. It appeared that people chose to stay cooped up in their homes until the storm ended. Made sense. Although the wipers sloshed the water back and forth like a madman, her vision was compromised by the storm's intensity.

"Where are you Billy?" she asked. Desperation was setting in. "I wonder if anyone saw you this evening, but who?"

Lightning cracked in the distance and lit up the sky. As she flinched, her hands let go of the wheel. The car careened to the right and hit the curb. Totally shaken, she fell forward onto the steering wheel and sobbed.

Sometime later a knock sounded on the window. Her makeup had run down her cheeks and her eyes were puffy and red. Keeping her head lowered, she hurriedly wiped her face with her closed fist before peeking up. To her surprise a man was standing alongside the car, an umbrella in his hand.

"Mrs. Gallagher, is that you?"

Her chin trembled as she spoke. "Detective Duncan, I didn't recognize you. Billy's missing. I've been out looking for him. Doctor Bob's out looking, too."

"Head home," he said. "Perhaps Billy made it back while you were gone. I'll follow you."

After pulling into the driveway, she sighed. The red bicycle was not in the usual place and the windows were shrouded in darkness. She dashed inside, but found it empty and silent, just as she had left it.

"What do I do now?" she asked him.

"Let me phone the station." After several rings, someone picked up. "Hey Phil, the Gallagher boy's missing," relayed Detective Duncan to his colleague. "What? Second child in a week? I didn't know—been on vacation. Uh huh. Uh huh. Sure thing."

The Detective assured her that he and several others would be driving around looking for Billy, but he suggested that she get some rest and someone, if not him, would be in touch.

Doctor Bob phoned an hour later and said he had had no luck. In fact, he wondered how Billy would be able to ride on a bicycle through such a powerful storm.

By ten o'clock Maggie collapsed in the rocking chair on the porch of her home, a cup of black coffee in her hand. She took a sip before setting it down upon the wooden floor beside the chair. *Where are you, Billy?*

A car would approach the house—she'd stand and peer over the porch rail, hoping someone was bringing Billy home, but each time, the car continued on. Once she finished the coffee, she went to the kitchen and poured another cup. Then she stepped back to the porch and waited…and waited…and waited…for her son to come home.

Billy crept forward to see who was crying, but he stopped in mid stride. His flashlight had caught sight of a large crevice on the right-side of the path—one misstep and down he'd fall. Alice chased a white rabbit and fell through a hole, but unlike Alice, Billy didn't think Wonderland was down there. He hugged his back to the wall on the left side and moved slowly and carefully.

"Shut up. All you've done is cry." A husky voice surged above the silence.

"I want my mommy. Please, mister."

A lantern lit up the space, so Billy turned off his flashlight and edged closer to the light. A little girl cowered on the dirt floor of the cave and towering over her was a burly man with his legs planted wide.

His nostrils flared as he taunted the child. "Mommy, mommy. She wants her mommy." He bent down, shook his outstretched finger at her and sneered. "Your uncle will pay a bundle to get YOU back. You're his pride and joy. Ha ha ha ha,"

*Her uncle? Who's her uncle?* Billy wondered.

He held up his phone and hollered, "Ten o'clock. Damn. No messages. Why's it taking so long to get that ransom?"

"Please, Mister. Let me go," the little girl cried.

"You're getting on my nerves, kid."

Billy leaned back against the wall, keeping very still so he would not attract the man's attention.

*I may only be ten, but I can tell that something is very wrong.*

The man picked up his phone and dialed. Billy edged closer to hear what he was saying.

"Pick up, Skinny. Pick up." His fingers were nervously drumming against his leg. "Finally. What took you so long? Uh-huh. You're getting the ransom at noon tomorrow? I thought it was tonight. No screw ups, you hear me? Okay, call me as soon as it's over. We're going to be rich!" He slid the phone into his back pocket.

Billy's left elbow began to itch. To scratch it, he had to free his right hand of the flashlight, but as proceeded to switch it to the other hand, it dropped. Thud!

"What the hell?" yelled the man. "Who's there?"

Billy's hand shot out and grabbed the flashlight to his chest.

"I said, "Who's there?"

Every muscle in Billy's body tightened. The man held up the lantern with his stubby fingers and glimpsed Billy huddled against the wall. "What have we here?" he hissed.

"Don't hurt me, Mister. "I won't tell anybody anything," Billy pleaded.

"No, you certainly won't." The man moved closer…and closer…and closer.

"What are you gonna do?" asked Billy, his chest heaving in and out, fear exploding inside him.

The man reached out to grab Billy, but instead, he was forced to raise his hand against a blinding light.

"I can't see," he cried and stumbled backwards. A scream pierced the air and an eerie silence followed.

Billy extended his upper body and aimed the flashlight down into the crevice, careful not to fall. At the bottom lay the man in a facedown position—arms spread wide, legs twisted, and his head tilted sideways. Billy's eyes bore into the lifeless figure, fully expecting the man to jump up and grab him by the throat, but he didn't.

*I think he's dead. That's how they look on TV.* His stomach clenched, and his face went pale. He inched backwards and huddled against the wall.

"Where's the man?"

Startled, Billy's head jerked. For a split second he had forgotten about the little girl. "Gone," he uttered, softly.

"Is he coming back?"

"Uh-uh." He'd never been at a loss for words before, but he was scrambling to understand what had happened.

"Who are you?" she asked. "Are you a friend of the mean man?"

"No. I'm Billy. What's your name?"

"Hannah and I'm five." She held up her hand and spread her fingers wide.

"I'm ten," he said. "Who was that man, Hannah?"

"I don't know. I was playing in the yard and he grabbed me."

"I heard him say something about your uncle."

"My uncle's the mayor. My mommy and I are visiting him."

"They must be very worried about you." Suddenly, he realized that his mom was probably worried about him, too.

"Do you know the way out?" Hannah asked.

"Um, not really, but follow me. We'll go this way."

Billy held onto the little girl's hand, as they ventured further into the unknown recesses of the cave. When they had walked a goodly distance, Billy sighed, "I'm tired. Let's stop and rest."

"Me, too," she said.

As the two children slept on the floor of the cave, their intertwined arms for pillows, the batteries in Billy's flashlight began to dim.

Maggie Gallagher must have drifted off at one point, because when her eyes opened, the sun was poking above the horizon and the storm had moved on. She checked the side of the house—no bike. Billy's bed had not been slept in either. Her cell phone showed no new messages. After calling her boss and explaining the situation, she scrolled through her contacts for the number of Billy's school and was connected to the principal, a stylish woman in her forties, who had known Billy since Kindergarten.

"Billy's missing, Mrs. Montgomerie. The police are out looking for him."

"I know," she replied. "Doctor Bob dropped DaQuan off and then stopped by my office. How are *you* holding up?"

"I'm trying to remain level-headed, but it's hard, since I have no idea where my son went." Her lips began to tremble, but she took a deep breath to steady herself. "I'd appreciate it if you could spread the word. If anyone has any news about Billy, they can call Detective Duncan."

"I sure will. We'll keep you in our prayers."

"Thanks."

Unable to sit still and do nothing, Maggie drove into the downtown, hoping someone had seen her boy. The big clock that hung on the front of the town hall, chimed nine times. The first person she caught sight of was Silas Baird, sitting on the bench outside the barber shop, whittling with his pocket knife.

*If anyone has seen Billy, it's probably him. He sees everything that goes on in this town. You'd think the man had ten eyes and ten ears.* She pulled over and rolled the window down.

"Did you see my son last night?" she asked Silas.

"Sure did. Was on that red bicycle of his. Wasn't raining yet."

"Did he say anything?"

"Nope. Miss Fullerton saw your boy, too, but he didn't say nuthin' to her either. Just smiled.

"Thanks," she whispered.

"Ya know, ma'am. Your boy talked a bit to The Mayor, but I got no idea what he said to that there dog."

She shook her head and breathed deeply. *Talked to The Mayor? Pigs can't fly. Dogs can't talk. Just another dead end.* Although she was not a church-going woman, she folded her hands, peered upwards and cried out, "Lord, where is my son?"

She drove up and down the streets, past the school on the southside, the library, the mayor's house and along the woods near Tottie River. There was no sign of a red bike or her lost child.

Suddenly a succession of high-pitched rings resounded from her purse. Her hands rummaged through the contents, desperately trying to locate her phone, which appeared buried somewhere amongst the clutter.

"There you are," she said, removing the device from its hiding place beneath her wallet. Hurriedly, she pressed the button.

"Hello?"

"Mrs. Gallagher, this is Detective Duncan. Has Billy returned yet?"

"No, he hasn't. I'm out looking for him right now. I can't just sit home and wait, Detective. I did find out that Silas Baird and Miss Fullerton saw him pass by on his bike before the storm, but he only talked to The Mayor, as if that does me any good."

"Didn't you say he was going over to DaQuan's? Have you spoken with him or his folks?"

"I got a hold of Doctor Bob late last night. I may be wrong, but I got this feeling that it wasn't what DaQuan did say, but what he didn't say."

"Sounds like I need to talk to Billy's friend."

Hannah rubbed her eyes. "Where am I? She saw Billy on the floor beside her. "Oh, I remember now. We fell asleep in the cave." She reached over and picked up the flashlight that lay in Billy's lap.

Her finger pushed the red button up and down several times, but nothing happened.

"What's going on?" asked Billy, sitting up, not yet fully awake.

"The flashlight doesn't work, but there's a light coming from somewhere. Look. Over there."

Before Billy could answer, Hannah had sprung up and disappeared around the curve at the far end of the tunnel.

"Careful. Don't fall," he called. His left hand slid across the wall to steady himself, as he advanced in Hannah's direction.

"Look at them, Billy. Aren't they beautiful?"

"Wow!" In front of him were clusters of flowers like none he'd ever seen—glowing petals in brilliant colors of red, yellow and orange—fires of radiant light. "Truly amazing" he said. "I wonder how they grow without sunlight."

"Your flashlight doesn't work. We can use these flowers to help us see," said Hannah.

"My flashlight doesn't work?"

She shook her head. "Nope."

"Pick three," directed Billy. "I'll take three, too. Then we better get going."

Before long the tunnel had gotten so narrow the children had to step sideways to maneuver through it.

"Are you sure this is the way out?" Hannah whimpered. "I'm scared."

"I'm not sure about anything anymore," Billy scoffed. Then he turned his back on Hannah and whispered, "Dad, are you there?"

Billy heard the voice and wondered if Hannah could hear it too, but he didn't think so.

*Yes, Billy. I'm here.*

"What should we do, Dad?"

*Billy, you need to go the other way…the same direction that you entered the cave. When you get back to the fork in the path, be sure to stay on the right. Trust me.*

"Okay, Dad. If you say so," Billy answered softly. Then he turned and faced the little girl. "Hannah, we're going back the other way."

Soon they passed by the glowing flowers and added one more to their beautiful bouquets. When they approached the crevice in the floor where the man fell, they cautiously inched around it. Billy couldn't resist looking down. *Whew! Dead as a doornail. Good thing.*

"Do you have something to eat?" asked Hannah. "I'm hungry."

"I don't think so," he said, but for some reason the bag seemed heavier. Grabbing the bottom, he flipped it over and let the contents spew out. He gasped. *Dad, did you do this?* On the ground lay a variety of snacks: cheese, crackers, gummi candy, peanuts and drinks in a box. They loaded up their pockets and munched as they walked, unwilling to waste time. As Hannah took the lead and was rounding the next curve, Billy stopped to tie his shoe. When he finished tightening the loops, a deafening scream split the air. His feet took flight, like a firecracker, and he found Hannah, standing stiff as a marble statue, staring upwards at the ceiling of the cave. The flowers she'd held so carefully, were scattered on the ground.

"W—W—What are those?" Hannah pointed.

"They're bats," he replied.

"It's not Halloween, Billy. Why—why are they there?" she stammered.

If you squat down and be still, they won't hurt you," commanded Billy. When she didn't comply, he grabbed her by the shoulders and forced her down. "Now, close your eyes."

Hannah sprawled out on the dirt floor, covered her head with her hands and refused to move a muscle. Billy, on the other hand, enjoyed watching the furry mammals taking flight, their outstretched wings fluttering overhead. When they had disappeared, he announced, "All clear. Let's go."

Hannah didn't budge.

"Come on," Billy said, as he hoisted her up and brushed the dirt off her clothes. After gallantly retrieving her flowers, she shuffled along beside him, clinging tightly to his arm.

"Tell me more about that awful man," said Billy. "I've never seen him in Kyleighburn before."

"He was mean and pushed me into his van. He talked to someone on his phone a lot. Do you know anyone named Skinny?"

"No. That's a funny name."

"Uh huh."

"Hannah, we should be out of here real soon. I bet my best friend DaQuan is wondering…"

"What's that noise?" she interrupted, squeezing his arm.

Billy hollered out, "My arm! Let go Hannah.'

"Sorry, Billy."

"I don't hear anything," he replied. "Hey, if you're still worried about the bats, they're long gone." Of course, he couldn't be sure, but he hoped that they were—for Hannah's sake.

Tired from the long ordeal, Hannah began dragging her feet, as if her shoes were filled with lead. Billy grew impatient.

"You're too slow." He began to speed up and drifted away from her.

"I know, but…I don't want…to walk…anymore."

Certain the bats were eyeing her from above, Hannah stared upwards, as she plodded along. All at once her foot struck a large rock positioned in the middle of the path. Down she went—boom.

"Ow!" she wailed. "My leg! My leg! It hurts! It hurts!"

Billy looked back. He saw the rock and a trail of blood oozing from a big cut on Hannah's leg. "Can you get up?"

"No…please don't make me," she sobbed.

"I could go find help," he said, "but I don't want to leave you by yourself."

He slunk down against the wall of the cave and sighed, "Will we ever get out of here?"

After speaking with Doctor Bob at his office, the two men agreed to meet at the school, so Detective Duncan could have a word with DaQuan.

Doctor Bob, known as quite the jokester in the town, exited his car and immediately accosted the Detective with some mid-morning humor.

"Hey Detective Duncan, why don't cannibals eat clowns?"

"I give up," replied the Detective.

"They taste funny. Get it?"

"Good one," he answered, but considering the situation, Bob's enthusiastic wit took Detective Duncan aback. As they walked toward the school, he caught a glimpse of funny man Bob. *Good grief, the man is still grinning. Maybe he missed his calling and should have been a comedian.*

As they entered through the main doors, Mrs. Montgomerie was standing in the hallway waiting. The Detective had notified her of their impending arrival.

"Gentlemen, follow me, please."

When they reached the classroom, she knocked and proceeded to open the door. "Please excuse the interruption, Miss Boyd, but it is important that I speak with DaQuan."

The teacher nodded. DaQuan arose from his seat and glanced around—everyone was staring and whispering. "What'd you do, DaQuan? You're in big trouble, man."

He sucked in a quick breath when he saw a policeman and his dad standing beside the principal.

"Good morning, DaQuan. I'm Detective Duncan." He shook the boy's hand. "I'd like you to accompany us to the principal's office. We'll talk for a bit. You haven't done anything wrong, so don't be afraid."

"Why's my dad here?"

"It's always good to have a mom or dad present when I talk to kids. Is that okay?"

"Sure, I guess so."

Detective Duncan took-in DaQuan's demeanor. *The boy looks nervous. Look at him biting his lower lip and fidgeting with his hands. Maybe it's nothing. After all, he'd been pulled from the classroom in front of the other kids.*

"Dad, is Billy still missing?" he asked, as they drew closer to the main office.

"Yes, he is."

Once they were seated, Mrs. Montgomerie closed the door and Detective Duncan took charge.

"DaQuan. Be honest with me. You know where Billy went last night, don't you? We want to find him."

"Son," said Doctor Bob. "Tell the Officer what you know. He might be hurt."

"We were, um. I'm not in trouble?"

"Not at all," said the Detective.

"Well, we were 'sposed to go up by Tottie River…and dig there. We've already found a few arrowheads." His eyes shifted toward his dad. "I had to go to my Grandma's instead."

"Do you think he went there last night?" asked the Detective.

"Probably," he answered.

Then he turned to Doctor Bob. "Is it okay if the three of us go check out the site?"

"Sure thing," he replied.

Detective Duncan drove the pair in his squad car to the outskirts of town near the river. DaQuan climbed out from the back of the vehicle and immediately began walking north alongside the grove of trees that overlooked a barren field to the west. The two men followed. Mud sloshed over their shoes as they sank in the soft earth, but they trudged forward. The Detective took notice of how the boy pointed to every tree he passed.

*What the hell's he doing?*

"There it is. See the red paint we sprayed on the tree trunk," shouted DaQuan. "If we walk twenty paces west, we'll be at the site."

He counted off. "One, two…nineteen, twenty."

After grabbing a broken branch, he stooped down and began swirling the stick through the mud, hoping to find a clue. It didn't take long. Something familiar was protruding from beneath the squishy ground.

"Hey, this is Billy's spade. I'd know it anywhere. There's a weird looking B on the handle. He carved it with his pocket knife. See."

DaQuan showed it to both men.

"Dad, Billy would never leave his spade here. He was careful with his tools. What do you suppose happened?"

"If he was here, he would've needed to take cover from the storm—fast. Any idea where he'd go?"

"I dunno," replied DaQuan. "We never got rained on when we were here."

"One thing we do know is that Billy *was* here. That's a start," said the Detective. "Thanks for your help, DaQuan... and Doctor Bob."

"I want my friend to be all right."

The Detective withdrew the phone from his pocket and checked the time—ten-thirty. "I'll take you two back to the school, as soon as I make a call to the station and make arrangements for a crew to come and search the area."

Within the hour a half-dozen officers and some volunteers from the town arrived at the site, intent on finding the missing ten-year-old boy. Billy's mother was asked to remain at the police station and wait for any news that became available.

Maggie Gallagher checked her watch—twelve noon. She glanced up and down the hallway from her chair at the police station. People flitted here and there, but not one person had stopped to give her an update about the search for her son. True, they hadn't been at it very long, but the waiting had become unbearable.

*I can't just sit here.*

When an officer walked by, she called out, "Excuse me, Sir. Is Detective Duncan around?"

"Let me check, ma'am." When he returned, she was told that he was nowhere in the station. She rose up, tightened her purse against her chest and left through the main door. As she passed several parking meters and even her own car—a sense of hopelessness enveloped her. She considered going back home to double check the house, but her feet seemed to have a mind of their own, tugging her toward a brown brick building known as The Drug Store. As she entered, a bell tinkled above the doorway. Joe, the bartender, busy replenishing bottles of liquor behind the bar, lifted his head and caught sight of his newest patron.

"What's your pleasure, ma'am?" Joe asked.

"A whiskey sour…on the rocks," she answered, hoisting herself onto the stool and tossing her purse up on the counter.

"Coming right up," he said.

Throughout the town of Kyleighburn police sirens were heard from the east to the west. Someone had been apprehended stealing a suitcase that Marino Esposito, the town mayor, had stashed behind the school—ransom for his niece. He'd done as he was told and placed one hundred thousand dollars in small bills into the case, with one exception—he had called the police, despite the harsh warning not to. He had faith in Kyleighburn's Finest, the modest police force that cared for the people in his small town.

As he sat impatiently in the front seat of the police cruiser parked near the school, a myriad of questions swirled through his brain. "Who's the guy that kidnapped my niece? Where is she? Is she hurt?"

Detective Duncan opened the door and slid into the driver's seat. "It's Stuart Dawkins, Mr. Mayor. He was caught red-handed with the suitcase. Keeps insisting he hasn't done anything wrong. Said he was walking by and saw it sitting there."

"That beanpole plumber? You've got to be kidding. Any news about my niece?"

"Sorry, sir. She wasn't with him." Detective Duncan started the car and weaved through the crowd of curious onlookers that had gathered along the street. "We aren't sure if he took Hannah and also Billy Gallagher. Once Dawkins is taken downtown, Officer Big Bubba Buchanan will interrogate him. There's no doubt he'll get Stuart to crack and eagerly confess. The guy's a good plumber, but he always struck me as being a follower, scared of his own shadow."

"A follower? You think there was an accomplice?" asked Marino Esposito.

"Could be," sighed the Detective. "Here's your house."

"Duncan, what am I going tell my sister about her sweet child?"

"Nothing right now, Mr. Mayor," he said. "but someone will keep you posted."

The mayor stepped out. His sister rushed out the door and threw her arms around his neck. The Detective pulled away.

Back at the station, Detective Duncan retreated to his office—a stack of paperwork littered his desk, but none of it was important enough to take precedence over locating the Gallagher boy. A note by the phone indicated that someone had checked the Gallagher home at 11:45, but the boy was nowhere around. He stepped out, closed the door and left the station on foot, eager to walk off his frustration.

He raced up one street and down another, deep in thought. *Why would gentle Stuart kidnap an innocent child? The mayor had money to pay the ransom, but Mrs. Gallagher probably lived from paycheck to paycheck. Why Billy? That is, if Stuart took Billy, too?* He rubbed his chin, unable to make sense of it.

His feet carried him to the middle of the downtown. Since he hadn't bothered to eat lunch, he entered the café, sat inside one of the booths, and placed an order for a sandwich and a diet beverage—all the while mulling over the facts of the case. *Billy had seen Silas and Old Lady Fullerton…and The Mayor. Yes, The Mayor. Damn, he wouldn't put anything past that dog. He was one smart canine.* He laughed and shook his finger in the air. *You know, maybe talking to that dog was worth a try.*

When his meal arrived, he devoured the sandwich and downed the drink as if he hadn't eaten in days. Then he stood up and cleared his throat. "Ahem. Attention everyone, has anyone seen The Mayor, the furry one?"

"Not me." Those two words echoed throughout and bounced off the walls.

*On to the next place. Maybe I'll have better luck.*

He darted across the street and headed into The Drug Store. *Look at all the people "drinking" lunch. Surely, someone in this place knows where The Mayor is.* That's when he noticed her sitting alone at the bar.

"Mrs. Gallagher, what are you doing here?"

"I'm having a drink, Detective. Crazy isn't it? My husband drank, beat me and left me. Now Billy's gone, too. I figured it might help soothe my worn-out heart." She stirred the drink several times with the tiny straw and took a sip. At the end of the bar, Joe was holding up three fingers.

"Call a taxi for Mrs. Gallagher, Joe. She needs to go home."

Joe nodded.

"No, no, no. My car is parked down the street."

The Detective put his arm around her shoulders and handed her ten dollars for the fare.

Then he climbed up onto a wooden chair and called out, "Has anyone seen The Mayor?"

"If you're talking about the dog, he was crossing the street over by the courthouse about ten minutes ago," answered one of the patrons.

The Detective ran the three blocks toward the courthouse. Resting on the cement steps, was The Mayor. "Bingo," he cried out. He crouched beside the dog and leaned in close to his ear.

"Mayor, listen. You saw Billy last night. He's missing, and his mother is heartbroken. Do you know where he went? You're the only one that can help me. Please Mayor." The Officer sat on the step, watched the cars drive by and waited, hoping the dog would respond.

Fifteen minutes later The Mayor rose up and took off down the street. Detective Duncan followed close behind. *Take me to Billy. Find Billy.*

The Mayor trotted east, past the shops, and through the neighborhoods toward Tottie River. When he turned sharply and headed south, the Detective heaved a deep sigh. "Gracious, how far is that dog going?" His feet ached and sweat dripped off his face. His uniform was sticking to his skin, wet and grimy. He pictured himself in shorts and a manly tank top, a much better choice for the police work he was doing that afternoon. Unfortunately, that kind of attire was not regulation, so he shrugged his shoulders and accepted the fact that feeling like a wet fish was part of the job on such a hot day.

The Mayor stopped abruptly, tipped his head back and howled. Then he turned and stared directly into the eyes of Detective Duncan.

"What have we here?" he sang excitedly.

*It made perfect sense. Billy had ridden his bike through the storm looking for shelter and found one of the many caverns that made up the topography of Kyleighburn.* But just as quickly, the grin was replaced with a frown. *When it stopped raining, why didn't he return home?*

He retrieved his phone from his back pocket. "Lieutenant, I have news. The Gallagher boy—I've got a lead. Send some able-bodied folks out to the cave entrance by Tottie River. Maybe a doctor or a paramedic in the bunch. Yes, that sounds like a good idea. I'll be here waiting."

Once he had finished the conversation with his boss, he turned to thank

The Mayor, but the dog had vanished.

"Billy, I'm tired. Do you think it's bedtime yet?"

He held up his watch. "No, it's three o'clock." Then he paused before continuing. "It must be Friday afternoon. I missed school today which means I didn't take my spelling test. Maybe my teacher will forget about it."

"What's a spelling test?"

"You put letters together to make words. I'm in fourth grade, almost fifth. I know lots of words. Do you know how to read, Hannah?"

"I know cat. C-A-T. Next year I go to Kindergarten at the big school. Want to hear me sing the ABC song?"

"Sure."

After she finished, Billy said, "Let's play a game. I'll say a word and you tell me what it begins with. If you get it right, you get…" He reached into the bag. "a gummi bear. If you get it wrong, I get it."

"I'll try. Billy, my leg still hurts."

"Try not to think about it. What does dog start with?"

"D?"

"You're right."

"Can I have a red one, Billy?"

"He opened the bag and emptied it into his hand. There was only one red in the bunch.

"Here," he said.

The game went on. When Hannah didn't want to play anymore, Billy counted—he had four. Hannah had eight.

"You win, Hannah. By the way, how's your leg now?"

"It hurts bad when I move it. Are you tired, Billy? I am." She laid her head against Billy's shoulder and dozed off.

Billy thought about leaving Hannah, so he could go for help, but once again he decided against it. A familiar voice penetrated the stillness. *"Billy, it's me. You're going to be fine. It won't be long now."*

"Is someone coming, Dad?"

*"Yes, Billy. Soon."*

"Hannah, someone will be coming for us soon. We're going to get out of here."

Hannah stirred. "Okay." Then she drifted back to sleep.

A motley crew of four gathered at the mouth of the cave armed with necessities such as: rope, first aid supplies, and tools.

"You fellas all know each other?" asked Detective Duncan.

"Yep, we're good," they echoed. Their flashlights lit up the entrance, as they searched for clues.

"Look," shouted Chuck, one of Kyleighburn's veteran firefighters, dressed in blue jeans, a red T-shirt and sporting a Carolina Panther's cap on his head.

His flashlight revealed an impression in the dirt, about three inches wide, beginning at the entrance and stretching deep into the structure. Beside it were shoe prints, relatively small compared to his own.

"See the zig zags inside the print? Looks like tennis shoes—kid-size," he added.

"I'll bet those are wheel tracks from Billy's bike and his footprints," Dax, a local paramedic, surmised. The colors in his flowered Hawaiian shirt were so bright, the men teased him about being able to glow in the dark. A full beard covered the lower half of his face.

"I wouldn't rule it out," Detective Duncan replied.

"Over here are more tracks. Some of these are very small, and some are quite large. I'm not sure if they are fresh or made some time back. One thing's for certain—all the tracks are going in, but none are heading out," observed Micah, an outsider who recently moved to town. His blue long-sleeved T-shirt matched his blue eyes.

After walking a short distance, Chuck declared, "Hey, Duncan, no more footprints."

"Dax bent down and examined the dirt beneath his feet. "The earth here is harder than up by the entrance, which might explain why there's no tracks. Let's keep going, fellas."

Eventually, they came across the fork in the path.

"Assuming Billy came this far, which way might he have gone?" asked Chuck, heaving a long-winded sigh.

Micah walked a short distance on the left and returned bearing a gift. "Lookee here, Detective. Potato chip bag. Billy's, perhaps?"

He took a whiff. "Smells like potatoes, oil and salt. Wait a minute, there's a chip at the bottom." After tipping the bag, it fell into his palm. He broke it and everyone heard the *snap!* "Sounds fresh to me. I'd say that's a good sign. It belongs to someone who's been here recently."

Dax wandered down the right-side path. When he returned from the short jaunt, he shook his head and said, "No tracks. Let's go left."

Narrow passageways made for a rather treacherous and slow-going journey. One behind the other, the closely-knit group plodded forward till a red bike came into view.

"It's Billy's. He's here somewhere," said Detective Duncan. "Billy. Billy, are you there?" Adrenaline pulsed through his body, but the exhilaration was short-lived when there was no reply.

"How long do you think we've been down in this underground city?" asked Chuck. "I sure could go for a smoke right about now."

"You're not serious?" asked Dax.

"Naw, just kidding. Gave up that bad habit years ago."

Micah flashed the light onto his watch. "We've been down here a little over an hour."

Detective Duncan called out again. "Billy! Billy!"

The echo of a child's voice could be heard in the distance.

"Billy, is that you? It's Detective Duncan."

"Help."

"We're coming, Billy," the men chanted.

As they meandered forward, darting about through the twists and turns, Billy came into view—standing before them with tears flowing down his cheeks.

"You found us. Oh, I can't believe it."

"What do you mean—us?" asked the Detective.

Billy stepped aside.

"That's Hannah. The awful man brought her here. I stayed with her. I didn't want her to be alone."

"What's wrong with my leg, Mister?"

Dax examined Hannah's leg. *It's probably a hairline fracture.* He patted her head and said. "You're a brave girl. Your leg might be broken."

"Are you gonna take good care of me?" she asked.

"You betcha," he answered.

After opening the First Aid Kit, he removed some splints to stabilize her leg and avoid more damage. Then he carefully placed his hands beneath her and swept the little girl into his arms. "Come on kiddo. Your mom and your uncle will be thrilled to see you."

"As for you", said Detective Duncan, staring at Billy.

"I know, Mom must be madder than mad."

"No, not at all." he replied. "In fact, she's more worried, than mad. You have no idea how happy she'll be to see that you're safe."

"Did the man bring you to the cave like he did Hannah?" Micah asked Billy.

"No, I found this place when the storm came. I decided it might be fun to go exploring. That's when I found Hannah with that awful man." He hung his head for a moment before looking up and announcing, "I killed the man who took Hannah."

"What are you talking about, Billy?" asked the Detective.

Billy led them to the crevice and explained what had happened.

"There." Billy pointed. "I shined my flashlight at him. He fell."

All four men peered down.

"Who is he?" asked Billy.

"Your guess is as good as mine," Detective Duncan answered, scratching his head.

Although the exhausted Detective could've gone home and slept for the next twenty-four hours, he returned Hannah to her jubilant mother and uncle before taking Billy to the station, where his frantic mother eagerly waited for him. Maggie Gallagher flew up from the chair and wrapped her arms around her son before planting a big kiss on his cheek.

"Oh, Mom. I'm too old for that mushy stuff."

She laughed and said, "You're not that old."

Detective Duncan patted Billy on the back. "You saved Hannah. You're a brave boy."

"Thanks a lot, sir. By the way, there's one more thing. It's about my dad."

"What about him?" his mom asked.

Billy described the encounter inside the cave, including the fact that his dad was dead. His mom narrowed her eyes and shot a quick glance over at the Detective.

"You don't believe me. Do you?" Billy grumbled.

She shrugged her shoulders and frowned. "To tell you the truth, Billy, it does sound farfetched. Don't you think so, Detective?

"I suppose it does, but stranger things have happened around here. Tomorrow I'll send some men out there to investigate. Then we'll know for sure."

Long after Billy and his mom left, the identity of the dead man was revealed, setting the station abuzz with speculation about what would happen next. Duncan's next stop was to see Big Bubba Buchanan.

"What did you find out from Dawkins?" the Detective asked.

"Not much. The guy isn't talking—insists he's innocent. Wanna take a stab at questioning him?"

"Sure. I've got a bit of information you didn't have a few hours ago that should rattle his cage."

"Go for it," said Big Bubba.

Detective Duncan walked down the hall to Stuart's cell where he found him lying face-up on his bunk, checking out the cracks in the ceiling. When the lock rattled, Stuart sat up, dangled his legs over the side of the bed and asked, "Who are you?"

"I'm Detective Duncan. I thought you'd like to know that we found Hannah. The man who took her is dead."

"Oh?" Stuart's face turned pale. "He's really dead?"

"You know who he is, don't you?"

"Why should I?" asked Stuart, heaving a deep sigh.

"Because he's your brother. We took his prints—wasn't hard to find a match. He's got a lengthy police record covering five states. He left Kyleighburn about fifteen years ago, didn't he?"

"Maybe."

"When did he come back?"

Stuart said nothing.

"He called you Skinny. It's true Stuart, you are tall and skinny."

"I'm not that skinny. I hate that name."

"Do you like being a plumber?"

"It's okay. Been doing it for twenty years."

"I'll bet you'd like to live in a house instead of a trailer."

"Sure."

"Was it for money, Stuart? You let your brother talk you into kidnapping an innocent little girl for money? That's mean, really mean."

"I'm not mean!" he shouted. "My brother said he wouldn't hurt her. We'd split the money. I wouldn't need to live in that broken-down trailer anymore. I could buy anything I wanted. Maybe even get me a girlfriend. I'd treat her right—be able to buy her nice things."

Stuart's body hunched over and he began to sob. "Oh, God, what have I done?"

That's all the Detective needed to know—case closed.

Three days passed. On a Monday evening Detective Duncan paid the Gallaghers a visit.

"He was there, Billy, just like you said. I knew your dad before he started drinking. He was a good man."

"Thanks for saying that."

"I guess you haven't seen today's paper." The Detective picked up the newspaper on the step, turned to the front page and handed it to Billy's mom.

"Oh my, look at this." she exclaimed.

**BILLY GALLAGHER SAVES MAYOR'S NIECE IN KIDNAPPING**

"The article says you're a hero, Billy."

"Wow! I'm famous." Billy beamed. He looked up at the sky. *Dad, are you proud of me?*

"Yes, you are." His mom wrapped her arms around him and hugged him tightly.

"Remember, don't kiss me, Mom."

Billy was quite the celebrity. If he was spotted walking down the street, people rushed over to shake his hand or pat him on the back. Many of the town's children, especially those younger than ten, wanted to grow up and be like brave Billy Gallagher. Even Gerald Winslow Franklin found it necessary to honor Mrs. Gallagher's request regarding her mortgage. It wouldn't be in the bank's best interest to foreclose on the mother of the town's new hero.

A few weeks later, as things were settling down, an envelope arrived in the

Gallagher's mailbox from the Triple Crown Life Insurance Company. Inside was a check for one hundred thousand dollars made out to Margaret Gallagher.

"Look, Billy. We're going to be all right." She held up the check. Tears rolled down her cheeks. "Your dad did love us, you know."

"I know," he answered. Then he took off running, out the kitchen door into the back yard. He sat beneath the tree, crossed his legs and reached into his pocket. He pulled out a wrinkled photograph, taken on the day he caught his first fish, a six-inch sunfish, which his dad helped him reel in. In the snapshot Billy was holding up his rod with the fish dangling from the hook and his dad was showing off his own catch—a striped bass. He touched his dad's face with his finger and whispered, "If you can hear me, thanks for everything."

A gust of wind rustled through the trees, tousling Billy's hair, followed by a sudden calm. A faint voice danced through the air like a song, "You're my son. I will always love you."

Friday, June 17

## What's Up

- Doctor Bob will give a lecture on healthy eating and weight loss at 7 p.m. Monday at the E.P.P. Scott Library meeting room.
- The Boy Scouts and Girl Scouts are combining to host a dunking booth at the Fourth of July celebration at Magnolia Park. Balls will be three for a dollar and the scouts are promising plenty of local celebrities will be sitting on the shelf.
- Farmers market is 9 a.m. to 2 p.m. Saturday in front of City Hall.
- Tuesday's children's hour at 10 a.m. at E.P.P. Scott Library is a reading of Neil Gaiman's "Fortunately the Milk" by librarian Delilah Chandra.
- The photos taken Saturday at the car show will be available for viewing after noon Monday at The Kyleighburn Kylter office. Come look over the photos we shot at the event and put in your order.

Friday, June 17

## Public Safety

Reports from Police Department, fire departments, Sheriff's Department; 6 p.m. Tuesday through noon Thursday.

- Speeding charge, Jerry Kowalski, Tuesday
- Speeding charge, Jerry Kowalski, Wednesday..
- Fire in dumpster, Thursday, City Hall. $200 damages. Thursday.
- Two-vehicle collision, no injuries, Main Street and McTeague Avenue. Thursday.
- Speeding charge, Jerry Kowalski, Thursday.
- Brush fire, Magnolia Park, minor damage. Wednesday.

# Friends for Ever and Ever

Iliana Navarro

## Joe & Cali C

THE GENTLE FOG LIFTED from Kyleighburn. The sun rose, and a serene silence surrounded the town as the morning arrived. The stray calico cat stretched, licked her short orange and black patchwork fur. She paced around the back door, waiting for the human to show up with food.

"Meow…meowww." she said as she jumped to the cement landing and scratched the wooden door frame that led to the kitchen.

"All-right…I hear ya," Joe said as he opened the back door, holding a cup of coffee, on top of the cup a folded newspaper with pieces of leftover tuna fish. Carefully he placed the newspaper on top of a stack of floor tiles. "Whoah, you are hungry! Mangia, mangia!" he said and smiled at the calico cat.

She immediately began to devour the food. As she was eating, she thought, *Don't understand human but smell food.* She stopped and purred in thanks. *Human saved me from dark cold water and feeds me…purr purr … before I clean myself, I will clean his hands.*

Joe chuckled, "Ha! You can't lick off my tattoos, but thanks anyways, much appreciated." He patted her head and picked up the newspaper, crushed it into a ball and hurled it at the uncovered trash can. The cat looked at the newspaper ball and leaped towards the trash, hoping there was something left.

Leaning against the door while sipping his morning brew, he sighed and said, "You know, you need a name. Something I can remember. After all, you and I have been hanging out for a while, like buddies. What can I call you? Hmmm…you are a calico cat…let's see…."

It took him awhile. Since the almost-drowning incident, his mind just slowed down big time. While the cat was going through her clean-up routine, he looked at her. *At this stage of the game I just live and experience as much as I can. I like her—fished out of the lake, almost-drowned, like me.*

*Tomorrow's Thursday,* his thoughts went on, *no to work, yes to fishing.* Fishing relaxed him. After a couple of hours, catch or no catch, he would pack his makeshift gear and bike home, content and in peace.

"You are a calico…. Hmmm not C-cat." he said and kept on thinking.

By this time Kyleighburn was bustling with activity. People were on their way to work, shops ready for customers, traffic rolling by, the busy-ness of everyday life. The cat looked towards the alleyway and the street, ready to leave.

Suddenly he said, "Ha! I got it! Cali C! Yep, that sounds good to me. Nice, short, and easy to remember."

Cali C purred as in agreement, with a full belly it was time for a nap.

Joe heard the school bus stop and realized the day was moving on. He said to Cali C, "Time to go, today is Senior Tourist Day. Yep, this town sure needs the money, even though they're not great tippers."

Bending down and with a mysterious tone, he said, "Cali C, wherever you go, whatever you do," he looked intently at her and shook his hands, "Do not go near the caverns! Strange things happen at that place." Wiping his hands on his jeans he got up and went in to begin his workday. He didn't mind, but not on a Thursday. No. Never Thursdays-ever was his mantra for now.

## Attack of the Humans!

Cali C stared at the door and turned. What human said sounded dangerous. She scampered out of the alley, down the sidewalk, thinking *humans strange…they shake and wave their front paws when bad things are going to happen.* The human that threw her from the dock waved the front paws too.

The trash truck turned the corner, Cali C stretched and scampered on to the library, ready for her nap. Arriving at the tree in front of the building, she curled up and wrapped her tail around her, closed her eyes and purred in contentment.

Cali C woke up to a human voice.

"Ahhh, Tommy look at the pretty calico!" Lillian Esposito said.

Tommy ran toward the cat saying, "Mommy! I want kitty!!"

Cali C looked up. She saw chubby hands and feet coming towards her. She went into flight mode, up the tree, to the highest limb she could find. Crouching from her perch and looking down she heard the little human.

"Mommy, kitty go…Oh Mommy." Tommy pouted as he stopped and turned, pointing at the tree.

Lillian walked towards him, looked up and saw the calico crouched, staring intently at them, hissing in attack mode. A move on their part to climb the tree would give the cat the go-ahead to jump straight at them and claw their efforts away. She decided not to continue.

In a soft motherly tone she said, "It's okay. I'm afraid we scared the kitty. Let's go in the library and look at kitty books." She knew Isabel, her out-of-control teenager, would soon be home, and alone. Lillian was trying to prevent the 'home alone' situation. Isabel was very creative in many ways, especially ones that grounded her for life. "Remember we have to go home before Isabel, or else she'll be sad we aren't home in time for dinner."

Tommy held her hand and looked at the tree. "Ahhh, I want kitty."

She looked at him, looked at the cat and said, "Well, maybe we can go to the shelter tomorrow and look for one, okay?"

He smiled, "Yeah, okay. I like very much." With that settled, they walked away towards the library, up the steps, and entered the building.

Cali C watched as the humans entered the large building. When the door closed, she crouched and carefully crawled down. She sped away from the library, weaving in and out of the bushes towards the heavily wooded area. *Humans... Hiss, hiss, they put you in a box to be dumped, or dress you!...* "Meow" *...hiss, pull your claws out, bad things happen... hiss... hiss.*

"Meow"*...one human feeds me, with dirt on his hands. He doesn't touch, gives food, talks, meow...* "Meow" ...one human good.

The rays of the noontime sun intensified, and the lunch time crowd cleared out of the streets. Cali C kept on towards the woods. By now she was ready to continue her nap, with no interruptions.

## A Confrontation

She was looking for a good napping spot.

"Arf…Arf…" Then came a whimper, another bark, and a growl! This startled her

"Meooww?"…" *What is it, don't want it near, nap now*, she thought, but her curiosity got the best of her. She saw a hole and heard the same whimpering cry. The hole was dark and had a different smell. Before she could jump to higher ground, the stones beneath her shifted. Losing her balance, she tumbled down the dark slimy hole.

Grasping and clawing, she tried to reclaim her balance. The damp and slimy ground didn't help her at all. Rolling into the cave, she bumped into a hairy lump.

It barked. "Arf…Arf" and gave out a long whimper. The lump had stopped her roll. She slowly looked around and tried to figure out where she was and who or what was the lump. *Lump not happy.*

She checked herself, some patches of mud in her fur and some scratches from the small stones she encountered on her way down. She stretched and walked around the lump, smelled it. It was breathing. All of a sudden, she felt a wet nose. Looking towards the wet feeling, she saw big eyes and fur.

"Meow, meow…," Cali C sniffed the lump, and it moved and whimpered. *A dog, hmmm, strange, not chasing me. Let me try to move him.* She crouched and pushed with all her might but all it did was sit down half-way. They stared at each other; the dog panted. She tried to move him again, but he lowered his head between his front paws and whimpered.

*Not good, no hurt, scared, last try,* she thought. Backing up and placing herself in attack mode, without hissing, she pounced on his behind full force with claws out. He let out a howl like a wolf acknowledging a full moon and jumped from the half-sitting position. He stood up, shook his fur, looked at his behind, and barked.

Face-to-face, all they could do was sniff each other suspiciously. Trying to find out what they were like by smell, just in case one was larger than the other and not too friendly. It was unfamiliar ground; both Cali C and the dog were hesitant to move. Cali C took the initiative to explore by crawling around the dog. She padded a little distance away to get a better look.

Suddenly a sharp bright light lit up the cave. A strong pleasant fragrance came from the vines that lined the walls surrounding them.

"Meow... meow." Looking at the dog, Cali C beckoned him over.

The dog wagged his tail. "Woof!" The bright light shone on, and he was able to look around. *Wet, slimy, can't be worse off near the cat, near light.* Squinting his eyes, he scampered over towards Cali C.

They huddled there together. The brilliant rays of the light bathed them. They could smell the sweet aroma of the vines. They felt the rays of the light, but a strange energy made them shudder. It was the electrical shock that made them jump, shaking their furs. With wide eyes they looked at each other.

The dog barked, "Arf...Arf," He thought, *The Mayor. You?*

'Meow." *Cali C,* returning the question with her thoughts. They were able to communicate! She licked her fur and wondered what had happened with the light and the smell of the vines. She couldn't figure it out, but one way or another, it sure changed them

There was an eerie stillness as they sat trying to figure out what happened. A hum broke the stillness, then a buzz...buzz...BUZZZZ! BUZZZZ!! A cloud came towards them. The sound startled them, and without hesitation they ran and crawled around and over the vines, past the light. The cloud hovered over them then continued on its course, following a breeze out of the cavern. BUZZZ...the cloud passed them, out a hole and into the woods. Stopping, scared, they crouched, too tired to move. Cali C looked at the dog who called himself The Mayor, panting, trying to catch his breath. She felt the breeze and slowly followed it to the hole.

The Mayor barked, "Woof, woof." He thought, *BEES.*

Cali C turned her head, "Meow, meow". She felt strange, the same way as when the light shone on them. Her fur stood up, and looking at the dog, she understood his thoughts.

She glanced at The Mayor and looked at the hole. She sniffed a few times and began to dig her way out. The Mayor began to dig away the small stones, leaves, and small branches blocking their exit. Finally they crawled out into a wooded area near the lake. They shook their furs and tried to lick themselves clean. Exhausted but hungry they walked around sniffing for food. They stopped when they saw a trash can near the old pier by the lake.

The Mayor took the initiative and jumped at the can. It fell and out rolled a mish-mosh of leftovers, a buffet of assorted half-eaten food items. They devoured half a ham sandwich, a hot dog and even a piece of fruit. It was getting dark, and with full bellies the afternoon adventure began to take a toll on them. They looked for a safe place away from the lake or pier, in case teenage humans decided to grace them with their rowdy presence. At this time, neither of them wanted or needed any contact with humans or other animals. Cali C and The Mayor settled in for the night between the bushes and large stones that surrounded them,

## Peace Out!

"Ping, ping."

It was a text: "On our way home, running a bit late. Mom."

*Perfect timing,* Isabel thought. She checked her list—all done and ready to go! This time for good. To them, she was too much trouble, both at home and at school. So much trouble, they'd suspended her for good and were sending her away. The decision was made. Mom and Dad, also known as Mayor Esposito, had sat her down and had the conversation.

Her dad said, "This is too much! You are out of control! Of all things, Isabel, a fire!!! At the caves, with all those woods!"

Isabel answered, "I was curious, I wanted to see what was inside, why people disappear!"

"Curiosity killed the cat, you know. This time you are the cat and you killed any possibility for home schooling." He paused, took a deep breath and said, "You are off to boarding school, yes! A rigorous curriculum, with discipline and counseling."

The news shattered her. She walked silently out of the kitchen. She had no words, no tears.

For Isabel this was the worst thing her parents had done. *Adults are all the same. Don't fix the problem. Let's not find a solution. No just send the problem away, let a stranger try.* According to her parents, she had two weeks before departing from the home front. During her 'home solitary confinement' as she called it, leafing through a magazine, she saw a beautiful vacation ad. It read, "Explore, discover, see what the world has to offer." The picture had a smiling young woman, backpack on her shoulder ready to travel.

Isabel thought, *I love to explore, discover. Heck, that's why I get into trouble…hmm, I could do this!* And so the plan began.

For the last time she looked around, a mental picture for her memories. Gathering her belongings and getting her bike from beside the back door, she pedaled as fast as she could towards the woods and the cave opening near the lake. She had to reach the lake before nightfall and camp out at a safe spot she'd found by the old wooden pier. Before sunrise she would leave her bike near the cave opening and make it look like she fell in the cave.

It takes twenty-four hours for a missing person report, maybe shorter, since her dad was the Mayor. By that time she planned to be on the early morning bus out of Kyleighburn. *Freedom never tasted so good.*

Arriving at her destination she settled down, opened her backpack and found a sandwich.

She mentally went over her plan, then rolled out her sleeping bag. She thought, *a new adventure unfolding.* The reflection of the full moon on the lake and the surrounding trees made Isabel sleepy. She curled up and fell asleep right away, forgetting to set her alarm.

Joe got up before dawn, dressed and went to feed Cali C. When she was nowhere to be seen, he set out on his bike looking for her.

He thought, *she never misses a meal. I hope she's all right.* This was not a good thing, especially on Thursday, his day off. He pedaled around the alleys, near trash cans, calling her name. No response. He even had a can of tuna with him, in case she needed a nudge. Arriving at the woods, walking towards the lake and the old wooden pier, he heard a commotion.

Cali C crouched, hissing. A smallish dog who looked a little like the town pup, The Mayor, barked and circled a teenage girl, not letting her through.

The girl tried to get away from them, then the cat hissed.

Isabel had a sudden flashback. After school at the lake one time, hanging out with her friends, she saw a calico cat and had an idea.

"Let's teach the stray to swim," she told her friends. But they'd left her for fear of being caught and having the death of a cat on their hands. Bored after a couple of tries and some scratches, Isabel left the cat to fend for itself.

Now, trying to move, she looked at Cali C and said, "Wow…move, cat…you survived! It's true cats have nine lives, but if you don't move now, you might end up with only eight. Move! I have a bus to catch!"

The animals were quick and slowed Isabel's getaway. Then Joe had an idea. He opened the tuna can, walked in the clearing and said, "Cali…Cali C, here girl look what I got!" Cali C stopped, looked around. She hissed one more time and ran to her human. She smelled the tuna and began to eat, then she jumped into his arms and purred.

The Mayor said, "Arf…Arf." *Human friend?*

Cali C purred back. *Friend, no friend other human.*

This all gave Isabel a chance to run towards Joe's bike, grabbing it to make her getaway. She had to make up for lost time.

Taken by surprise, Joe ran after her, shouting, "Girl that's my transportation, get back here!"

Cali C and The Mayor joined the chase, through the woods and following a trail, leading them to town. Isabel saw the bus stop, crossed the street and looked for bus Number 7. Before boarding, she looked for a place to stash the bike.

She heard a loud, tired, exasperated voice. "STOP, girl, don't move!! Give me back my bike!!"

Isabel looked across the street, at the bewildered man, the hissing cat, and the dog barking at her. Throwing the bike near a bench, she boarded the bus.

Joe couldn't believe it. All he wanted was find to Cali C, then go fishing. He sighed, picked up Cali C, and crossed the street. Exhausted he sat on a bench, staring at the last window of the bus. It was just too much for him.

The bus began to move, and he saw the girl at the window waving her arms at them. Not a good-bye wave but more like good riddance. Isabel made a sign on the window with her fingers, while mouthing the words, "Peace out."

Cali C hissed and looked at The Mayor, his tongue out, panting heavily,

"Meoww." Hiss... hiss... *human wave arms...* hiss, *no friend, human push me in water...* hiss... *good human save me.*"

The Mayor barked in agreement, "Arf, arf," *understand.* "Woof," *Cali C, big change at cave, The Mayor know more.* "Arf, Arf."

Joe picked up his bike, scooped Cali C and The Mayor into the big front basket and pedaled steadily and slowly towards the trailer park. He looked at both of them and said with a smile on his face, "What a Thursday, almost lost my bike, but it ended on a good note…a banner day after all. Found you both, and now I have two best friends for ever and ever!"

# On the Steps

Susan Turley

SHE CAME AND SAT BESIDE HIM on the library steps as he watched the fireflies dance in the park across the street, a silent presence for several minutes before she held out her hand and introduced herself.

"Hope Landreth," she said with a smile.

"I know," came the quick reply. "How are the bugs?"

"I keep telling you..." she cut off the indignant cry quickly and looked around. She knew they were being watched. If they were being watched, they might be heard.

"They're not acting normally, if that's what you want to know. I can't figure what's going on with them."

He nodded but didn't speak.

"I know you're Micah, but I don't think I ever heard your last name."

He shrugged.

"Can you tell me about the cavern? No one wants to talk about what you all found."

He shrugged again.

"I don't know if I've ever met a chattier man."

A third shrug, but this time he did respond. "I don't chat. I only talk if I have something to say."

She leaned back and watched the sky, breathing in the sweet odor of the honeysuckle that nearly covered the deserted building next door. The vines covered the front, so she'd never been able to see if there was a sign, but she thought the two-story brick structure had been a store, with apartments or offices on the second floor. She had noticed that sometimes there were lights moving around inside.

"So you won't talk about the cavern?"

This time he didn't shrug but hesitated before he answered. "It's complicated and it's late. Are you sure you want to do this now?"

As the question ended, she heard the scuff of a shoe and a cleared throat from her left. As Micah rose from the step, she looked over her shoulder and saw a man approaching, his face a mask in the purplish glow of the streetlight. Shadows covered his lower face and the light emphasized his shiny forehead.

Like most of the town, she didn't like the banker, but he was friendlier to Micah than she expected. She'd seen the man interact with others. He was adept at pretending to like them while his contempt was obvious. This was genuine.

Gerald Winslow Franklin clapped the slender handyman on his left shoulder as he grasped Micah's right hand.

"Good to see you tonight, Micah. Are you telling Ms. Landreth about what we found today?

"She needs to get in there to see our big find—right up her alley."

She listened as the two men chatted without revealing any details, then the banker excused himself and walked away.

She looked back at Micah as they waited for the banker to disappear. He tapped his right hand against his thigh in a familiar rhythm and remained standing next to her. She looked up into the deep blue eyes, hoping he would sit down again and explain everything.

The hand was gentle on her shoulder. "We'll talk tomorrow, miel," he said softly, and was gone into the night without a sound.

# Special Delivery

RJ Minnick

MORRIS BACKED HIS MINI into a parking space and unplugged his charger, tossing the untethered cable onto the passenger seat and pocketing his phone. Locking up his car, he stood alongside to get a read on the area.

Quiet, no, soundless. Like a grave. Even the kid riding the bike a block away seemed able to speed around without adding a decibel to the noise level of Kyleighburn's silent streets.

Each vivid leaf of every tree stood out in still relief, motionless, poised in zen-like anticipation of the next event. Trees spread off in three directions across a small park whose border he'd parked along, then surged straight up in towering layers of the radiant verdure that earns spring green its name. The air hung heavy with mimosa and gardenia and honeysuckle with a hint of some other flower he couldn't place—oleander! There it was, growing in two giant manicured bushes flanking the stone steps to the library.

The building opened in twenty minutes. He plunked himself on the steps to wait, ready to scrutinize passersby for resemblance to the sketch weighing down his pocket.

Playing in his head was his contact's terse phone call outlining his assignment.

"We just want you to find this character. Bring him in. It's protective custody. Two-way protection, true, but if he's who or what we think he is, he'll need protection. And if we're the ones giving it to him, maybe he'll give a little back. KnowwhatImean?"

Morris could almost see the ash drop off the guy's inevitable cigarette as he jabbed home his point. Oliver had never been able to quit.

The guy, the character Oliver spoke of, wasn't dangerous. But he did seem to be turning up in a lot of places with accelerating frequency, particularly in North Carolina. Kyleighburn was only the latest. His features were unusual, and there was some kind of concern for his health. He was the sort of mild-mannered guy that people pulled away from, that somehow seemed strange, off, queer, and Oliver and his Under-Studied Science Regiment were convinced he was of use to them. They'd zeroed in on this last known location and recruited Morris to fetch. It wasn't his usual kind of case, but his bank account was leaner than usual, and Oliver's was the one government agency he trusted.

The sketch Morris carried was of Abel, the guy he'd been hired to find. No literal photo existed. No last name was known. This picture was done by a street artist who hung around downtown turning out drawings for the occasional coin. Abel had apparently been mowing the park, and she'd been struck by the paleness of his skin in this sunny climate. She'd sent an image of the drawing to a friend and Oliver's crew had picked up the likeness in transmission. Morris needed to find the artist and see what else she could tell him.

He heard the snick of a door unlocking and turned to see the library door open. A quick run up the steps and he was able to slip inside and follow a swirling cloud of fabric to the main desk. He arrived at the counter as the petite young woman pulled a stepstool up to the working side of the counter and climbed up, one dainty foot after another, and greeted Morris with a huge smile.

"Good mornin', sir. I'm Delilah Chanda." She paused. "I should be Delilah Chandra, but my parents dropped the 'r'. Thought it looked too Indian," she said, tossing her overlong dirty blond ponytail with its dark roots over one shoulder where it tangled with the flowy fabric of her dress. "What can I do to help you today? If you're looking for a particular book, I can help you find it. Well, of course, I can. After all, that's what librarians are for isn't it? Of course we also deliver programs and help with the computers and community resources, and even direct the way to the bathroom for mothers with screaming children who've had too much chocolate." She stopped to breathe, and then she grinned at him. "Now what would be your question?"

However loud she was, every word came out with a smile as clear and broad as a Carolina beach.

He leaned across the counter and pushed the sketch to her. "My name's Koadh. I'm an investigator. I'm looking for this man, and I wonder if you've seen him around? I've been told he came to Kyleighburn a bit ago."

She drew it closer and studied it, starting at the left top corner and scanning it inch by inch, her head moving slowly as she examined every penstroke and space it encompassed. Her body suddenly a study in stillness and quiet, her mind seemed to trip through possibilities, much like checking her own interior card catalogue. Finally she looked up.

"Nope. Don't recognize this guy."

Morris reached for the picture, but she laid her be-ringed hand over it, and a radiance poured over her pert face.

"I do recognize the strokes of the artist, and lucky, lucky, she's here today. She's in the back room arranging her display carrel, getting it ready for next week. She brings in new art all the time and the patrons love it. Some of them even buy it. I think it's awfully special and—," she was backing off the stepstool as she talked, proving to even the greatest nay-sayer that she could indeed walk and chew gum—or in this case, talk and climb down—at the same time. And if anything, her vocal volume increased as she headed toward a back room filled with tables and chairs and five carrels lining the outer walls.

"Tatianna! There's someone here who'd like to talk to you! Tat!" Her robes were swirling again, obscuring her figure and making Morris think of clouds of random smoke from colored fireworks, whirling away to some exotic destination of their own.

"Shh, Delilah! People are supposed to be reading!" a slender figure in khakis topped with a rough linen peasant blouse came forward, but the woman was laughing, as clearly there were no people back here. No patrons at all, so far as Morris could see. It may simply have been too early. And so it didn't really matter that the delightfully-named Delilah erred on the side of raucousness.

Suddenly Morris relaxed, and this assignment seemed accompanied by an engaging assortment of perks.

"Tatianna Claflin-Brouilliard, meet—meet—This is Koadh. He's looking for the man whose picture you drew mowing the lawn over at the park. You know, the one you told me about because you were curious that he had no tan? This—Koadh, here says he's looking for him, although he didn't say why. Are you going to tell us why, because I am sure that must be just so interesting, Mr.—"

"Koadh. Actually it's Morris." He smiled at Tatianna as she stepped forward and took the drawing from his hand. Her hair was a short cap of red streaked with purple, but it looked somehow just right, and she moved with an attractive lithesome ease. "Can you tell me something about this guy?"

Delilah moved closer, too, as if to get one more look, but the bell at the front desk rang. "Oh, poo!" She headed for the front, hustling more than floating this time, and Morris turned his attention back to Tatianna.

"Do you remember anything?"

The artist was shaking her head, causing the purple strands in her hair to shift like errant ribbons. She frowned at the picture, turning it back and forth as she spoke. "He was just mowing that day while I was out drawing." Her voice trailed off and she raised her head sharply. "Where did you get this?"

Morris felt his face go red. "I—that's just the picture they gave me to show around."

She lowered her head, but kept her eyes darting back at him, as if checking to see if he'd suddenly grown horns or something equally evil. "I'd finished a picture of my friend Micah—he's everyone's friend it seems, but don't get Delilah going on him. She has a huge crush, and when she gets started, well..." She grinned, sapphire eyes twinkling.

"Can't stop, right?"

"Exactly. But, anyway, I'd just finished his picture when this guy came into view and—,"

"By the way—excuse me—how did you know his name is Abel? Didn't he give you a last name?" Oops.

"All right. That does it. How do *you* know I knew his name was Abel? I didn't tell you that. And I want to know exactly where you got this—"

Tatianna waved the drawing at him. "Who are you exactly? What do you want with him?"

*There are some cases a PI just shouldn't take, no matter how good the money is,* Morris thought. "That's sort of confidential. You know, how things are today." He could feel the perspiration at his brow. That's where it always showed up first. Next it would start prickling his scant beard. "It's—just, well it's just…I'm here to make him a job offer. A very good job offer. That's why they sent me in person," he added, then turned a brilliant smile on Tatianna.

She ignored it, looking at the paper in her hand and saying pointedly "My drawing prints out well, doesn't it? I suppose I can tell you what I know. It isn't much. But," she threw him a dark glance, "Things are just getting back to normal around here. You're not going to cause him any trouble are you?"

"Oh, no, no," he hurried to say. "Back to normal? What kind of normal?"

Tatianna was turning away. She rustled through the things on the table for paper and pencil, and Morris finally noticed the clutter and mess strewn across it. Mats and glue and paper and cutters—scissors and Exactos and old-fashioned pocket-knives. Two folded frames waited to be assembled. And the wall of the tiny carrel was already partially hung with photographs and pencil drawings. One depicted a large bee on a sort of vine decorated with flowers in 1960's style. The colors were shades of puce, occasionally dotted with a brighter, flamboyant fuchsia. The effect was, he supposed, what they used to call psychedelic.

"Looks more like something Delilah would've done," he commented, trying to tease a laugh from Tatianna.

He was halfway rewarded. She smiled slightly as she handed him a scribbled piece of paper. "It's mine, but I drew it for her. She brings so much joy into Kyleighburn's life—even if it is a little noisy—I wanted her to have something as loud as she is. Don't tell her, though, she doesn't know it's for her."

Morris glanced at the paper. She'd written a phone number, along with the words 'Kyleigh B&B' on it, and a small rectangle with lines and dots through it. She reached up and pointed a finger at each item.

"There's a phone number you'll need. Kyleigh B&B is located out on Lighthouse Road, right where you turn away from town to head out to the river. And that's a map of the park where I saw him, not the one across the street. This is the big park. This circle is the statue, here's a grove of trees, and here's where I was, and Abel came out from here." She pulled her finger back from its dance around the paper.

"Does he live at the B&B?"

"No. But he does odd work for them, I think. Micah would know, and *he* does do odd jobs for them. You can find him or leave him a message there. He'll get back to you. He's pretty reliable. I think. The phone number," she blushed again, and Morris felt a lightening in his chest where he expected his heart was.

"The phone number is my uncle's house. Cell phone reception around here has been spotty lately. If you want to get back in touch with me, check here or call my uncle's. If I'm not there, they'll take a message."

"Thanks. I might need to get back with you again." Morris pocketed the paper. Nodding toward the drawing of the flowers he said, "Too bad we don't have real flowers like that. It would be spectacular."

Tatianna rolled her eyes towards the picture and back to Morris, her mouth opening to speak.

"Glad we don't have those bees, though. Thanks, Tatianna."

Before she could say anything, Morris was leaving the building. She shrugged and went back to framing and hanging her work.

Morris hustled down the library steps, pausing to inhale again the wonderful fragrance of oleander. Finally, there was life on the street. A couple of cars cruising by, as quietly as possible, it seemed to him. This town was made for electric cars, he thought. Their near-silent hum would fit right in.

A dog barked and another answered. Small-town life. Dogs run free; there were two on the other side of the street, trotting along as if they had a business appointment downtown. Behind him he heard the click of claws on concrete. He was turning around to see when he heard the abrupt snap of jaws shutting.

He jumped to make sure that snap hadn't connected with anything of his, but he felt no pain, only a little foolish as he spied a rather scruffy but dignified-looking brown dog a couple of steps above him. He snapped again, and again, pausing to regard Morris between snaps.

Then Morris saw what he was snapping at. Bees. Very large, vivid yellow-and-brown bees with dark visible veins in their over-sized wings and what Morris would swear were two-inch stingers. Morris was allergic to bees. A half-dozen of the beasts were hovering over the oleander. One crawled out of a blossom as Morris watched and launched himself toward the park, flying slowly like a troop-laden C-17. He passed another bee coming from the park, zeroing in on the beflowered bush.

Biggest damn honeybees I've ever seen, Morris thought fervently—and incorrectly. He shuddered and turned towards the dog.

"Thanks, buddy," he said, and headed toward his car. He tossed around the alternatives. He should check the park, he supposed. It was right here, and so was he. But—bees. He stared at the park, one lone large tree atop the grassy knoll in the middle of his field of vision. He swore he saw movement at its bark. Bees!

He started the engine. Damn giant bees! Where'd they come from? The thought of being stung by one of them was terror-striking. He better drive out and find this B&B. Better odds of getting results there. No need to randomly check the park when he had a real lead at hand.

Kyleigh B&B was a white clapboard building with a classic wraparound veranda; honeysuckle and hanging baskets and rocking chairs filled it with an old Southern sense of welcome. Morris peered at it from his car. Windows indicated a four-square floor plan, a window in each of two outer walls to each room. The kitchen was probably on the first floor at the back. He sat for minutes, watching, thinking, wondering what sort of approach he needed to take.

Outside, behind a bush, lurked a figure, watching back.

Morris was right about the kitchen. "Hello?" he tapped at the screen door. "Hello? Okay if I come in?"

"Sure, son. How can I help you? Can I get you something to drink?" A middle-aged woman in jeans and an orange sweatshirt with cut-off sleeves wiped her hands with a dishtowel. Food preparation was clearly underway. Chicken lay on a broiler ready for an oven. Fresh bread was stacked on the table, still in their loaf pans, and lettuce, celery, and tomatoes that looked to be garden-plucked formed a low pyramid to one side. A pitcher of sweet tea sat on one corner, flanked by glasses filled with ice. Already the woman moved to fill a glass, saying, "My name's Biannca. Here."

"Thanks." Morris savored the sweet icy liquid slipping down his throat.

"So, what else can I do to help you?" Biannca asked, switching tasks to salt and pepper the chicken and rub it with herbs. She was sliding it into a heated oven before Morris answered.

He coughed once, and stroked at his beard, scratching the patch of skin that still hadn't sprouted. Then he pulled the drawing from his pocket. "My name is Koadh. I'm looking for the man in this drawing. I understand maybe he does some work for you occasionally. Do you know how I could get in touch with him?"

Biannca peered at the photo, dusting off her hands. "Sure, that's Abel. He doesn't work here regular; just when I need an extra hand. We're not real busy right now, so I haven't seen him in a week or so."

"You have another handyman. Micah, I think?"

"Micah, sure. He's a good guy. Good worker, too. He's a pretty good friend to Abel. Maybe he can help you locate him. That's how we usually do it."

"How can I reach Micah?"

"He's due to come in this afternoon and do some trimming. If you want to wait around—"

"Actually, I wondered if you had a room available. I've come in from out of town to find this guy, and I need a place to stay."

"Sure. We have a couple of vacancies. Things have been slow over the last few months. A couple of the supervisors for the lighthouse work stay over here, but we haven't had any newcomers in a while. Come on, I'll sign you in."

She led him back through to the front of the building to a credenza that served as a front desk.

"Here, there's a room that overlooks the lighthouse. It was beautiful when it lit up. Although with the work going on, they're not lighting it right now."

Morris nodded. "That would be fine." He focused on the information on the guest card he was filling out. A P.I. had to be cautious what he put on paper. He wrote in his P.O. box for his business address, and his cell for his phone number. License plate: MRS KOD. All public knowledge. He hesitated over the 'miscellaneous' lines, as he called it, one of those sections of three lines for the visitor to add information they want the proprietor to have. But, given those humongous bees—'allergic to bees' he scribbled, 'but fond of honey.' Biannca would get a kick out of that, he decided.

He followed Biannca to his room, expressed his pleasure at its spaciousness and decor, and set about moving in for the indeterminate time it would take to complete his mission. He'd stashed his few shirts and jeans and one pair of slacks (always packed in case he had to attend something 'formal' and now bearing long-term wrinkles and creases that might never hang out) and put spare shoes under the bed and his blender and smoothie fixings on the dresser next to the decorative pitcher and washbowl and antique perfume atomizer. He fingered the edge of the pitcher. At least he hoped it was meant to be decorative.

Across the water of the toddling Tottie as he was privately calling the river, activity was underway at the lighthouse. He could hear the banging and clanging of heavy equipment, and the wrench of metal on metal. But nothing seemed to be actually moving. Weird. He shrugged and looked down, closer to the inn. No one was paying him to investigate the lighthouse, and his curiosity didn't work that way. He wasn't like some of these journalists who acted like they had a bee up their butts.

Below him was the driveway. A green pickup rolled up and parked off the pavement. A tall young man with shoulder-length dark hair climbed out of the driver's side and circled to the back to pull out a shovel. He shouldered it and headed around the back of the building. Micah? Alone, whoever he was. Morris would still have to talk to him. He left the window to grab his wallet.

A solitary slender figure jogged up to the truck and opened the passenger door. Morris headed downstairs as the pickup door shut with a thunk. The jogger peered into the back of the truck and pulled out a rake and a chain—a necklace of thick rustic links connected by a design made of two-to-three inch square metal nails. He paused to pull the necklace over his head, then trailed the first man's footsteps to the back, carrying the rake in his right hand, adjusting the chain against his shirt with his left. The designer nameplate always caught. He tugged at it, centering the name precisely on his chest. ABEL.

It was on his way downstairs that Morris got his brilliant idea. He was used to getting at least one a week, so this probably meant his quota was used up for this trip.

"Ms. Biannca! Hey! Ms. Biannca, could I speak to you for a minute?"

She hustled in from the kitchen, dishtowel in hand. "Sure. What is it?"

"Do you suppose it would be possible for me to invite a guest for dinner tomorrow night? I'll pay for her meal, of course."

She grinned at him. "Ah, a young woman already. Who's your anticipated guest?"

Coloring briefly, he said "I thought I'd ask Tatianna?" He waited for her nod. "I met her this morning. She said she's the mayor's niece?"

"Mhm. She is. Staying with him for a bit while she gets her life together, she says. She's been around here pretty frequently of late. Don't worry about the food. I'm glad to have her over."

"I was counting on that. Thanks." He set out to his car and pulled out his phone and Tatianna's note. He dialed the number, not sure what exactly he was going to say—or why, for that matter. It was, he figured, one of those P.I things to do. And, like happens when the lucky P.I. gets all the girls, Tatianna answered the phone.

"Hello?" Her phone voice was light, tentative. Well, she wouldn't recognize the number.

"Tatianna? It's me, Morris. The detective. We met at the library? Remember?... Um, no, not a mustache.... Never mind. I found the Kyleigh B&B. Biannca's a good hostess. She's said—uh, yes it is a beautiful river. Biannca said—Oh, the lighthouse, too? Yes, I'd love to see them. But— yes, but—about—Tatianna, Biannca said I should invite you to dinner for tomorrow." Phew! Okay, small white lie about who said what, but at least he'd finally asked.

She answered right away. "I'd love to. And I'll bring my sketches. Is my uncle invited, too? He's been under such pressure lately, and what with that incident with our little cousin a while back, and his own daughter taking off, and the sight-seers and expeditions, well, Kyleighburn's been a lot of work the last few years. He could use a nice meal. —What?... Oh, I'm sorry, his secretary says he has a meeting. So, it will just be me.... Maybe that's enough?"

He could picture her ducking her chin to speak directly into the phone, her wild red-and-purple hair combed all business-like but twirly at the ends, the nape of her neck rising above a collarless shirt.... Wait a minute. This was supposed to be a way to get chummy with everybody, not get a date. And Tatianna, good-looking though she might be, was not his target. His goal was to get Abel to leave town with him.

His tone grew brusque. "Tatianna, I'm sure your presence will be enough to entertain—er, delight everybody. I'm going to see if I can round up Micah, and maybe Abel, too. It would be great if he came so I could tell him about that job. If you see him around town, would you pass that along? I really am on a deadline with this."

"Well, sure. If that's what you want." Tatianna's voice was flat. Apparently he'd burned that bridge before he crossed it. On the other hand, she said she was coming. Morris never had done too well at juggling business and a social life. Which would explain why he had little of either.

Things looked brighter the next day. He checked the park where Tatianna had drawn her picture of Abel. This park was smaller than the one at the other side of the town, with fewer trees, but a lot more oleander bushes. The flowers on these bushes were even larger than the ones at the library. Their colors ranged from violet to fuchsia with hot pink in the middle. He looked around for bees, but the coast was clear. He meandered along the dog path, watching where he stepped, especially when he realized he was following what must be the only dog walker in the whole town, a young kid with at least ten small dogs in tow and one hugely large Great Dane who seemed to relish the cluster of mops and hotdogs scurrying at his feet. He peered under bushes, finding leftover blankets but no bits of paper or other rubbish, just blankets under a few bushes. Maybe there was a small homeless problem, and some church or other stocked blankets under bushes where people could find them and use them. Or, maybe they were abandoned from picnics gone bad.

Unfortunately this wasn't helping him find Abel. He tried Tatianna's number, but all he got was a loud-voiced man who kept shouting, "No, no one is here. No, Mayor! No dogs!" He checked in at the library to see the amazing amorphous Delilah who couldn't help him with finding Abel but who recommended he get some sparkling cider for the dinner because that was Tatianna's favorite, and he should think about shaving that spiky beard. She hoped the two of them would get together because they made such a cute couple, and then maybe they could double date, Morris, Tatianna, Delilah and Micah. Or maybe Abel, if Micah really wasn't available. Morris lost track of the conversation after that stopper.

Unable to make any other progress, he headed back to the bed and breakfast around three. Biannca had been successful in reaching Micah, and he was sitting alone on the veranda when Morris drove up.

For a second, Morris thought he'd found Abel. Micah was slender practically to the point of emaciation. Only his biceps and forearms hinted at his strength. And Abel was supposed to be pale of skin. Could they be related? Was that why Micah seemed to have befriended the man? Then he remembered the comments Biannca had made about Micah the previous evening.

"Micah's a funny bird. Hard worker. Always ready to help. You don't always see that in someone so young. But that's another thing." She bent down to put away a pot in a lower cupboard. Morris was talking with her under cover of helping out with the dishes. "I call him young, but I'm not really sure how old he is. He keeps to himself, but that means everyone in town talks about him all the more. And to hear tell, Micah could be anything from 17 to 30."

"How does that work?" Morris asked, drying off a large salad bowl and passing it to Biannca.

"Well, take Mayor Esposito. He is constantly sayin' how Micah worked for him as a gardener one summer, seven years ago. He insists Micah's the boy who climbed the tree to pick the wild muscadines from the vines that had climbed the trunk of a long leaf pine."

"Is he that boy?" Morris asked.

Biannca shrugged. "He hasn't said. Delilah would have us believe he's her long lost crush from college, a guy who hung out at the main campus library where she was interning. Age-wise that makes more sense, but so far as I can see, Micah isn't paying any special attention to Delilah. And then Kevin Hamm is convinced they were lab partners back in high school and acted together in the school musical. Kevin Hamm is 34 if he's a day, and I don't think Micah is anywhere near that old. Besides, he only turned up in town a few years back. I met him just before Kyleighburn went through its changes." She sighed, wiping out the sink and taking the towel from Morris to hang up. "Like I said, he's a good worker. But he's pretty tight-lipped. I don't think anyone really knows him well. Good luck getting anything from him."

Morris raised an eyebrow, and Biannca shook her head at him. "I don't mean he won't be willing to help, but I always feel he's trying his level best not to share anything. He's all right, but I don't know how much he'll tell you."

"What does he have to say about all these people who think they remember him?"

"That's just it. Nothing. Nice guy, but nothing to say."

Morris shrugged off the conversation from the day before and exited his car, shoving his hands in his pockets as he approached the veranda. "Hello there."

Micah rocked his chair a couple of times and stretched his lips in a smile. He used one hand to draw his long hair over one shoulder. And kept rocking.

"I take it you must be Micah," Morris said, holding out his hand.

Micah took it and stood, taller than Morris by four inches. A grin finally broke through his reserve. "Sorry," he added. "Didn't mean to seem like I was ignoring you. I was calculating how many mulch bags I'd need tomorrow. I hate doing math in my head. And it shows. Sit down with me."

Morris took up the rocker next to him. "Mulch, huh? You working on a garden back there?"

"Sort of. Biannca has taken it into her head that she wants to keep bees. The ones around here are particularly friendly. They don't mind giving up their honey. And it's as smooth as it is sweet. Doesn't need much refining. And we need to have flowering shrubs nearby to help keep them producing nearby."

"I saw a couple downtown going back and forth between a park and the bushes at the library."

"Oleander. Biannca's already got enough of those. But they don't really help the bees produce honey, so she needs some other kinds ranged around where the hives will be. Wildflowers, clover, Buddleia—er, that's butterfly bush, dogwood. They were going to add azaleas, too, but I put them off that. Poisonous."

"Poisonous! Azaleas?"

"You can die from honey made from too much azalea nectar. Beekeepers generally keep azalea far from their hives and make sure their bees are kept in good supply of something they like better."

They rocked for a minute while Morris pondered this. "How do you know so much about all this, Micah?"

"I've picked up a little here and there." He ducked his head and gave a sly little smile. "Actually, I spent a semester or two up at NC State. They have a good program, and they let me work there as well."

"And when was that?"

Micah laughed a little. "Back a ways. I get that a lot around here."

"How long have you been here?" Morris asked.

Micah sighed. "Look, detective, or whatever you are, I moved here a few years back. About a month or so before the lighthouse went down."

"I heard somebody in town is sure you went to college with him." Morris could kick himself for not having more details. He couldn't ask questions properly without original information. "Did you run into anyone you knew from Kyleighburn up at State?"

Micah shook his head. "I must have one of those faces or something, detective. People are always claiming they know me from somewhere."

A flash of light came from the island. Capgen's Isle, it was called, home to the ruins of the defunct lighthouse. It had been replaced years ago by channel marking buoys, and when it quit working, it was abandoned and left to fall into ruin. Or at least until a few years ago, after whatever happened to it.

Morris could see the wharf where the workers docked when they went out to the island. Two figures were walking along the dock right now, looked like supervisor-types, maybe headed their way. Behind them was another flash, maybe from work they were doing behind the building they were leaving. Welding, maybe?

"So, all your work here is getting ready for bees for Biannca's honey?" Morris asked Micah, his eyes still focused on the work site.

"Pretty much. I'm nearly done with re-locating the hives, and we've—I've got most of the flowering shrubs in, and seeded the surrounding field with the wildflowers. Biannca's still after me to put in additional oleanders, but I don't see the point, really. Why more oleanders just for flavoring honey?" He chuckled at the vagaries of clients.

He didn't sense Biannca coming up behind his chair.

"Now you know I stand by my honey, Micah. And that oleander is what makes it special. You know those bees are crawling all over those bushes now."

"That isn't how it used to be, Biannca." Micah protested.

"I know, I know, but it's how it is now. And everybody says they love my purple oleander honey, and I'm not about to stop making it. Well, canning it, preserving it—whatever it's called. And you know I appreciate all the hard work you've done. Dinner will be at the usual hour. The lighthouse crew should be done soon, and Tatianna just called and said she was headed out here. Just wanted to let you know."

Morris glanced at Micah. "I don't suppose you've seen Abel around anywhere. Biannca told you I was looking for him, didn't she?"

"Actually I heard it from Delilah. Mind if I ask why?"

"I've been hired to convince him to come work for the government in some medical research."

"You're a head hunter? I thought you were a detective." Micah's demeanor shifted slightly, and his eyebrows raised.

Morris squirmed. This story sounded thinner every time he told it. But it was true! It just wasn't *all* the truth. "I make a living as a P.I., Micah. And that's a pretty uneven living. Sometimes I take on other jobs to supplement. Some of them are pretty weird gigs. This is one of them."

Micah chuckled. "Any gig that involves the government is pretty weird."

"You got that right."

"Who's got what right?" The voice came around the corner of the house, followed by the appearance of two dark-haired workmen wearing hard hats, one guy skinny and lanky, the other built with the svelte proportions of a Hollywood actor. The lighthouse supervisors.

"Hey, Micah."

"Hey, Dean. Jerry. How's work at the lighthouse?"

"Goin' all right. Gotta get us some other help out here," said Dean, coming up the steps to the veranda. He reached out and shook the men's hands as he elaborated. "Art's okay, but he needs direction at every turn. And Simon, he never says a word. Silent. I never know what he's thinking. That's not good in a crew, you know."

Jerry piped up, his voice kind of strained and gangly. "Hey, Dean! What about Johnny and Tim? They're *really* strange. Sometimes, sometimes I think they're really killers in disguise, ya know? Or maybe they're zombies."

Morris's eyes widened. "What kind of work are you all doing over there, anyway?"

"Just your basic renovation and repair," began Dean.

"Nah, don't let Dean fool you. It's way more important than that." Jerry nodded authoritatively and puffed out his chest.

But then a little red car pulled up, and Tatianna climbed out... with Delilah.

"I hope you don't mind," Tatianna said, gesturing toward Delilah.

All the men waved her statement aside while Biannca's shoulders shook with silent laughter. "I'll have the supper on the table shortly. You all can bring drinks out here if you like."

Delilah hustled herself up on to the veranda and called out, "Just let us know if you need any help Ms. Biannca. I love to help out, you know. Why one summer I helped Mama serve four weddings, and you know how much work that can be, don't you? Hi, Jerry, isn't it?" She slid her eyes sideways towards Micah in a move that told Morris she was looking to see the effect she had on him. She shuffled a little closer, too.

Micah, however, was involved in asking Dean something about the lighthouse. Morris heard something about flashing lights before Tatianna approached him quietly.

"Really. I hope that was okay. She kind of cornered me about where I was going tonight."

"Seriously, it's okay. The more the merrier! And Biannca seems okay with it. Maybe Delilah will get the others talking." He smiled at her immediate giggle.

"If only in self-defense," she said. "But, Delilah is a good person. She has her faults, but she's also got a good heart."

"I think that's pretty obvious to anyone who meets her. Just as it's obvious you are a talented artist. Did you bring those sketches?" Morris had a sudden desire to see what she'd drawn.

Over at her car, Tatianna pulled a brown cardboard portfolio from the back seat. It was only about twenty inches long and a little frayed at the edges, but she unwound its cord with business-like precision and pulled out a sheaf of drawings. Some were charcoal, some pencil. One was a more detailed and elaborate watercolor that she said she'd done as a composite from some of the drawings. The watercolor carried a border of delicately executed flowers reminiscent of the ones Morris had commented on at the library yesterday. She pulled one from the back of the pile forward.

"Here, this is a few days before the collapse. Well, maybe a few weeks, I'm a little hazy on the dates. But, you can see here, even though it wasn't functional, the light tower was intact. The walls went all the way up, and they were pretty sturdy. I watched the high school football team climb up and down them like rock walls for cross-training. They held up fine and no one ever got hurt. You can see how it is now."

Morris squinted into the sun to see, but most of his view was blocked by where Micah stood. Still, he could detect differences.

"Tell me what the most noticeable changes were," he said, pulling out a second drawing for reference. This one appeared to be shortly after things had fallen, based on rockfall and the whitecaps she'd included on the water. He frowned as she explained and pointed things out to him.

"These windows are broken, and the ironwork came down. The tiled courtyard must have exploded, because see here? Those are the tiles that were scattered everywhere."

Morris pulled back. "Wait, what? Exploded? What the hell happened out there?"

Tatianna took the drawings back, shrugging as she did so. She was shuffling them together when Jerry walked up behind them.

"Wuh—oh. Oh Dean! Dean, I think we have a pro-b-lem!" He circled his arm over his head, pointing down with one big finger at Tatianna's head.

"A problem?" Dean asked, sauntering over and lighting a cigarette. "What sort of a problem could the lovely Tatianna be causing?" His charm didn't erase the concern Tatianna saw darkening his eyes. She shook her head tightly, just once. "Let me see what you all are lookin' at," he said, pulling a drawing from her hands. "Oh! This is from before the collapse. Um-hmm. Um-hmmm." He shook his head in appreciation, his dark curls bouncing as he did so. "I said from the very day that I met you that you were as talented as you are beautiful." Without another word to her or Morris, he clapped a hand on Jerry's back. "Come on, let's go clean up to eat."

Delilah hustled in behind them and fetched some sweet tea and lemonade for everyone, returning to the veranda with glasses and pitchers. "Biannca says fifteen minutes." She handed glasses round. "Has anybody tried Biannca's latest batch of honey? I don't think it's as purple-y as the others."

"Purple-y?" Morris asked, smiling and sipping his tea.

"Yeah. Like the oleander. All her honey tastes purple-y now. That reminds me, I wanted to ask her what she does to the honey to take out the poison."

Morris choked and spat out a stream of tea. "What? What poison?"

Micah ducked his head and turned away.

"The oleander poison. Everyone knows oleander is toxic." Delilah looked around at the others. "Don't they?"

"Toxic? Biannca's been making her honey for at least a year now. No one's got sick, have they?" Tatianna worried.

"No, but I was helping Billy Gallagher with his project in the spring, and we were looking up flowering shrubs—"

"Whoa up, Delilah. I think you're scaring Morris here."

"It's kind of a question," said Morris drily. "Micah told me about azaleas being poisonous, but he spoke like oleander is okay. So, is it toxic?"

"Everything I saw says it is," Delilah insisted.

"Okay, yes, Oleander is toxic." Micah raised his hands up in defeat. "*But* Tatianna is right. In all the time Biannca has been making her honey, no one's got sick. And I know for a fact that Biannca got the honey tested. *And* besides, there is no oleander nectar. So the bees aren't adding that to the honey."

"But—but, then why are they flying to the bushes and crawling around the flowers? Why is the honey purple, like most of the oleander flowers around here? And how are they pollinating the bushes?" Delilah drew breath to continue, but Micah held her off.

"The flowers produce pollen, not nectar. There is no oleander nectar to go into the honey. As to why the bees are hanging around the flowers, it probably has to do with the size the flowers have gotten to and the fact that they're the same bright colors as the flowers in the—in Tatianna's pictures. It's got to be the color that attracts them."

Delilah furrowed her brow and looked at Micah. "Really?" was all she could say.

"Really," said Micah, clapping a hand on Morris' shoulder. "And besides, who can argue with success? Like Tatianna says, no one's gotten sick from Biannca's honey. It's the bees Morris has to watch out for, right Morris?"

"All too right," Morris agreed.

"Dinner!" came the call from the kitchen.

They paraded in, arranging themselves around the table, Morris in front of the window that opened on the view of Capgen Isle, Jerry, and Dean across from him and the others scattered between. Biannca set off passing the food, and conversation began anew, although the nasty oleander seemed to have vanished from the list of topics.

As they tucked in, Delilah turned to Jerry. "Dean and Jerry! That's so funny! It must be fun to be named after famous people! Do a lot of people comment on it?"

"Famous people? Oh, you mean where we got our names. My mother named me after the milkman. He's very famous in our neighborhood. All the ladies liked him a whole lot! Would you pass me the ketchup?"

Delilah blinked several times then turned to Dean.

"What about you? You know who I mean, don't you?"

Dean took his time answering, glancing at Jerry a couple of times before he did. "Well, it is kind of fun. 'Specially after I found Jerry here. He caught on right away. He does love his sausages. Said it was too bad he wasn't named Jimmy 'cause then we'd be Jimmy Dean and people would get it sooner."

Delilah blinked again and muttered down into her food. "Sometimes it doesn't pay to be a movie buff."

Jerry was gesturing with his knife and fork. "Dean's right. I love my sausage. But, you know what? I love Dean more. I do, yes I do. He keeps me out of trouble all the time, a-l-l the time. The other day, he kept me from falling down this big hole we're trying to fill. I nearly stepped right into it, and he yelled and he pulled me right back!"

"Really!"

"Jerry, not now, we don't want to bore everyone with business—"

Morris spoke up, "Hey, I'd love to hear about your work on the island. I understand you're renovating?" He gestured over his shoulder toward the window behind him. Through it was a clear view of the island, the lighthouse, some cement trucks and the wharf. Stacks of broken tile were scattered around the remaining base of the lighthouse.

Dean poked Jerry as two figures came out from the lighthouse courtyard carrying a large wooden packing crate.

"Wha— Oh! Oh, yeah, well, Mr.—Mr.—"

"Koadh. Morris Koadh. What were you saying?"

Dean broke in smoothly. "He was saying that our work is actually pretty boring, Morris. We watch over crews that are pulling tile, laying bricks. That hole he referred to is one that opened up when the foundation collapsed and opened a hole in the courtyard over the cellar. There's a lot of debris in there that makes working it dangerous."

Jerry nodded vigorously. "Yeah. That's it. We're trying to rebuild it, but we're not making much headway. There's a lot of concrete and tile that's rock hard. It's beautiful. Oh, boy, is it beautiful. It's got this sort of starry design and there's a pattern. Tell him about the pattern, Dean."

The men set the packing crate down and pried it open, lifting out a large round disk-like object a couple of feet in diameter and about a foot thick.

"You tell him, Jerry. I'm going to have some more of Biannca's roast. You did a wonderful job here, Biannca."

"Mr. Koadh, you should see that tile. And we're being real careful with it, aren't we, Dean? Because we don't know what might happen if we don't handle it just right. Isn't that right?"

"Oh? Why?" Morris glanced up from his plate.

Dean spoke up. "We're still trying to figure out why everything happened at once, or if one thing caused another. Of course, any kind of work around a damage site can be hazardous."

"What were those light flashes I saw earlier, when you were leaving the island?"

Dean and Jerry looked at him blankly, then lifted their shoulders in a synchronized shrug.

"Must have been a reflection off the water," added Micah. He shrugged, too. Then Tatianna.

Delilah watched Morris, drawing breath as if she were about to say something, but he'd half-turned toward the window to get another look.

"Here, Mr. Koadh. Have some turnip greens." Biannca held a serving platter to his right, and he turned back to the table to help himself. Biannca caught Dean's eye as she set the dish down.

Now the two men on the island were joined by a third, and the three of them began to scale the lighthouse wall. A cement mixer sitting to one side started to turn. As close as the island was close, no sound made its way to the mainland. The three men disappeared over the broken top of the wall. Seconds later a thick beam of light, faint in the slow twilight of summer, rose from behind the wall to point straight into the sky.

Micah glanced at the window once more and hurried to speak.

"Morris, can you tell us something about this job you're seeing Abel about? I mean, if I know more about it, I can explain it to him better."

*Why did people always ask him the wrong questions,* Morris wondered. "I can tell you a little about it," he hedged, thinking furiously.

Delilah scooped up some salad from her plate. "Is that why you were hunting him down at the library? I thought maybe he'd done something bad. There's been a lot of strange things happening all over, hasn't there?"

"No!" shouted Morris, Micah, Biannca, and Tatianna all at once.

Dean and Jerry stared out the window, Jerry poking Dean in the arm.

"Dean. Oh, Dean! I think we have a problem," he whispered loudly.

"Yeah. Yeah. I think we do. 'S'cuse us, folks." He threw off his napkin and headed for the door, Jerry lunging behind him.

Micah glanced over his shoulder and then called Morris's attention to the table of food. "Unless, of course, Delilah is referring to the fantastic growing season we've had here in Kyleighburn."

Morris looked at the table blankly. Food? Yeah, food. That would work.

"I don't know how much you folks know about Abel, and the—the—my client couldn't tell me much about him, but apparently he is some kind of food expert or something? Something to do with ways to feed large numbers of people nutritiously and sustainably, I think. I guess he's got some kind of great reputation or something."

Micah replied slowly, as if thinking about what Morris had said. "Abel's knowledgeable about food, I'll give you that. That's why he's such a help with the gardening here. But he's a quiet dude. How did your client hear about him?"

Morris shrugged and surreptitiously wiped his brow. "I'm just the delivery man. I'm supposed to make the offer and bring Abel in—I mean, provide transportation if he accepts."

"What if he's not interested?" Tatianna asked.

Whose side was she on? Morris wondered. Then he realized. Oliver had said to bring Abel in. He didn't say what Morris was to do if the guy didn't want to come.

"Well, I expect we'll just have to see, is all."

"I'll talk to Abel. If he's agreeable, we'll be by in the morning," offered Micah.

"Thanks. Thanks." Morris nodded and returned his attention to his food. "Ms. Biannca, if I haven't said it already, this food is marvelous. You are a great cook."

Micah and Biannca exchanged another look.

"Are they doing all right, do you think?" asked Delilah, nodding her head toward the window. "They sure took off out of here fast. I haven't seen Dean move that fast since the field day race last year. I love field days don't you? I don't participate in the games, but I love cheering from the sides."

Tatianna chimed in. "I remember that race. I came in third. It was a lot more difficult than it sounds," she explained to Morris. "They added some obstacles in the middle and had us leaping and climbing and dropping off walls. Dean nearly beat me, but I got past him." She nodded her head sharply and popped a bite of food in her mouth.

"How did you avoid the bees during your race? They'd have made me run faster!" Morris laughed.

Tatianna frowned. "The bees never give us much trouble at all."

"But they're so big!"

"Not really," Tatianna argued. "If you measure them, you find that they're really only about thirty percent larger than the largest honey bees. Their stingers are disproportionately long," she added mischievously, squinching her eyes at her.

"You're a braver soul than I, woman."

Suddenly there was a loud clap and rumble, as if thunder were passing through. Morris jumped and ducked his head in response. "What the hell was that!" He held up his knife and fork as if to fend off an unseen enemy.

They all sat, eyes down, hands still. No one spoke except Biannca, who said serenely off-topic, "I've got a surprise for you, Mr. Koadh. I held back some of my oleander honey. There will be some in a jar on the counter tomorrow for your smoothie. Or perhaps you'd like to take some when you go up for the night? Micah, would you bring in that jar next to the cookie box in the kitchen?"

Micah rose to fetch the honey as the others resumed eating.

"Wait. Didn't any of you hear that noise? Was that thunder?"

"I didn't hear anything," Delilah said, setting down her fork after a last bite of potatoes.

"Unh-unh, me either," said Tatianna.

"Maybe you're just over-tired, Mr. Koadh. A lot of people hear things funny when they have worked too hard. Had a lot of caffeine today?" asked Biannca.

"You all really didn't hear that?" Morris asked, thinking how there were those three espressos he'd had in the car while he was driving around town all morning. "Maybe I should head up to bed early. Say, Micah, what do you think? Will I see you and Abel tomorrow?... Thanks," he added, accepting a small octagonal jar that looked like a large jewel, filled as it was with a thick amethyst-colored liquid.

"We'll have to see. Abel may not be interested in leaving Kyleighburn. He's never lived anywhere else."

"Oh, really? I had the impression from my client that he'd lived all over. Certainly he gave me several references of places to look for him. Kyleighburn was simply the latest on the list."

"He's traveled well enough. But he's never shown a desire to live anywhere but here. But, hey, who knows, maybe you're making him an offer he can't refuse!" Micah clapped him on the back.

Morris stumbled forward, nearly dropping the honey jar. He hadn't wanted to see it that way, but Micah was right. Abel couldn't refuse.

The thought was still with him when he set the honey jar down on the nightstand in his room. It was troubling to him, in a way, although he still felt he could trust Oliver more than any other Fed he knew. Oliver would make sure Abel—whoever he was—was looked after. And the incentives Morris had been authorized to offer should be enough to tempt any scientist into accepting. Morris wasn't in any way supposed to act coercive. It was a peaceful assignment, relying only on detecting, not action.

Morris sighed. The thought, which should have relaxed and calmed him was having no effect on him whatsoever. In fact, it disturbed him to think about how grateful he was that this assignment was essentially a safe bet, a moneymaker with no potential for physical harm.

He plunked himself down on the springy bed and pulled off his socks and shoes. One shoe dangled a moment before hitting the floor. Out the window he could see the bulky shape of the lighthouse, now shrouded in darkness. Running lights were visible moving across the river on a diagonal line from the island's dock to the one at the B&B. Dean and Jerry headed back? Why *had* they gone out there? And what took them so long to return? It might be unrelated to his case, but Morris' curiosity was being piqued, and for once he allowed it. But he was tired, so he'd think about it and maybe ask more questions in the morning.

He completed his evening routine and set his phone alarm, setting his phone alongside the jar of honey so he wouldn't forget it in the morning. Anticipation of seeing what the 'purple-y flavor' they referred to was all about made him smile. He reached over and took the jar and unscrewed the lid.

He held it to his nose, sniffed. Sweet. Floral. Visions came to him of the flowers Tatianna drew. With one finger he drew out a dab of the radiant syrup, licking it off his finger delicately, like a cat. The taste was potent, and now, added to the visions of Tatianna's flowers came memories of violets, and the fragrance of lavender and lilac. The sensation was overpowering. Bursts of purple flower-shaped fireworks exploded in his head. His eyes slid closed, and he fell backwards on the bed in a complete collapse into slumber.

"Let's face it," said the diner across from him. "Morris, you're a wimp." He forked some food off the plate and caught it in his mouth. "A wimp you always were and a wimp you will always be."

*I should feel insulted.* "I like being a wimp," he said instead.

"Because it's easy-peasy!" sing-songed the diner. Peas spewed out of his mouth and spelled out the word EASY-PEASY on his plate in vivid green dots.

"Not always so easy," contradicted Morris, feeling the lie burn on his tongue. "You should see some of the jams I get into...."

"Jams! Jams! I see no jams!" screamed the diner as his eyes flew off his face. He lifted a biscuit smeared with peanut butter and jelly and stuffed it into his mouth. Orange juice poured over his head in a giant waterfall and all dissolved into a field of giant fuchsia flowers.

Morris woke in a sweat. His sleep-shirt was soaked and he hastened to check his shorts as well, but they were fine. He'd only been asleep a half-hour, one of those pre-sleeps he had sometimes when his mind was weighted down.

He didn't really want to delve into this battle now. What the diner in his dream said was all too true. Had been true a long time. What was changing, however, seemed to be how Morris felt about it.

He rose and went to the bathroom for a towel and a drink of water. A look in the mirror showed him tousled hair and a bit of a flush on his face. Maybe his eyes looked glassy. He tilted his head back and forth. Maybe a little bloodshot, too. He raised a bottle of water to his lips and put it down in immediate response to the recoil his stomach made. He shuffled back to his bed.

Okay, he didn't feel too well. Anxiety, probably. That would account for the damn dream, too. He wished this were the first time he'd had it.

He sighed, turning to find a comfortable fetal position he could rest in.

So what if the dream was right?

*Yeah, I'm a wimp. Heck, I'm comfortable being a wimp. I can sleep at night because I'm alive to sleep. Although, there are perks to not being a wimp I could do with.*

Because, he had to admit, being a wimp and taking only safe jobs like this one seemed to be, just wasn't glamorous. *Where are the blondes, the redheads, the dolls, the babes who can't get enough of my company?*

He sank into nebulous distractions of what this might—what this ought to look like.

And re-awakened twenty minutes later feeling hot and thoroughly unsatisfied. He groaned and rolled over to his back, staring at the ceiling.

Now the argument itself was stuck in his head.

*I'm fit, basically. I could learn all that stuff that would let me take on harder jobs. I could learn those martial arts you read about. Some of them were created for guys like me. Wiry, not brawny. Yeah, learn all those pressure points and balance stuff. And I'm not a bad shot. Pretty good in fact. It's not like I lack skills. I don't lack skills.... I'm pretty good.... I just don't....*

A low-grade fever pushed him back into sleep. Somewhere he could feel wheels turning and pinpricks of needles and light....

The orange waterfall was back. Morris stood at the top of it, feet barely touching the tumultuous liquid. He knew, he *knew* that if his feet sank in, the motion and force would drag him down and pull him over the edge, into the maelstrom that awaited at the bottom.

The bottom. He couldn't see the bottom from where he hovered. He stretched his neck, his Adam's apple pressing against his skin, to peer down, sure he could find the bottom if only—

His foot dipped into the juice and was sucked in up to his knee. His arms flailed, windmilling as he fought back. He couldn't go down there! He'd never stand a chance! He'd die! He'd die!

This time he awoke with his arms and legs wound up in the sheets. The sweating was gone, but his stomach still spiraled, catching up to the waking world. He groaned.

He didn't lack skills. What he lacked was physical courage. He had moral courage, he was pretty sure of that. Decisions about right and wrong had never been difficult for him, nor had he shirked from acting on them. Well, to be truthful, he'd never really worked at that part of things much. But at some concrete inner level, he was pretty sure he could do it. It was partly a matter of resolve—to pay attention to life around him and do something about it. And if he could beef up his moral courage and his skills, maybe that would give him the physical courage he....

This time he slept. The fever subsided, his stomach calmed, and the pain in his head that he hadn't even noticed was repeatedly awakening him, floated away.

The next morning looked fresh to his eyes, and he hummed, looking forward to the smoothie he'd make with the honey and some banana and other fruit. He hoped his blender wouldn't wake any of the other residents.

His phone sounded. The number was not one he recognized. Tatianna? He thought with a sliver of hope. Not that anything he'd contributed last night would have impressed her into calling.

"Hullo?"

"Morris? Micah. I'm here with Abel. We'd like to come by and discuss this offer you're talking about making to him. He—uh, he might be interested."

"Fine, that would be great. Listen, if you don't mind my breakfasting while we talk, come on out now, why don't you. I'm eager to meet Abel."

"We can do that. In fact, we won't be more than fifteen minutes. See you then."

Suddenly Morris was in business. He glanced at the smoothie fixings. He'd get that ready in a minute. More important now was to find the brochure Oliver had created legitimizing this offer he was making Abel. Everything the brochure said was guaranteed and true. He'd receive a handsome salary, a home, and a good place to work. The only thing was, this offer and this job didn't officially exist anywhere for anyone else. It was all for Abel, to bring him under Federal protection. The two-way protection Oliver had referenced.

Morris felt his stomach clench and his resolve flinch. Ignoring it momentarily, he arranged the papers and blended his smoothie. He poured it into the matching shake cup and went downstairs, folder in one hand, smoothie in the other.

"What is it you think, Micah? Is this what I should do?" The slender man called Abel had a light baritone voice; those few who'd heard him speak had commented on its pleasant tone.

Micah put the pickup round the turn a bit faster than usual. There was a slight lift to the right side as centrifugal force took its effect. He shook his dark head at Abel.

"That's not one I can answer for you. You'll have to follow your own guidance on this one. To be honest, I don't exactly trust anyone connected to the Federal Government myself. However, that doesn't mean working for them couldn't be useful to you and yours."

Abel appeared to ponder this seriously, in his heart as it were. "I'll have to think about this deeply after I hear the actual offer."

"Another meditation topic, huh?" Micah's words had the cheerfulness of familiarity.

Abel chuffed with a tiny smile. "I grant you could call it that."

The three men stood on the porch: Morris finishing off his shake, a caterpillar-shaped strip of foam caught on his upper lip; Micah shuffling from foot to foot, surreptitiously observing how each man reacted to the other; Abel's face open, curious, and placid.

"Aah." Morris wiped a forearm across his mouth to rid it of the foam. "Why don't we sit down inside, gentleman? I'd like to go over things with Abel here and explain just how good this offer is. It is," he waved his arm broadly in the air, gesturing the others ahead of him, "a stupendous offer." He tripped going over the threshold. "Mmm, 's'cuse me."

"You okay, there, Morris?" Micah steadied him by the arm.

"Yeah, yeah." Morris felt sweat springing up on his eyeballs. His hair felt feverish. He blinked. Maybe he wasn't over last night.... "Please, uh, Abel, Micah, let's sit down here at the table. Abel, Abel—uh, excuse me," and he turned his head to belch.

Abel eyed Micah uncertainly, but he sat. He reached over to Morris for the folder, but he took him by the wrist instead. "Mr. Morris Koadh, please. I will look at the folder while you get a drink of water? Then we can talk. Micah, get him some water, please. And see if Biannca has any fruit juice, would you please?"

Abel slipped the folder out from under Morris's hand and began to read, ignoring Micah's questioning look.

Morris's head bobbled in agreement and he slumped into the chair. He could feel himself zoning out. He tried hard to lock his mind onto a word, a math problem, anything to try and focus. At last a jingle wormed its way into his inner ear.

Hefty, hefty, hefty!
Wimpy, wimpy, WIMPy!
Hefty, hefty, hefty!
Wimpy, wimpy, WIMPy!

And in his mind he saw garbage bags dancing through the streets with big burly men in aprons. Fighting to keep from sleeping, he stirred and groaned. "Oh, God, not again." His stomach lurched.

Abel closed the folder and felt of Morris's temple. "He's running a fever, Micah. A bad one. I think he's about to go delirious."

Morris raised a hand, one finger pointed up. "Courage. Must have courage."

Abel looked up at Micah. "Does he mean me?"

"I don't think so. What did you think of the offer?"

Abel frowned. "Help me move him to the sofa." Micah moved instantly at his friend's tone. Together they half-walked, half-carried the detective to the parlor and eased him onto the lumpy couch. Abel began examining Morris, touching his temple again and grimacing. "Hotter." He lifted one eyelid. "Rapid-onset jaundice." His hands moved on to probe and prod the detective's abdomen. There was the vibration of a rumbling belly, and Morris moaned at the touch.

Spears in the belly. They were poking him with spears in the belly. They were on fire, too. White-hot-tipped spears, poking him all over.

"Stop! Stop!" The stabbings moved from one place to another instantaneously, as if zooming around him of their own accord, the action creating a buzzing sound.

It was the bees! It had to be the bees!

They were after their honey! They wanted it back!

Abel sat back, his knees folded under him. "I'm not sure what's wrong with him, Micah. We have to take care of him. I need to figure out what is wrong."

"Abel, it's not your responsibility—" began Micah.

"It is. We are all each other's responsibility. I need to take care of him. Let me concentrate."

Micah ran his hand through his hair and began to pace. The unexpected made him nervous. Which was saying a lot considering all they'd been through in Kyleighburn. But those were things he'd understood, people he'd worked with, projects he'd been part of. This visit from an outsider wanting to remove one of his—his men, Abel. He didn't know what to think about it, and he wasn't sure what Abel was going to say.

Despite everything, he didn't want Abel to leave.

Morris groaned again and rolled to drop his head over the side of the couch and spew a small cascade of brownish liquid onto the floor. Micah watched as Abel took a cloth and wiped the man's sweating brow, then grabbed a towel to cover the putrid mess.

"Have you any idea what was in that drink of his?" Abel asked, never taking his eyes off Morris.

"Not really. Although Biannca said something about giving him some honey for a smoothie this morning. Could be that's what this is." He left the room briefly and returned with Morris's glass. "Looks like it. Here, what do you think?"

Abel sniffed it. "Nothing unusual. Banana, milk, strawberries," he wrinkled his nose, "kale, and the honey. Nothing lethal there. Certainly nothing that could cause this! His fever's rising, rapidly. 103 I think."

Morris clawed at the air. The bees, he had to shoo the bees away!

"Don't paw the air so, dear." His mother's voice chastened. "You'll only make them angry. Don't be frightened. They don't want to hurt you."

But he was burning up. He could see the numbers, great big red numbers rising and flashing over his head. 103... 104... 105... 108... 110.... That was impossible! He must be dying! That was why his mother was here. Oh, God, what she must think of him!

Micah whirled around. "The honey. The oleander honey. Could it be toxic after all? Did we poison him? Could he be dying?"

Abel shook his head. "No, no. The honey is fine. The bees render it harmless. Once they knew they were adding toxins from the oleander contact, they re-engineered the honey. That isn't the problem."

"Then what is?" Micah paused. "And what is he doing?"

Morris had returned to flailing the air and pulling his head into his chest as if he were a turtle.

"He looks as though he were trying to shoo away flies," said Abel slowly.

"Or bees," said Micah, bouncing on the balls of his feet. "Morris is allergic to bees. He's mentioned it more than once."

"And the bees wouldn't know about that. When this honey was made, Morris was not present in Kyleighburn yet." Abel beamed.

He turned back to Morris, kneeling alongside the prostrate body on the sofa. He touched Morris at various pressure points along his arms and legs. At each touchpoint, movement stopped, and the muscles relaxed into a deep state of stillness, as though each individual one went to sleep. When Morris was quietened, Abel motioned to Micah to push a large ottoman alongside where he could sit and still reach Morris's temples.

As his body had stilled, Morris's flush had receded, his temperature had dropped, and now his body was in a cold sweat. He had probably emptied his bladder, too, noted Abel. Not surprising. Gently Abel placed two fingers over each of Morris's temples. Assured his position was comfortable enough to maintain for a long time—just in case—he lowered his head and closed his eyes. Awareness of Biannca's comfortably shabby parlor receded. He was engulfed by a hot fog of noisy color.

"Mama! Mama! Don't leave me here. I'm sorry! I can't do it! Mama!" They were anguished cries, and Abel recoiled from the anxiety they portrayed, but he didn't let go. Numbers rose through the fog like helium balloons expanding faster than they could fly. Abel turned his attention that way. Morris was on his knees, beseeching the air before him as if a person stood there.

Abel watched and recorded in his mind the perilous image, simultaneously searching the fog and the depths of his own subconscious for the solution he was sure existed.

Morris rose to his feet, stretching his arms for balance. He recalled his earlier contemplation, about his wimpiness. Again he felt the shame. Again, he heard a chorus of "Wimpy, Wimpy, WIMPy!" Now he also felt defiance. A defiance at the lethargy that had allowed the status quo to become the tenor of his life. A defiance over the idea that he could not change. He could, he could! He had the moral courage. He could develop the physical skills! He could amalgamate the two; he could fix things. It wasn't partly a matter of resolve, it was *all* a matter of resolve. His hands resolved into fists at his side.

Abel smiled to himself. There it was! That's what he'd been searching for. Like a surgeon using micro-tools, Abel nicked a line and tripped it over, re-establishing a connection that looked well-worn with time if not practice. It had taken both of them, but quietly, deep inside Morris, change began.

Abel rocked back on the ottoman, his slender hands paler than before. Morris's breathing was perfectly even, his color up, and his temperature steady at 98.6.

There was a flutter of Morris's eyes, but he didn't wake. That concerned Abel a bit, but he knew things wouldn't happen all at once. His examination had revealed some unresolved issues that only Morris himself could clear up. But the incremental changes that had already begun were reassuring. He motioned Micah aside for a conversation.

"He'll be all right. It may take a little, but he'll come 'round. I tweaked a few things. Successfully, I warrant." The satisfied expression told Micah everything.

"You're going to do it, aren't you," he said, no intonation of query in his voice. "You're going to go with him."

Abel looked at the floor, a smile playing over his lips. "I have to, you know. It's what we've been planning for, isn't it?"

Micah's shoulders heaved with an uncertain resignation. "Yes, I suppose it is. But, well, I'm just not sure. This part of things seems so foreign to me. I've been with you all a long time. This kind of decision is above my pay grade."

"That's the thing, Micah. That's the thing. You're moving up to that pay grade someday. You have to be able to handle these kinds of decisions. And you can. It's what you were born to do. Just like I was made to serve. We all, Micah," he put a hand on Micah's shoulder, "we all have our calling in this life, no matter how long it lasts."

Cloaked as he was in his stupor, Morris felt panic. What if his moral courage led him into a dilemma where physical courage was a necessity? He would fail of course. That had always been the problem. It was the problem for most ordinary people, which was why his flaws hadn't set him apart from the crowd. He wasn't particularly or obviously wimpy (even if he did think of himself that way). He was just ordinary. A lone worker bee who somehow managed to make himself his own boss, doing his job in competent, unspectacular, but solid fashion.

But it wasn't glamorous. And while adding glamor to one's life may not be a particularly admirable goal, it actually meant more than that to Morris. In order to add the glamor he envisioned, he'd actually have to improve as a person. With a not-so-bad character, a moral compass that was reasonably steady, conquering his physical fears would strengthen and develop him into a better, more useful human being—who happened to be involved in a glamorous profession. (There's that word again!)

His limbs stirred of their own accord, and he sank into deeper contemplation. His breathing steadied once more. Abel moved over to check vitals.

"His heart rate is stabilizing," he told Micah. "Sooner than I expected. Micah, you need to re-examine the guidelines. Talk with your father if need be, and learn from him how things are handled. You need to be prepared."

"What about you? I thought interference was against the guidelines?"

"What I am doing is *correcting*—,"

"No you're not." Micah regarded him without blinking.

Abel, whose words were never hasty to begin with, drew out them out like stretched spider-thread. "You can see what I'm doing. Aah. I hadn't realized that. Now I understand why things are taking this direction. I reiterate. We all have our callings. You cannot ignore yours. Nor I mine."

He made his way to the kitchen and filled a glass with water. When he returned, Micah was staring out the window, his back toward Morris. He turned at Abel's entrance and watched as Abel cautiously roused Morris and forced sips of water down him.

He paused, setting down the glass, wiping Morris's chin and relaxing his arm to allow him to lie back. He had to pull his necklace back to keep it from poking Morris in the eye. Momentarily, the detective struggled to sit up.

"Mr. Koadh, how are you feeling?"

Morris nodded, rubbing his throat. Its interior felt swollen, and it burned from the vomiting he'd done. The slender man nodded at him pleasantly.

Only this close to him and feeling a little more coherent did Morris realize Abel's eyes had an Asian shape. They were a vivid hazel, with the green component more predominant than most. Morris spotted the necklace that Abel wore like a name plate, as if to help people tell him apart from others, but before he could ponder it, Abel distracted him.

"I've given your offer more thought. And, I'd like to come work for the 'Feds' as you succinctly call them. I think I could be of significant service. Research falls in line with my calling."

It was sort of an odd way to refer to it, but at least it sounded like he was coming with Morris. Good! He could use the fee Oliver promised him. And he felt confident about turning Abel over to him. Of anyone, Oliver would do his best to make sure Abel was treated properly.

"Well, I'm sorry to take you away from your job here. I know Biannca and others here depend on you for your help."

Abel laughed. "Someone will come along to take my place. My job here isn't rocket science after all."

The three men laughed together, if for different reasons.

Next morning, Abel appeared at the B&B's door, suitcase in hand. They loaded up and were gone from Kyleighburn by nine. As they passed by the bushes, Micah stepped toward the lane and waved good-bye to his helper.

"Is he okay?" came a whisper from behind him.

"How does he look?" came another

Micah waved the owners of the questions forward.

"He's fine. You know, I think this is how it was supposed to work." He handed them each necklaces similar to Abel's, but with their own names attached. Charles slid his over his neck and tucked it inside his close-cut brilliant white shirt. Bakkir's hung outside his dashiki, glimmering against the fabric's pattern.

"Bakkir, you need to deepen your complexion," Micah said, beginning instruction even before the car was out of sight. "Use some of that cream I gave you, until the change becomes permanent. Charles, a moustache would be appropriate, I think. A little clichéd, but appropos. And you both need to gain a little weight. No one is as thin as you all. Let people see you eating more, the weight gain should make sense."

Bakkir and Charles nodded, Charles writing a note to himself: "Stop shaving, think of British writer Agatha Christie's Belgian detective Hercule Poirot."

Micah finished, "We'll go to Biannca's for breakfast, and I'll introduce you. And then, we need to talk."

"Speaking of talk, Micah," said Bakkir. "I hear they've decided to move you—forward?"

Micah gave a mild smile. "Up. They'll move me up. When I'm ready, that is."

"They're giving you a posh sort of title, Micah. Hope it won't make you forget yourself, *mon ami*."

Micah laughed. "I didn't think they were given to titles. Must be a new thing. What did you hear, Charles?"

"Let me think a moment. It was long... ah! *Oui!* I saw the printout on the job description. You, *mon ami*, will be the new, the very first, Chief Project Personnel Placement Officer. *Est-ce formidable, n'est-ce pas*?"

# Purple Honey Baklava

## from the Kyleigh Bed & Breakfast

*From the creative cookery of the innkeeper's kitchen owner, Biannca O'Hare*

## Baklava

- 1 pound pistachios, coarsely ground, (optional: set aside some for garnish)
- 1/2 - 1 teaspoon ground cinnamon, to taste
- 1 cup panko breadcrumbs
- 1 pound unsalted butter, melted
- 16 sheets phyllo dough (fresh or thawed from frozen)
- ***note,** *keep covered with a damp towel during preparation so it won't dry out*

## Purple Syrup

- 3 cups sugar
- 8 ounces fresh Kyleighburn purple oleander honey *
- ****CAUTION,** only oleander honey made by Kyleighburn bees has been proven not to be toxic. No other honey made from oleander flowers can make that claim. Oleander is a toxic plant with NO edible parts. If Kyleighburn purple honey is not available, use 8 ounces sourwood or clover honey, colored purple if you so desire.*
- 1 1/2 cups water
- 1 - 2 tablespoons fresh lemon juice

Pre-heat oven to 350 degrees F. Combine nuts, cinnamon, and bread crumbs in a bowl.

Brush a 9x13 inch baking pan with melted butter. Layer 10 sheets of phyllo in the pan, brushing each sheet with melted butter as you layer them. Sprinkle a fourth of the nut mixture over the 10th sheet of dough. Add 4 sheets of phyllo (each spread with butter); sprinkle the 4th with the second quarter of nut mixture. Repeat twice more. Layer the last 10 pieces of phyllo on top of the last layer of nuts, then brush extra butter on top. Cut the baklava into 1 1/2 inch strips, then slice again on the diagonal, also 1 1/2 inch wide, to make diamond shapes. Bake until golden, about 1 hour.

While it's baking, bring the sugar, purple honey, and water to a boil in a saucepan over medium heat and cook, 10-15 minutes. Add the lemon juice and boil 2 more minutes, then cool slightly.

Pour the syrup over the warm baklava; let soak, uncovered, at least 6 hours or overnight. Garnish with the pistachios.

# The Expedition

Susan Turley

THE EXPEDITION TO THE CAVERNS below the town seemed like a dream just hours later and a lot of the details have faded, so I was telling Hope the truth when I said it was complicated. I remember leaping about the cavern, jumping onto and off of ledges, crawling and swinging through the vines, tucking and rolling as I fell from impossible heights.

I remember more details from before the expedition, including going to three grocery stores before we ventured into the caverns, twice to one of them, to get everything I wanted to take along. Foster's didn't have any sandwiches; the Meat Market had sandwiches, but not the potato chips I was looking for. I found the chips at Food Galaxy, but they were out of the citrus green tea I had decided to take along for everyone. I remembered I had seen the tea at Foster's, so I had to go back there.

Janine Foster, the owner's 18-year-old daughter, smiled at me when I walked through the door, just as she had half an hour earlier. "I knew you'd be back, Micah," she said. "Just like I know that we sat next to each other in Bible school when we were five."

I shook my head, as I always did when someone in Kyleighburn tried to make that kind of connection to the past. "We never went to Bible school together, Janine. I'm older than you and I've only lived here for the past six months."

She frowned but let it slide and rang up the drinks. I was a little surprised when she wished me good luck on the expedition.

"Small town gossip," she said. "Everyone knows everything."

Passing Jefferson School on my way to the river, I noticed that the school's lighthouse needed a touch up. The paper whirligig on top of it had faded from the sun and the paint on some of the handprints on its white sides had run. Evidently whoever had sprayed the fixative to preserve the prints had been in a hurry and done a sloppy job. Probably Stuart, the jerk.

I looked down at the sidewalk and realized I was standing in the top space of a chalk-drawn hopscotch grid. The outline was smeared, green, yellow and blue lines faded but still visible. The game had been abandoned abruptly, maybe during the morning's brief thunderstorm, with two markers left behind, a hacky sack in the six square and a Hello Kitty candy tin lying on its side in the three box.

I picked up the two markers and left a sticky note on the wall saying that I had rescued them. I also picked up a stubby piece of green chalk that I thought might come in handy in the cave.

I hadn't been invited on the expedition, but when I turned up on the beach outside the cave entrance, no one seemed surprised or resentful. They looked grateful when I pulled out the food and drinks I brought along.

Doctor Bob was there, but just before we walked into the mouth of the cave, his phone buzzed and we got a line of Herman's Hermits' "I'm into Something Good." The call was from the hospital; a colleague had an out-of-town emergency and the doctor was now on call. That was a shame, since we would need him later.

He did leave us laughing before he walked away and I wondered again where he got the corny jokes. I talked to him several times most days, and I never heard the same joke twice.

He smiled down at the mayor and said, "This man goes to a psychiatrist and says, 'Doc, I'm really depressed. I have the urge to bark and scratch and wag my tail. If someone throws a wad of paper, I start to chase it. I turn around three times before I lie down. I feel like I'm a dog.'

"'I see,' said the doctor. 'And how long have you felt this way?'

"'Since I was a puppy.'"

Joe started out with us too, but turned back after about twenty feet, before we got far enough inside for the light to fade. He had started shaking after two or three steps, turned green after several more and finally just stopped. He huffed out a breath, drew another one in through his nose, and raised his right hand to his mouth, grasping the stud in his lower lip and turning it. I could read the tattooed letters on his knuckles—LIFE.

He huffed again, twirled the stud again, then turned and looked back at the river through the mouth of the cave. The sun glitter made him squint as his face reddened, and he looked as sheepish as was possible for a big, tough, pierced bartender. He just stood there for a moment before he stuttered out a few words "I did... I... I didn't know I was claustrophobic." Then he sighed, we told him goodbye and he headed back into the daylight.

That left four of us to walk into the dark, moving into single file as the corridors narrowed and turned to the right. It seemed to be the right direction.

We were led by the mayor, Marino Esposito, who was dressed as casually as I had ever seen him, in slacks and a long-sleeved T-shirt. Even that plain navy shirt had the embroidered family crest that he wore on everything. I had my suspicions about the design, a black ram's head with a green wine bottle leaking red wine in front of it. By the relative size of the two items, my suspicions were that one of his ancestors had cut them from different wine labels to make up the design.

I came next and Elizabeth, a town council member, followed me. Although she was obviously a woman, wearing flowered dresses and heels when she wasn't delivering mail, the residents of Kyleighburn persisted in calling her the mailman. I had met her a few times, once changing a flat on her mail truck when I happened by, but I didn't have a good feel for her personality. She had at least dressed appropriately for the expedition, in jeans and sensible shoes. I still don't know her last name.

Next was the town's new bank manager, Gerald Winslow Franklin. I did have a feel for his personality and I was in agreement with many of the townspeople. We didn't like him. He was arrogant and officious. I didn't bank with him, he ignored me. Unlike Elizabeth, he hadn't dressed appropriately. He was wearing an expensive silk suit, thousand dollar Christian Laboutin shoes and a gold watch that probably cost more than I made in a year. Some people had taken to calling him G.W.F., and Mrs. Upjohn, proudly Welsh in the Scottish town, eschewed the initials and called him Gwif. Never did find out why he was along.

Actually, there were five of us. Following behind was The Mayor, the scruffy terrier that lived in Kyleighburn but belonged to no one but himself.

As we walked, we argued about the color of the glowing flowers on the vines that twined on the walls and ceilings of the corridors. Elizabeth said, "What is this color? I was going to say purple, but that's not exactly right."

The mayor (Marino, not the dog) called it lavender. G.W.F. said mauve. The Mayor didn't express an opinion.

I am a trained artist and I know my colors and I knew that the flowers were puce. "They" were always careful to say puce. And when I say puce, I mean the brownish, purplish dark red that defies most people's description. Puce.

I was surprised at that color the first time I saw it. You don't see it often in nature. But there are rare colors even in nature. Chartreuse is another one you rarely see. There are flowers of many colors in the caverns.

It took three tries to find the main cavern. Marino insisted on leading and refused the piece of chalk I had picked up on the way. After thirty minutes of walking, the mayor (Marino, not the dog) halted so suddenly that I ran into him, and The Mayor yipped as someone stepped on his paw.

"Watch it, kid," Marino snarled.

I just grinned.

The reason for the sudden halt was a wall, draped with the vines and the glowing puce flowers. The five of us turned around and started back to the last junction, the mayor fussing the whole way because he was now bringing up the rear. The corridor we were in was too narrow for us to change places and let the grumbling town leader... lead.

After returning to the last junction and turning right at Marino's insistence, we walked for another 30 minutes before we began to see light ahead. We emerged from the labyrinth into the riverside cove where we had started.

Marino wouldn't meet anyone's eyes, looking belligerent and mumbling about it being my fault. No one said anything. We reversed direction, heading back into the cavern, Marino waving me into the lead. The vines were thicker and ropier as we worked our way through the corridors and across several caverns. Some of the flowers were pink, blue or yellow, or even multi-colored. There was one small cavern with chartreuse flowers and another with an orange-yellow that looked like cheddar cheese, not as bright as mustard, but close. As I said, not the colors you see in nature.

At one point, I stopped the group because I thought I heard movement in the cavern we had just left. We stood quietly, but heard nothing but our own harsh breathing, and moved on.

There was a red bicycle lying on its side in one of the caverns. I knew that Billy, my young buddy from the park, had been riding a red bike that got lost when he was involved in the rescue of the mayor's niece. I wondered if this was his lost bike.

In another cavern, we found a human skull lying against a wall, but it looked so brittle we were afraid to touch it. A nearby leg bone looked too short for an adult so we wondered if we had found the remains of a parent and child. On the wall above the skull, someone had painted a squash blossom, which still glowed a bright yellow in the dim light of our flashlights and the glow of the puce flowers that filled the cavern.

I had begun using the chalk, marking each turn in light green so we could find our way back to the cove.

As the vines grew thicker and the flowers larger, we made one more right turn and stepped into the biggest cavern we'd seen. The domed ceiling wasn't that high, but since the cavern was under the hills of the forest, this was the highest ceiling in the labyrinth.

The room was filled with the twisted vines, climbing the walls, hanging from the ceiling and draped across the floor. They made it difficult to see what else might be there. The flowers here were all puce and their glow reminded me of the light of a laptop or a TV screen seen from a distance. Some blossoms were almost six inches wide.

The strongest glow came from the center of the room. G.W.F. immediately jumped forward and started tearing at the vines, grunting with the effort. He was yelling incoherently, but between the other sounds, you could hear him gasping, "No, no, no." Although we hadn't seen thorns on the vines, I could see blood on his hands almost immediately. I pulled him away from the rough vines and he stood for a moment with his head hanging, blood dripping off his long freckled fingers.

"What the hell are you doing?" I hissed at him, and The Mayor growled in agreement. We were suddenly buzzed by a squadron of bees, larger and more aggressive than any I'd seen before. They didn't sting, but they seemed determined to keep us from harming the vines or moving farther into the room.

Two of them hovered over G.W.F., buzzing back and forth in what was an obvious and agitated conversation. He tried swatting them away but I grabbed his arm and calmed him down, without giving in to the desire to punch him.

"Leave the bees alone. They've never stung anyone, but you're giving them good reason to now."

The two insects pulled away as the agitated banker calmed down, keeping a wary eye on the thousands of bees still swarming nearby. He stared down at his bleeding hands.

"Why did I do that?"

Shrugging was beginning to be a bad habit I would have to try and break, but a shrug was the best answer I had for him.

I pulled the first aid kit from my backpack and quickly cleaned and bandaged the cuts to his hands. The bees that had threatened him moved closer and hovered just behind my shoulders. I could feel the tiny breeze from their gauzy wings.

Marino and Elizabeth had walked away a few steps and were talking quietly while they waited for the doctoring to end.

I watched the mayor reach out and gently take hold of the vine. The bees continued to buzz around my head but seemed to accept his careful handling as he moved the section of the thick, ropey brown stems aside, clearing a little space that led toward the central glow.

Marino handed the section of vine to Elizabeth, who took a step back and laid it on the ground. He then reached out and took a new section, pulling carefully, making sure his grip didn't damage the flowers and moving it aside before stepping forward again.

The swarm moved toward the two of them but halted when The Mayor yipped gently. I looked at the dog, who gave me a head cock and a smile.

"You ready?" G.W.F. gave me a look I couldn't interpret but I nodded and moved over to the space that had been cleared by Marino and the mailman. Now I was thinking of Elizabeth that way myself.

I was surprised by the sudden sound of the banker's voice beside me. "Thanks for fixing my hands. I don't know what came over me."

I fought—and won—against another shrug. "This is a weird situation. I guess you just freaked out."

This time he was the one who shrugged. "I guess that's all it is. I don't usually lose control."

There was a long pause and then he spoke again as he handed me a section of vine that he had moved out of our way. "I know people don't like me but I don't understand why. I'm really a nice guy. Everything I've done was for the good of the community."

He looked at my face, which I tried to keep neutral but must have shown some exasperation or incredulity, then looked down at the furry wrinkled brow of The Mayor.

"No, really, the investment in the trailer park wasn't the best way to go and I tried to explain that to the owners. That friend of yours, the tall guy, kept telling me they shouldn't expand the park. They wouldn't listen and everyone got mad at me. And look what happened. The park collapsed, three people died and everyone blames me."

I couldn't dispute that but was surprised that Abel had talked to him.

"What do you think they should have done?" I asked him.

A cry from Elizabeth interrupted us before he could answer. She and Marino had reached the center of the room, where the flowers were even larger. We moved to stand with her and Marino, and I picked up The Mayor. The short-legged dog was having trouble getting through the ropey vines, which kept catching at his multi-colored pelt. I started when I felt something cool and moist touch my chin and realized that he had licked me.

What was glowing in the middle of the room was a beehive, standing about four feet high. The bees around it were huge, and I was wishing Hope was there with us.

That was it, though. All the build-up, all the anticipation for what was just an ordinary item grown larger than normal.

Marino was the first to say anything. "Well, that's boring. I expected...."

We all looked at him. His chin jutted forward and he rubbed a dark, hairy hand across his face and then through his hair. "More, I guess. I was expecting a big secret. A buried treasure, a mysterious ship, just something else. Exciting."

Everyone nodded, sharing the letdown. When I laughed at the "Goonies" reference, Elizabeth and G.W.F. were obviously puzzled but I didn't try to explain. Marino was smirking. He always smirked but I was pretty sure he knew why I laughed.

Suddenly tired and hungry, we walked back out of the center of the room to a clear spot and sat down to eat our sandwiches and chips and drink our tea.

Marino started talking about destroying the beehive. "I wonder if there's methane or other gas in here," he said. "Maybe we could burn it."

I was astounded. "Why? It's not causing harm."

He glared at me, immediately belligerent and talking over me.

"It's not normal. I've never seen bees or a hive that looked like this."

I tried again. "The bees are unusual but they're not dangerous. You even have an expert in place to help. That insect specialist. What's her name.... Is it Faith?"

He snorted and backed down a little. "No, and it's not Charity, either. It's Hope. I guess we should get her down here to see what we found."

I nodded and he dropped the subject.

Then we followed the chalk marks back to the cove exit and headed back to town.

ꕤ

That's a nice story, isn't it? Suspense. Mystery. Anticipation. Letdown. But that's not what really happened.

Some of it is true. The people, the Mayor, the dead-end corridor, the bicycle, the skull and leg bones below the painted squash blossom. We really were led back to the cove and had to start over, even though I knew the exact route.

G.W.F. did tear up his hands trying to rip a way through the vines and we did all maneuver through the vines to the center of the room. But it wasn't a huge beehive surrounded by the glow of the puce flowers in the center of the room.

I had been in the caverns a number of times. Now that others had seen it, I could retrieve Billy's bike; it had been replaced when the town honored him for rescuing the mayor's niece but we could fix it up and give it to another kid. Abel had repainted the squash blossom just two months ago after we noticed that it had faded.

Abel's an android I've been handling. That's my real job and it's why I'm in Kyleighburn. I come from a long line of handlers, reaching back some 500 years to the Aztec and Spanish ancestors on my maternal side and farther back to the southeastern tribes that later merged with English, Scottish and German settlers in the early days of the European invasion of North America on the paternal side.

Even with all the tradition that more than 500 years had passed down to me, I didn't know what was in the center of the vines. But this time when I looked at the beehive that the others saw, there was a moment when the feeling from the presence felt more like a greeting and I could almost see what was really there.

We handlers aren't supposed to see it any more than uninitiated strangers can. We know it communicates with us. We know it creates the androids. We are connected to it but we don't know what it is.

I had been helping other family members with androids as long as I could remember, but Abel was my first solo assignment.

The North American coordinator, Emmaline, had called me five months earlier. "I've finally got an assignment for you. Kyleighburn, that little town in North Carolina that's been locked since 1880 or so."

She waited a second for the request to sink in. "I didn't know they were going to mess with the lighthouse. They broke the lock and we've got one active android already."

Handlers are a loosely organized group, mostly members of families that have been involved for hundreds of years. I was surprised to be promoted since there were more experienced handlers waiting for assignments.

Abel was unlike the other firsts I had worked with. He wasn't resistant to trying new things, but he expected me to explain why he needed to do them.

The androids have plenty of knowledge but don't know how to use it.

He wanted details of human life explained in minute detail. I would walk into the cavern and he would be waiting with questions.

"Micah, why do people jump out of airplanes that are functioning normally?"

"Micah, why do humans have different languages?"

"Why do high school students bully other students?"

"What does 'the n-word' mean?"

So I would have to explain that some humans enjoy the thrill of falling that is parachuting, how humans developed society and language, that bullying was a way for people who felt powerless to gain some status, and that some humans hate others who are different from them.

Along with the struggle to answer questions to his satisfaction, I struggled to get him to change his appearance.

"You're not getting darker fast enough," I told him two months ago as I was unplugging him from the puce flowers and waking him up. I had got him pretty far along on most of the other important things, such as genitalia and excretory functions.

"You don't need to be as dark as me, but you aren't dark enough. Your height is enough to make you stand out."

He wouldn't tell me why he wasn't interested in making that change. "It will be all right, Micah," he said every time I brought the subject up. Stubborn, just like every android I had known.

My triplets were destined to be males. Abel was five months old, Bakkir was three months and Charles was just barely a month. The first was the hardest, then that one helped with the second and they both helped with the third.

Then Abel surprised me by showing up in town just after Charles was generated.

The presence in the caverns creates the androids. The vines are circuitry and the different colors of flowers are responsible for different functions. Some days they need to be plugged into puce flowers, other days only red or chartreuse will work. The colors are different in different sites. I'd never seen chartreuse flowers at any other site, and there were no turquoise flowers in Kyleighburn.

I was standing in front of the library one Saturday morning about a month before the expedition, talking to one of the McDougald twins, trying to peek at the titles of the books he had checked out and to figure out if he was Noah or Matthias. The two had widely divergent interests. Noah was interested in sports and gaming. Matt was dreamier and quieter and read poetry and science fiction and fantasy.

Noah it was, I decided, seeing the edge of a Minecraft book.

I asked him where Matt was but he took a step backwards and gulped before he could answer. I heard the robotic voice behind me before Noah was able to collect himself.

"Hello, Micah. I decided I should come and work with you today. Who is your young friend?"

I kept the annoyance out of my voice. "This is Noah McDougald. Noah, this is my friend Abel. He's just moved to town."

Noah had more presence of mind than I expected. He stepped forward and held out his hand. "Welcome to Kyleighburn, Mr...."

Abel smiled down at the eight-year-old. "Please just call me Abel, Noah. I'm sure we're going to be friends."

Two contractions in the same sentence. I felt a little sense of pride in spite of my agitation about Abel's sudden appearance.

We chatted with Noah for a few minutes longer and I could see him loosening up as he listened to Abel's explanation of some arcane baseball rule. I made sure Abel knew that Noah had a twin brother who wouldn't know who Abel was.

"Until we meet, he won't," Abel said. Another contraction.

It was too late to send Abel back to the cavern. He had been seen in town and had to have a place to stay. He could spend time with Bakkir and Charles, but he had to be incorporated into the world. Later that night, he confessed that the three had been sneaking out of the caverns and spending time in the old department store. That explained why people had been seeing lights in the deserted building.

"Bakkir found a... device that collects sounds from the air," Abel said, his eyes glowing. "People talk about things and music is played. It wasn't working but it is fixed now. It made me want to meet real people and learn more about them."

I questioned him about what they'd been listening to, hoping that the three of them weren't listening to AM talk radio, even though I was sure they would reject hate messages. Turns out that they all liked rock, although they argued about which era they preferred. Abel preferred The Beatles and '60s and '70s folk rock, Bakkir had a fondness for 21st Century alt-rock, and Charles liked everything popular since 1955 and was the only one who liked jazz.

Abel, who became my assistant handyman, was accepted into the community as easily as I had been, although no one tried to persuade him that they remembered him from the past. They worried about him and his pale skin, afraid he would suffer from working in the hot sun, and fretted about how thin he was.

Janine Foster always tried to get me to buy extra sweets for both of us, even though I assured her that we were eating properly.

Just today, she tried again, ignoring my protests. "I eat a lot, Janine, and Abel does too. We just burn it off."

She shook her head at me and forced me to take two packages of Twinkies, one for each of us.

As I started out of the store, she called me back. "I almost forgot, Micah. A couple of strangers were looking for you. A man and a woman. I mentioned that you might be at the boarding house or at City Hall."

She described my father and Emmaline. I wondered if I was in trouble over Abel's early emergence from the cavern or from the expedition two days earlier.

I still felt it was a mistake having the presence under the town. Most of the sites were remote, keeping the presence from affecting the uniniated. I think that's why the cult of The Mind had formed twice in the little town. Although it had disappeared again in the late '70s, there were still vestiges left, including people like Mrs. Daughtry, who had recently dragged Hope into her house and spouted her conspiracy theories—killer rugs were prominently featured.

The next three hours were frustrating. I tracked Dad and Emmaline around town, one or two steps behind them. I went to the library, they'd been there an hour earlier, and were headed to Foster's. I tried the boarding house, and missed them by 15 minutes, but Biannca didn't know where they were going next. City Hall lurkers said they'd just been there and were headed to the park. I gave up the search, left Dad a voice mail and sat down on the library steps to wait for them to find me.

Three people came by in the next half hour and told me about the pair looking for me. Marino had talked to them right after they started the search, and Matthias McDougald had met them at the library. And Doctor Bob encountered them in front of his clinic.

"I really like your dad, Micah," the doctor said when he found me sitting on the steps. "He liked my joke about the Pygmy father who told his son he was going on a hunt and would be back shortly."

"Did he say where they were going?"

He shook his head. "I think you'd be smarter to just wait here. I hope everything is okay," he said. I probably reacted to that since he grinned again and walked away.

Of course he'd figured out that Hope and I were related. If Dad had introduced himself as Michael Landreth, it would be obvious. I had never used my last name in Kyleighburn. I paid with cash. I only used my last name or credit card when I left town.

When I sat down yesterday with Hope at the coffee shop to tell her about the expedition, I greeted her as hermanita. We'd both been slipping over the past few weeks, but calling her "little sister" in public was pretty obvious. When I first came to town, before Hope was around, I often threw Spanish phrases into conversations.

I wanted people to take me at face value, as a wandering handyman who was staying in town for awhile because I was out of money and needed to save some up before moving on. I slipped sometimes, usually with the more educated people like Doctor Bob.

Then came the collapse of the trailer park and Hope's arrival to study the bees that swarmed from the hole. I didn't like having to ignore my sister. We were close, despite the seven-year gap between us and the fact that she had a different mother. She's not my little sister in age, just in size. She's a tiny thing, just five feet tall, and no one could look at us and suspect that we are siblings.

If she's a hobbit, I'm an elf. More than a foot taller with black hair and dark skin, I'm quite the opposite of my blonde sister. The only thing we share is the dark blue eyes we inherited from our Scottish ancestors.

We tried to be discreet. I didn't want rumors to start but we had to meet to compare notes. Hope had helped with androids her whole life but wasn't a handler.

Handling can be hard on families; my parents had a volatile relationship when they were together but working in different parts of the country helped keep the marriage functioning. Hope and I had both been home-schooled, which meant we could be passed back and forth between Mama and Dad.

It was hard when Hope left for college. We'd almost always been together, helping during the difficult first two months of a triplet cycle, or traveling during the times between cycles. Mama had only ever worked in the caverns in New Mexico, which produced a set of female triplets every three or four years, but Dad liked to move around and liked to keep busy, so he filled in when other handlers needed a break, besides keeping up with his own site in Tennessee, which produced every two years. He had both male and female triplets, even twice having a set of mixed gender.

I had helped with ten sets by the time I was 20. We knew to watch the thirds carefully. They tended to be more careless than the first, so most of the deaths were from injuries. Mama had two of her thirds die and Dad had lost three.

But my experience in Kyleighburn was different. Abel was less cautious than most firsts. He used contractions, he worked with dangerous equipment, he came out from the cavern early. I was glad that Dad and Emmaline were in town, because I wasn't confident in my ability to deal with him properly.

And if my first was as independent as most thirds, how would Bakkir and Charles act? This triplet set might be too much for a first-time handler. Were Emmaline and Dad here to take the site away from me? I didn't think I could step aside and let Dad take over. I certainly wouldn't be able to stay and be a helper.

Dad's gentle shake of my left shoulder brought me out of my brooding and I looked up to see two blood members of my family and one honorary one standing around me.

Their smiles were reassuring.

I stood and bowed to Emmaline. "Your highness. Have you come to relieve me of my duties for gross dereliction?"

She curtsied back. "No, my valiant knight. You have been ever vigilant and honorable. But it is inappropriate to discuss the kingdom's business in such a public forum. We must repair to a more secure location."

Despite her old-fashioned name, Emmaline is a slender fashionable 50-ish woman who dresses in suits or plain dresses and sensible shoes. Today, she was wearing a cream pantsuit with a rust-colored blouse, and brown shoes. A curly pixie cut had replaced the chin-length bob she'd had six months earlier.

She's all business when she needs to be but she was so close to being a family member that she was often playful with me when we weren't working.

The four of us went into the library and I tried to hide behind Dad so I wouldn't be buttonholed by Delilah.

Didn't work. She came bounding out from behind the desk and grabbed me.

"Micah, you never told me that Hope was your sister. Why not? Did you come here to be close to her?"

She went on, asking question after question without waiting for answers, until Emmaline's annoyance finally got her attention.

Delilah wound down in the middle of a tale about how she had stopped talking to her brother for six months after an argument. She never got to the reason for the argument. I'll have to ask her someday. Delilah's mannerisms may be annoying but she's so sweet I can't imagine her cutting someone out of her life. I really want to know.

We left the little librarian standing and moved into a small conference room. I offered to get drinks but Dad had Hope go get them while I filled Emmaline in on how Abel had broken protocol by coming out of the caverns before he had finished his training.

When Hope returned, the meeting turned to handler gossip for a few minutes, then Emmaline finally got down to business. "Micah, I've been communicating with the presence for the past several months about my successor."

I searched her face. "Are you okay? You're not old enough to retire. You've only been coordinator for 10 years or so because Edward held on for so long."

She quickly reassured me that she was fine and nowhere near ready to retire. "Edward wasn't the one who decided how long he would be coordinator. It's the presence that makes those decisions."

I wasn't sure she was telling me the truth. Could she be ill and just afraid to tell us?

"Your successor won't need that much training," I said, assuming that Dad was the choice, and turning to give him a mock salute.

He and Emmaline shared a brief smile before she leaned forward to clasp my hand.

"Michael isn't the next coordinator, Micah. You are."

I jumped to my feet. My mouth dropped open but nothing came out. I found myself peering into the corners of the room, searching the room for the swarm of angry bees before realizing that the buzzing in my ears was internal rather than external. I took a step away from the round conference table and felt my knees weaken.

Dad and Hope grabbed me and sat me down before I embarrassed myself by sprawling on the floor.

"Micah, you need to breathe." I heard the voices but wasn't sure I could obey them. I didn't want this responsibility. I knew what Emmaline's life was like. We hadn't known Edward as well, but I knew what pressure he was under.

"I can't," I said as soon as I had enough breath to speak and the three of them let go of me. "There are too many others who have more experience."

Emmaline shook her head. "That doesn't matter, Micah. It isn't a matter of seniority or experience or even of desire. You really don't have a choice. The presence makes the decision. It has nothing to do with anything but what the presence wants."

I dropped my hands to the table and waited. Head down, I let myself relax and opened my mind. The presence spoke to me then, words I have no intention of sharing with anyone. It told me what it wanted me to accomplish over the next few years as I prepared to take over from Emmaline.

"There will be changes," I whispered, still looking down at my hands. "The presence wants to accelerate creation of the androids. It didn't cause the re-opening of this site, but it is pleased that it has happened."

Emmaline squeezed my hand and I felt Dad behind me. I finally raised my head and looked at each of those beloved people.

"I need to talk to Mama. Can she come?"

Dad shook his head. "Her third is about to generate. She couldn't come for at least a week, even if I went to relieve her. I'm sorry, son."

I understood. She was at a critical point and had to be there for her new android. They were as clingy as a four-year-old for the first week or ten days. After that, they could cope with the help of the other androids or any handler.

"I know you want to talk with your Mama, but you need to go into the cavern now and talk to the presence," Emmaline said. "You know that the center of the cavern doesn't hold a giant beehive. Now that you are chosen, you will see what is really there."

She saw my reaction. "Have you seen it already? Oh, Micah, that is the way you know you are chosen!"

I told her about the shimmer I had noticed when I looked at the beehive. I had already known that the presence would show us something that wasn't there. I hadn't expected that I would see more than the others saw.

"You are very close to knowing," she said. "Much closer than I was right after being chosen."

I stood on shaky legs and felt childish and pathetic when I asked them to come with me, at least to the cavern entrance.

We walked warily from the conference room but this time Delilah kept her distance, merely waving from behind the desk and saying she hoped I would be alright.

I think the smile I gave her was more like a grimace, but I thanked her in a voice that didn't shake. Well, not too much.

We walked the half mile to the riverside and climbed down to the beach next to the cavern entrance. Somewhere along the way, The Mayor joined us. I picked up the scruffy little dog and carried him down the most difficult part of the walk. I again felt the cool moistness of his tongue on my chin as I set him down on the sand.

I walked away from Hope, Emmaline and my dad, into the cave at the river and through the corridors, past caverns filled with puce, red, orange, chartreuse and multi-colored flowers and the twisted vines that weren't vines. I didn't need chalk marks to guide me safely past the dangerous corridors or dead ends. The Mayor walked beside me part of the way before he stopped and sat down.

"Are you resting or stopping?" I asked, before he turned his head toward the entrance to the main cavern and yipped.

I left him behind and entered, slowly stepping across the vines toward the glow in the center of the room. Bees surrounded me, some landing on my head and shoulders. Their hums filled the cavern. The buzzing stirred the air around me. My bones throbbed along.

The glow of the flowers increased with each step. The air pulsed with the color almost as strongly as with the sound.

I could understand why I'd been told the presence had affected people so strongly in the past that the coordinator had locked the Kyleighburn site down. If those people had felt the energy and power I was feeling, it would have been hard to resist.

I stopped between one step and the next. My hands and face were tingling and I could smell ozone as small electric pulses began arcing between the bees, like little jagged bolts of lightning. I almost turned back but the hum urged me forward.

One more step. The pulsing stopped as I entered the open space. The bees still hovered but the ones I had carried with me lifted from my body. The flowers still glowed but the flashing stopped. The humming stopped. The lightning stopped. The smell of ozone dissipated and I could smell the flowers again.

There was a calm that almost drove me to my knees but I fought to stand there, calming my breathing, closing my eyes and waiting.

I felt a voice in my head. The presence had communicated with me for most of my life, but that had been more of a feeling, almost like instinct.

This was new. The voice said, "Welcome, Micah. Open your eyes and look upon me."

I held my position for three breaths—in and out, in and out, in and out.

As that last breath ended, I let my eyes open and I saw....

The words that were said to me will never be told, and the things I saw will never be described. I am chosen and I will lead.

Tuesday, June 14

# What's Up

- The E.P.P. Scott Library is offering an **exhibit of artwork** from students at Kyleighburn High School through Aug. 15. Artworks include, drawing, paintings, fabric pices such as batik and weavings, pottery and basket weaving.
- The **farmers market** is being held in front of City Hall from 1 to 4:30 p.m. Wednesdays and 9 a.m. to 2 p.m. Saturdays through Sept. 3.
- A **summer reading program** for all ages is being held at E.P.P. Scott Library and Kyleigh Books and Art. Signups are being held now. Everyone participating gets a totebag and a bookmark. Prizes will be given to those who read the most books during the eight-week program, in five different age divisions.
- **Bible School** programs have begun in most of the town's church. See Friday's church page for more information.
- Biannca O'Hare, owner of he Kyleigh Bed & Breakfast, will give a **cooking demonstration** at 4 p.in the small exhibit tent at the Fourth of July celebration in Magnolia Park, featuring her Purple Honey Baklava.
- The Kyleigh County Orchestra will hold **auditions** at Kyleigh High School at 5 p.m. July 1.
- Dr. James Mitchellson, a social science professor at Courtney University, will speak on **human trafficking** at 7 p.m. Wednesday at the Kyleighburn Police Department meeting room.

- The **Kyleighburn city council** meets Thursday at City Hall. At 6:30 p.m., a reception and awards will honor the town's police officers and local volunteer firefighters for their efforts to help citizens during the recent disaster. The council meeting will begin at 7:30 p.m.

## Public Safety

Reports from Police Department, fire departments, Sheriff's Department; 6 p.m. Thursday through noon Tuesday

- Fire, 2225 Main St., minor damage to utility building, Thursday.
- Drunk and disorderly arrest, James Miller, Friday.
- Vehicle crash, Main Street and Kyleigh Road, minor injuries, Friday.
- Four reports of lights in old Jacobson's Department Store building; one Friday, two Saturday, one Sunday.
- Vandalism of two school buses; estimated cost of repairs, $600; discovered Monday.
- Death investigation, probable natural death, 144 Kyleigh Road, James Miller, Sunday.
- Stolen bicycle, valued at $250, Magnolia Park, Sunday.
- Shoplifting, three 20-ounce soft drinks, two cans of energy drink and three candy bars, Foster's Grocery. Items valued at $11; Saturday..
- Fire, trash dumpster at Magnolia Park. Damage estimated at $500. Friday.
- Assault, Danny Foster of Foster's Grocery was accosted as he left the store at 6:15 p.m. Saturday. He shoved the attacker, who ran away.

**Tuesday, June 14**

# Former Principal Found Dead

## Police believe James Miller died of natural causes

*By Jennifer McTeague*
*Editor*

James Miller, 72, longtime Kyleighburn High School principal, was found dead Sunday in his home at 144 Kyleigh Road.

Miller, who struggled in the beginning of his career to overcome suspicion and ridicule because of his connection with the group The Mind in the 1970s, had been arrested on a drunk and disorderly charge Friday night.

He retired from the high school in 2010 after 20 years as principal. He began his career in 1980 as teacher at Kyleighburn's Jefferson School and became assistant principal at Kyleighburn High in 1988 and principal in 1990.

A news release from the Kyleighburn Police Department says Miller was found by Delilah Chanda, head librarian at E.P.P. Scott Library, who went to check on Miller after he failed to show up to teach Sunday school at Kyleighburn Baptist Church.

Police said they are awaiting results of an autopsy but believe Miller died of natural causes.

Miller is survived by two sons, James Jr. and Edward and a daughter, Michelle Foster, all of Kyleighburn; a sister, Marian Miller of Charlotte; a brother, Kenneth of Raleigh; and eight grandchildren.

Funeral services are pending.

Memorials may be made to Kyleighburn Baptist Church.

# Mayor vs. Mayor

Mackenzie Minnick

MANY YOUNG WOMEN AND MEN in (usually respectively) yoga pants and unkempt man-buns hold a misconception about Karma. They believe that outputting good vibes and intent to the general world will ensure that the world will return to them gifts and prizes based off of the amount of the aforementioned good vibes and intentions. There are those who hold the opposing view point. Both are incorrect. Karma operates on a cosmic ledger. If a Gargan on the planet Epsilon Eridani b kicks the equivalent of an Earth puppy, then Amanda in SoCal spills her Starbucks on her laptop as payment.

Marino Esposito, mayor of Kyleighburn, alias Marino "Pulverizer of 53rd Street" Esposito, alias "Boss", alias "the Defendant", was aware of this fact. The best way to ensure safety from the karmic ledger is balance. Do a little bad to do a little good. Burn down someone's house to build an animal shelter for fire rescues. Make Karma's math easy by having a consistent zero sum, and everything will work out how you planned. Just look at the yoga pants and man-buns. Those same people believe in things like harmonic crystals, vegan-only foods for their pets, and that vaccines cause autism. It's easy math.

For now, though, Marino was stuck at his desk, shackled to a rotary phone. It was the pinnacle of technology well over a half century ago. The faux-gold-plated piece of crap was also the most modern piece of technology Marino had found in the mayor's house when he bought it. Still, Marino was never one to shy away from displays of grandeur. It was a steady flow of negative karma to balance the accidental good. Again, easy math.

A thick heavy Sicilian accent answered the phone. "You, who call me on this, the day of my daughter's wedding, what would you ask of me?"

"Dah, your daughter has been married and divorced four times, two times consecutively. Just pass me to Mah." Marino pinched the bridge of his large, beak-like nose. Dah had lost a lot of his stature since he went a bit senile.

"I work my whole life, I don't apologize, to take care of my—" the voice faded away as someone took the phone away.

"Go sit in your study, dear, the McBrides are plotting again. Hello?" A sharp Brooklyn accent saved Marino a few minutes of lecture.

"Hi Mah, it's me." Marino said.

"Cubby! How are you honey?" the matriarch of the family responded. "How's the Southern life? Have those poor bastards stuffed you like a Thanksgiving turkey yet?"

"Mah, I'm fine, I just need to know if Dino has talked to you lately."

"Dino? Last I knew, he was lookin' around for a… trumpet."

"What? A trumpet? I didn't know the pillow-brain could play—" There was a knock at the office door. After a second, the door cracked open enough to allow a head covered in brown curly hair to stick out.

"No, no Cubby-baby, it's a… Oh, you've been away too long. No, I haven't heard from him." Marino looked up long enough to see the head, and waved it in. The door fully opened to show Tabitha Crumb, his trusted secretary. Although she stood at barely over five foot, the woman was chockful of legal and illegal knowledge. She was a middle-aged tome of secrets. Her pages currently read *Something is going on and you need to worry about it.*

"Look," Marino could feel the pain in his temples doubling. "He's supposed to be bringing a truck load of building supplies. Tell him to call me."

"Sure thing, Cubby. You got anything else you want?"

Tabitha crossed the room, skirting between the two luxuriant armchairs in front of Marino's desk. She picked up a legal pad and feathered pen that was left on the edge of the oak monstrosity. Tabitha scribbled something on the pad then flipped it around. *Debate in an hour.*

"No Mah, thank you—"

"Good, how long are you going to be in that tiny little town? You need to be with your family, not in some rinky dink hole with gun-toting hicks—"

"Mah, I'll talk to you later. Good bye."

"—who have no class, no culture, no nothing! It isn't safe!" The voice shrilled as Marino returned the handset to the switch hook with a satisfying *clunk*. He looked at the hastily scrawled message Tabitha wrote again.

"I'm running unopposed," Marino stated in the same manner that a child reiterates that Santa is real despite the insistence of a non-believer.

"Apparently there has been a write-in nomination, Mr. Esposito."

"How? I thought we had someone watching the ballots?"

"We did. There was a disambiguation regarding certain votes that wrote in 'The Mayor', and the officials have determined that the voters did not, in fact, mean you."

Marino leaned to the side and opened the bottom drawer of his desk. Tabitha betrayed her normally stoic expression to lift a single eyebrow, soaring it above her horn-rimmed glasses. From somewhere, Marino pulled out a bottle of whiskey and two glasses. He set the glasses down, and handed the bottle to Tabitha. As she dutifully poured out two glasses, Marino stood and paced the plush carpet of his office.

"Over a hundred people without a place to call home, and people want me to debate a terrier?"

Tabitha turned an armchair round and sat in it. On one of Marino's passes, she held out his glass. He reached one end of the maroon carpet, turned on his heel, and went back the other way.

"I should do it as it'll help get everyone's mind off the calamity—"

"But then you're wasting your time," Tabitha followed up, sipping appreciatively at her whiskey. "And if you don't do it, you risk losing to a stray dog."

Marino stopped pacing and stared at her. The woman looked like a cat, curled into the seat of the chair. *Cheshire*, Marino thought, *she knows what I'm going to do before I know it's an option.*

"Where the hell is Dino?" he spat out, though the answer was irrelevant. Dino would arrive, one way or the other, but if the building supplies for the trailer park came *right now*, Marino would have the election clinched. Tabitha didn't answer, only smiled wider. She could see the metaphorical screws being twisted into Marino's thumbs.

It reminded him of a certain doomsayer, Mr. Derry, who used to roam the streets back North. The Espositos couldn't rid themselves of the zealot, who only wanted to stand on the corner and commend any and all to the devil who will soon consume the world in wrath and hellfire. It was distracting for business, but taking any aggressive steps meant earning the ire of certain members of the public. Thus, they left Mr. Derry alone. One day, his mother called him for help. She had somehow broken both her legs by falling down some stairs while holding a crowbar and needed him to come back and take care of her. Sometimes, things work out. Other times, pretending to ignore the problem until you think of an indirect solution is the better way to go. Of course, certain accusations were made, but until there was proof, alleged was as good as "Never happened" for the State of New York.

"It's only an hour," Tabitha reminded Marino. He drowned the rest of his whiskey and set the glass down with a sixteen-ton sigh.

"Where?"

"Community center near Magnolia Park,"

A flash of a very large, very *unpleasant* image sprawling under the park crossed Marino's mind. There were some things not even Tabitha should know.

"Fine," he said, mentally filing the expedition as 'Alleged'. "Get the car started. Send a message to Lillian and have her meet me there with the kids. Tell them to dress Sunday Funeral, post-burial."

*Maybe something useful will come of this*, Marino thought. After all, Mr. Derry turned into a great advocate for disability rights. Five installed ramps and counting.

Marino arrived at the community center with fifteen minutes to spare. Instead of going inside, however, he sat in the car, watching the minutes get closer and closer to six. Being perfectly punctual meant a lot of hurry up and wait. To kill the time, Marino was trying to figure out why the people of Kyleighburn were making him do this. It couldn't be Karma, as the last thing he had done was ordered the shipping supplies stolen from a warehouse—

though something could have happened during the heist. *Mah's right. I've been away for too long.* Ten years, in fact, since Marino left the family business, wife and daughter in tow. Ten years since they came to Kyleighburn to hide from some of Marino's associates; in particular, the kind to shoot first and then shoot again to make sure. Mah kept pretending the heat was gone, but Marino knew that some "fine" folk held grudges until someone swung from a meathook in the freezer.

The clock turned 5:55. Marino opened the door to his black sedan and stretched out of the car. There were some fifty or so other cars in the darkened lot. Far more than Marino had anticipated. Something was not quite right.

He strolled through the door at six, and found himself behind a dense mob of people, bustling and jostling with each other to find an empty seat somewhere in the open room. Marino instead chose to place his hands into his pockets, hunch his shoulders, and loom. The effect was nearly immediate, with people parting left and right to make room for the mayor, and he promenaded to the front. As the way cleared, he could see two podiums. One had a very tall box in front of it. Marino took a position at the other one. A short and pudgy man dressed in overalls approached him.

"Evenin', Mr. Mayor," he said. "Name's Harvey, I'll be doin' the moderatin' tonight."

"Harvey Bells." Marino said. "You run a bakery, yes? Lillian has praised your sourdough."

"Er, that's right." Harvey looked nervous. Marino stared at him.

"Where is the dog?"

"Oh—uh, Joe is roundin' him up."

"Thank you," Marino turned his attention back to the crowd. He could see several of the town regulars there. Gerald, the banker was already sitting isolated in the seats. Delilah was swapping hot gossip with a few other women. Marino noted Tabitha was there among them, holding a very large, very official book. As he kept scanning, he spotted Lillian in a splendid black gown. Her dark hair was pulled up in a bun with a couple of strands of hair hanging loose. Isabella had on a school hoodie, with the strings drawn shut. Tommy was in his mother's arms. Marino waved them over. Lillian approached, flashing a bright smile at the crowd.

"What the hell are you thinking, Marino?" Lillian hissed. "Tommy was fast asleep in his bed and now we're standing in front of all these people just so you can talk to some dog? They do understand your position, right?"

"I didn't have any choice, Lilly, they want me to do this."

"It doesn't matter. You have a daughter and son that you need to attend to instead of some publicity stunt. Tell them 'haha', you get the joke, then we go home."

At that moment, Joe the bartender came in holding a terrier in his tattooed arms. The crowd cheered. Marino ushered Lillian off to the side then took his position behind the hardwood podium. Joe set down the scruffy dog and kept its attention by holding up a cooked hamburger patty. Harvey stood up.

"Hello, Kyleighburn. Tonight, we shall bear witness to the debate for the mayoral position. Our participants are the current incumbent, Mayor Marino Esposito, and challenger The Mayor, dog. Opening statements begin, followed by a Q&A. Do you understand, Mayor Esposito?"

"I do,"

"And you, The Mayor?"

The Mayor (the dog, not the man) barked. The crowd tittered. The mayor (the man, not the dog) sighed, and pinched the bridge of his nose, wishing to be anywhere else at the moment.

"Very well. Mayor, er, man Mayor, you begin. Since you can talk."

Marino composed himself and then looked out into the crowd.

"Everyone, I appreciate the spot of levity that we are having tonight, as these last several months or so have proven to be very difficult for our town. Ten years ago, Kyleighburn welcomed us with open arms. Nine years ago, I started my journey to repay that debt. I'm still working that off. Please allow me to get back to the job."

There were a few half-hearted claps. Harvey turned to the dog. Before he could even speak, The Mayor started to scratch at an itch behind his ears. The crowd laughed again, and there were a couple of cheers. Marino had a feeling in his stomach, similar to when a bunch of men carrying suspiciously long packages walk into a restaurant.

"...so if everyone could line up," Harvey was saying. "then we can begin the Q&A. First up, Mr. Pile."

"Thank you, Harvey," *Mr. Pile, age fifty-four, carpenter, still has yet to give back his neighbor's hammer.* "My question is for the mayor."

"Which one?" Harvey asked.

"Uh, the man. Mr. Mayor, can you describe in precise terms how you have the town's best interests at heart?"

Marino glanced at Lillian, who was wearing an expression of *I will personally kill you if you don't wrap this up*, which has come up more often than Marino was willing to admit. He smiled.

"Mr. Pile, everyone, as I said I appreciate the joke here. Life's a—a tough one." Marino was tempted to make the pun, but was never good at them. Besides, Lillian would have his head for soiling the ears of Tommy so early. "Let me go home with my wife and kids. I can take care of you all. If you don't believe in my capability, then I got a special tidbit for you. I have a shipment of supplies coming in to restore the collapsed area of town. I have personally seen to the securing—"

Marino was cut off by a sudden rise in jeers, primarily coming from Harvey, who had clearly forgotten the role of moderator. *And this is where they shoot me*, he thought. He made eye contact with Lillian and gave her the signal to leave with the children as quickly as possible. She took Isabel by the shoulder and melted into the crowd. Now was not the time for pictures.

"Hold on!" He projected his voice over the crowd. "What's going on?"

"We don't want you to tell us what you're doing for us!" a woman with far too much makeup on cried out. "We don't need you to tell us what our problems are. We want to tell you our problems!"

Marino tried to formulate a reply, but he had just realized that Tabitha was sitting behind the woman, and she was *grinning*.

"He listens just fine," Miss Fullerton said, her two chins wobbling. "he's just too damn suspicious! I tell Reginald that I was having a bit of knee trouble and might not be able to bring home a pumpkin for Halloween, next thing I know Esposito's at my door holding a gourd!"

"Wait, last year some thieves stole pumpkins from—" a farmer started, but Harvey jumped in before an incriminating connection could be drawn.

"That Mayor," he yelled. "The dog mayor could do a much better job than you!"

The crowd agreed. Someone started a chant. "Mayor! Mayor! Ruff! Ruff!" It was growing into a steady roar. With the metaphorical bullets starting to fly, Marino couldn't afford to shoot back. Instead, he started searching for an exit path.

He locked eyes with Tabitha, who still hadn't moved from her chair. *Get me out of this*, he thought, and tried to send that desperation to her. She sighed, then stood up on her chair. She held out her book so the title could be read: *Kyleighburn Archives and Laws*. She cleared her throat loudly, then opened her book to a tabbed page. The room was silent as she read.

"This article herby establishes that the position of mayor must be held by someone who refuses an offering of food or wine not once, but twice, before finally accepting if offered a third time. Section 3c, Mayoral Requirements, 1845."

There was a long moment of silence before Joe tentatively offered the patty to the terrier. The crowd breathed a small sigh of relief when the terrier hesitated. When Joe offered the patty a second time, The Mayor (the dog, not the man) nabbed the patty from his hand and chewed on it satisfactorily. Marino breathed a sigh of relief.

"Aw," went the crowd.

*Thank God for Tabitha,* Marino thought. But he couldn't celebrate yet. There were a lot of capable people in the center that night and someone was bound to realize that they could run instead of the dog.

"Everyone," Marino announced. "My apologies on your candidate being unable to run officially. However—" Marino elevated his voice to cut off Harvey raising his hand. "—I want you all to know you have moved my heart. I hear you, and I wanna offer an olive branch. A new position in the mayoral office, Minister of Advice and Suggestion, filled by mayoral appointment, shall go to The Mayor."

"Dog or man?" cried out a dozen people.

"The dog." Marino emphasized in a strained voice. Just then, his cell phone vibrated in his coat pocket. "The minister will now answer any questions."

"Minister! Who's a good boy?" someone shouted as Marino stepped away from the podium and made his way outside. When he finally checked his phone, he almost dropped it trying to answer.

"Dino! Where the hell have you been?"

"Ah, sorry Rino, tha boys and I had some problems tryin' to get to you. We couldn't find the turnoff until some tall, pale guy told us where it was. I'm telling you, tha guy looked like he was a ghost, I told Manny, see, I told Manny that if we pulled over for some spook and then got busted by some pigs haulin' a bunch'a stolen supplies, we'd be doin' a—"

"Dino! Where are you now?"

"Oh yeah, we're right at your house. Got two trucks full of stuff, just need to know where to go. Nice place, buddy, lots'a space and great view of that river, what was the name of it? Some Scottish thing? You know Dah's gonna get a heart attack if he thinks you're with tha McBrides—oh, I see Lillian, I'll go say—"

Marino hung up. He took a deep long breath of the cool air and looked upwards to the sky, out amongst the stars. Somewhere out there, Karma was making careful notes of the events tonight. *I'll need to get that dog a collar and bug it*, Marino thought to himself, and Karma put a simple little zero next to his name.

Tuesday, June 14

# Grocer Attacked

Danny Foster of Foster's Grocery Store told police someone tried to attack him as he was leaving the store Saturday evening.

Foster, who wasn't injured, said he shoved the attacker down and the person got up and ran away. The attacker wore a face mask and was dressed in black but Foster couldn't see the person's face or be able to give any kind of description.

"It happened so fast. I had just locked the door when this figure in black came rushing at me from around the corner of the store," Foster said.

"It wasn't even dark so it was kind of stupid. I can't give much of a description but it was a young person probably by the way they moved. I couldn't tell if it was a boy or girl, what race they were, anything."

Foster says he never leaves the store by himself with a money bag so the attacker wouldn't have profited by an attack.

"If I have to take money to the bank, I call Micah or someone like a coach or a football player to go with me. I've even called Doctor Bob or the mayor (Mariano, not the dog) if I couldn't find someone else to go with me."

Foster said the incident shook him, but seems insignificant now after the death of his father-in-law, former Kyleighburn High principal James Miller, who was found dead in his home Sunday morning.

"We knew he was not feeling well, and he hadn't been acting like himself for several weeks," Foster said, citing Miller's uncharacteristic actions Friday night, which led to an arrest for being drunk and disorderly. "My wife and her brothers had been trying to get him to go see Doctor Bob."

Foster said his store will reopen Wednesday after being closed Monday and today. He'll make a decision on closing when the family is able to make funeal arrangements.

# Canon

RJ Minnick

MICAH STOOD IN THE GARDEN, giving it a last once-over. Three months back, Biannca had changed her mind. The bees, according to her, needed peace and quiet to keep them coming 'round. So she'd requested he give the bee garden a complete makeover. It had been nearly ten years since he'd put the original garden in. The conversion would take a great deal of work, requiring as it did the removal of nearly a third of the plantings; since it would be the last one he did for her, he did a bang-up job of it. A rectangle of hedge and English garden encasing a Zen garden that acted as a courtyard for the row of hives. It was the capstone of a healthy relationship the once-itinerant man had with the village of Kyleighburn.

But now Micah Landreth would be off to further adventures in his on-going role as mentor and coordinator to a group of dedicated, ambitious individuals eager to serve the greater world. He was excited; he was nervous; but mostly, he was puzzled. The extent of his puzzlement finally revealed itself in a project briefing session.

"All right everyone, we need to get some work done. We don't have all that long before we deploy, you know that."

Doug raised his hand almost at once. "You always use the word deploy, Micah. It sounds so militant. Isn't that counter-descriptive?"

One of the guys in the back groaned. "Does it really matter? We all know what he means."

"I know, but it sets the tone, and we have all been taught how important that can be in our interactions," Doug replied placidly. As one of the older personnel, he'd been preparing for this a long time.

The first few team members had gone out as Micah was finishing the bee garden the first time. It took a while for them to get established. The first reports back from Abel on what outside conditions were like didn't come in for six months. Kyleighburn and North Carolina in general were a very small part of a very big world after all. It was even longer with Bakkir and Charles, both of whom were sent overseas. Then came the special orders for particular personnel. Demand was high for certain kinds of talent—diplomatic corps, educators, scientists, doctors. And there had been that dust-up over gender, which had required an executive decision from Headquarters.

They were so dismissive of names and things like gender, they wouldn't even respond to the question at first. At last a directive was sent out stating that gender didn't matter and HQ didn't want to hear any further noise about it. At which point, a number of personnel discussed matters amongst themselves and opted for the fluidity of assigning posts purely on talent and letting the individual deal with gender issues. Yes, it had taken all ten of the years to prepare, all of his previous knowledge first as a handler, then as the coordinating officer, but Departure Day was almost upon them.

Not only did his diverse team need to be prepared, Micah thought to himself, so did he. He needed to really understand his personnel if he was going to coordinate them effectively and report on their progress. He needed to understand their story as well as their mission. It was his objective to be the best Chief Project Personnel Placement Officer in existence—even if he was the only one.

"Okay, guys, okay. Look, I want these next few sessions to be a sort of bull session. I want us all to be at ease with each other, understand one another. Sort of be in each others' heads."

The room burst with laughter. Micah looked up at them and grinned, waving the laughter down with a shrug. "Okay, okay. I know how that sounds. I'll be honest with you. I know you all understand each other. Obviously that's at a level I can't share, not having your—heritage. So, I want you to explain to me, as best I can comprehend, who you all are, individually and collectively, and what you hope to accomplish."

Queen stopped examining her new-grown nails to speak up. "You are saying you want us to articulate our missions. This is with the hope of intensifying our focus?"

"That is what I hope it will do for you, yes."

"And what will it do for you, my friend?" this question came from India. She sat next to Queen, frowning as Queen brought out a nail file. "Ssst. Put that away. It ruins your image!"

Queen started to glare at her, but then she shrugged and pocketed the file and put a dedicated professional expression on her face. "Micah?"

He sighed. "Look. You all share a connection I can never be included in. But in order to serve with you, to serve you and our mission, I need to know what you're trying to do, and why you're doing it, and even how, if we can tell that this early. Roger?"

"What do you want to know?" he asked.

"Well, for starters… tell me more about your dedication to service. Why is it that all of you here in Kyleighburn want to go out and serve humanity?"

There was a collective sigh of patience from the group in the room who knew so much and could convey so little to their friend, protector, and officer. This was not going to be an easy meeting after all. And the next three days—and they all knew it was only three days, even if their leader was unaware—were going to be very, very full.

With that in mind, Howie spoke up. "Micah, how about for today, some of us meet with you and discuss that question. Maybe," he looked around the room, pointing, "Queen, you, and Yankee, Peter, Sierra, Foxx, and Edward and Tara. You all, plus myself and Uncle here. We'll talk with you about why we feel so strongly about the mission. The others can continue packing and readying their credentials and lists—"

"Wait, packing?" asked Micah, his eyebrows up. "Isn't it a little soon for that?"

"Well, we always like to prepare early," said Howie. "And some of us believe in prep redundancy. You know how emergencies are. Plus we have a committee working on finance that has to take a Swiss video conference in just a few hours. They have some figures to pull together, I believe."

Sugar nodded to Howie as she and George left the room together. The others not designated by Howie filed out, too, leaving a silent Micah to wonder, not for the first time, who was really in charge here.

He clapped his hands together and settled on the corner of a table at the front of the room. "Right. Of course. How about we all gather together closer, a little more comfortable, all right? Easier to talk. Right."

Howie caught Uncle's eye as they gathered round, and ceded leadership to him with barely a glance. The older-looking man remained standing and began to speak as the others sat.

"Micah, you've asked us about our career choice, our desire to dedicate our lives to serving others. It is a passion that has led us to offer our assistance to those living outside of Kyleighburn. Personally I have lived here my whole life, trying to be of help to people living here, teaching, lecturing, trying to educate people about events of the world. Now, I have a desire to further my contributions. Some of you may recall that much of my ten years here has been spent teaching at the local high school; recently I've added delivering lectures at the library, and even to visitors at the Kyleigh Bed and Breakfast.

"It's been noted that I have an authoritarian presence and a trusted manner with imparting information. Therefore, Micah has procured me a position with a rather large and wide-serving public news service. The plan is for me to move forward as quickly as possible, and attain a position as a trusted news anchor for the service. I can serve people well, I believe, by reporting facts in a trustworthy and believable manner, guiding them through calamitous times safely on to prosperity."

Micah raised his hand to pause him. "Just a comment, Uncle. You may want to dial back the pomposity. People love gravitas in their newsmen, but too much pomp and fancy language and you'll lose your audience."

"Noted, Micah. Now… ahem," Uncle paused. "I think then, no one wants to call their newsman Uncle. It is too informal and can have very negative connotations." He peered questioningly over his eyeglasses at Micah, who nodded. "Very well, then in addition to making my delivery more business-like I will use the name Walter. A long history of confidence and trust attaches to that name. It recalls a time of security and assuredness that what a viewer saw and heard was the truth, that it was the way the anchor said it was. So, Micah, I will assume duties as Walter Armstrong, if that meets approval."

"I think that will work. But maybe shorten it to Walt. Walt Armstrong." As the man formerly known as Uncle nodded in agreement and sat down, Micah recognized another speaker. "Sierra?"

"Micah, thank you. You all know I'm a recent comer to this party. It's taken me a while to try to get my act together, but, honey, I do think I've adjusted, don't you?" The tall slender female stood and strutted just a bit as she came to the front of the room. "My specialty is entertainment, but we all know how shallow a profession that is, unless of course, you do it right. If you are at the top of your industry, then you have a platform to speak from. But not everyone has a message that is productive for others to hear. Simply put, my goal is to use my influence to move people toward their goals, to help them figure out how to realize their own potential by seeing how I achieve mine." She walked back to where she'd been sitting, humming a little. When she sat, Sierra scribbled some words on a notepad, adding key signatures to what looked like a short verse on the page.

His head bent, Micah didn't call on anyone else who had hand raised or stared at him expectantly. This wasn't going where he wanted. At least, not exactly.

"Thank you both for sharing that with us. I know it gives me a clearer picture of what you hope to do. But, truly, I was hoping you'd each get into depth a little more about why you are doing this. What is your motivation?

A dozen sets of eyeballs stared blankly at him.

Finally Howie spoke up. "Micah, it's what we do man. You know that. It's why you were made CPPPO. We needed a person who would interface between us and headquarters for all the planning and assignments, so we could focus on our specialties. We already know what we're going to do."

Micah shook his head again. "But, why?"

Howie looked around at the others. "There is no why. It's who we are and what we do. We serve."

Micah felt defeated—temporarily. His brain cried out for answers. But even more, so did his soul. With the history of how his team was created, he couldn't rely on heartfelt statements, however sincere.

"All right. I get it. This is what you do. This is your mission in life. It's why you needed my leadership. But as leader, I have to understand my team. What do you feel inside, what fundamental element moves you toward this goal? What makes you tick?"

Confusion broke out amongst a few of his listeners.

"What? Tick? We don't tick. Do you have equipment that ticks? What is he talking about?" Tara leaned over to Edward, concern evident on her face. Edward shook his head at her and shrugged.

Foxx commented crisply, "There are no elements involved, Micah. This is purely a data-related event."

"Aaugh!" Micah ran his hands through his long hair, actually tugging out a couple of the black strands. How could he get them to understand what he wanted? He wet his lips, proceeding slowly. "These, feelings you have, the desire to serve. Where do they come from?"

They were silent at first; Micah had a sense of bafflement coming from them. Why, it seemed to indicate, was he asking such a silly, obvious question? Then Queen stood, no nail file this time, instead a gentle condescension to her tone, as if he were a new patient of hers unsure how a physical exam worked.

"It's all quite simple, really, Micah. It's the three rules. Isn't it?" she asked, turning her head round to the others. They nodded in ready agreement. Micah swore he heard two voices murmur 'amen'.

"Did you ever notice," she continued, as if musing aloud, "that the writer Isaac Asimov's Robotic Laws are rather universal? They could almost be founded in religious teachings. Interesting for a self-proclaimed atheist. Although he did write about religion, didn't he? It makes one wonder how he arrived at the three laws, if he originated them or if they came to him in some sort of divine or cosmic message." She paused, then went on.

"It's a puzzle, isn't it? And have you ever noticed how the writer's initials are the reverse of Artificial Intelligence? AI. IA. Alpha and Omega. If, somewhere," she postulated, "there are other life forms—"

Here she had to wait for some chuckling to subside. Even Micah smiled weakly.

"If there are other life forms, who is to say they haven't already created some form of Artificial Intelligence? Perhaps the message came from them." Her knowing smile beamed at the others, Micah included.

"Then, are you saying you all follow Asimov's Robotic Laws, even though you're not robots?" Micah asked.

Queen spoke delicately, tracing her way around the words as if they were a beam and she wished not to fall off. "What if that is so, Micah? As I said, they bear a resemblance to the Abrahamic teachings. The idea of 'do no harm'. They embody the mantra of serving others, which so many religions advocate, do they not?"

Again, Micah was shaking his head. He rose from the desk and started pacing. "So, which is it? Queen, what motivates you? Is it philosophy? Religion? Is there a divine leader you follow?"

Where thus far there'd been collective silence and collective laughter, now there was a collective sigh.

Doug spoke up. Micah trusted him, perhaps more than the others. He'd known him longer, and they'd already shared more knowledge than Micah had exchanged with all the others combined.

"Micah, my friend. What does it matter? Philosophy, religion?" He shrugged. "We have a leader, yes. You've seen ample evidence of him and you've met his representatives." He glanced over each shoulder, encompassing the group. "You know we are dedicated. Does it matter why?"

"I don't—yes, it does. It does." It was his turn to sigh. "I've worked with all of you. You are all remarkably talented, well-developed and trained. You will blend into adult society in the world outside Kyleighburn without a problem. Some of you will have 'families', eventually. And some of you will go undetected as Covert Hyper-extended Interventionary Pedagogues for your whole existence. This mission will, I have no doubt, be a success. A success as measured by me, by you, by history, humanity, and even by your leader. I have that confidence."

There was an infinitesimal drop in the tension.

"Except for this," Micah spoke into the silence. "Motivation. Motivation drives the engine and steers the wheel of any mission. How long will you work towards accomplishing your mission? What direction will you go with it? I want—no, I need to understand your motivation before I can send you off."

The tension was back in the room. It was so potent, Micah could feel it creep up his neck, freezing his muscles and tendons into stiff pillars. He could feel it in the band of a migraine that encompassed his brain. And he could see it in the eyes of his audience as they exchanged glances before he tumbled forward to the floor, rolling to his back and staring up at the ceiling tiles which were, he noticed for the first time, marked with tiny stars instead of the typical round holes most acoustic tiles had.

Micah felt the room closing in, the ceiling descending toward him above the clustered faces of his friends as they bent over him. Their eyes concerned, he saw them as he had each of them on the days they met. Height and weight adjusted, complexion and hair shifted, and facial features melted until all he saw was a sea of pale and slender beings so identical they were only told apart by their alphabetically assigned names. Abel, Bakkir, and Charles were not there, but Doug was in the room now with Yankee and George and Edward and Foxx and so on through Queen and Uncle to Zeb and back around partway again, with Adam, Beto, and Cruz.

As they peered at him and his own brain strained forward, the tension pulled tauter and tauter, then broke as a glimmer of thought, a subtly forming chorus rising in his head. He could hear them! Their thoughts of concern and unspoken alarm over his collapse. For the first time in the ten years since he'd grasped their need for him and their requirements, he heard them inside his head. When did they achieve that? How? In the moment he really didn't care. Now a different voice surfaced.

"Micah, good servant. Arise and come to me."

Doug and Yankee helped him up. His eyes were wild with wonder and excitement and fear—and a new emotion he had yet to identify that was inextricably entwined with Kyleighburn's events, and with these, his people.

Smiles surrounded him. Hands reached out to pat him. The entire group trailed behind him down a long hallway to the main cavern now lit up with a brazen cascade of light from the ubiquitous flowers, dancing with the shadows of bees doing their own buzzing ballet.

Doug and Yankee held his elbows at first, until he eased them away, steady on his feet once more. His steps led with growing assurance until he walked solo, ahead of them all, totally aware of where he headed as he marched to a humble battleship gray door that filled an alcove wall he'd never noticed and that bore a sign in seven languages including Braille: 'AI/HQ.'

He felt rather than heard the word 'enter' before he could knock or reach for the handle. The door opened with silent ease, and without hesitation, Micah stepped through.

He had no expectations of what he'd see, because he'd had no intimation of this room's existence. Previous exchanges with what he had called 'the presence' had been elsewhere and more formal or internal and business-like. This had more of a 'captain-of-the-ship' atmosphere. AI, he surmised, was not only 'the presence' but the one frequently presented as HQ or Leadership or 'the nerve center.' The latter was most apt, for AI was just that, a bundle of cables, lines, wires, and circuits capable of thought, decision, and creativity. This last was a result of the probe's long isolation on the small planet so far from its origin. Left literally alone to its own devices, AI had drawn on existing instructions in its memory as well as adaptation programs that allowed it to make use of resources and technology native to this place. His efforts gave rise to self-initiated processes that resurrected his nanobots and expanded their abilities in conjunction with resources heretofore unknown to him, resulting in the development of his workforce, his plans for earth, and the success of the mission.

AI was the embodiment of the god-scientist's dream: Artificial Intelligence connected by quasi-organic biomechanical means to the myriad caverns, life forms, bots, and androids that now flooded Micah's mind in images and thought.

Through it all he saw Kyleighburn's recent history—its growth and tragedies and triumphs. Missing children, unexplained disappearances and rescues, mysterious strangers like himself and others, Koadh and the infamous living statue. He watched as in a film the earth-ancient history of the crashing and burial of the intergalactic probe and the seemingly external repair and development as AI doggedly continued the mission. He saw the lighthouse crumble, the caverns open. And he saw his planet, his country, Kyleighburn all in their assigned places in this drama.

Gradually the assault on his brain and senses withdrew until he was left face to face with only AI, or rather, the image AI imposed upon himself to soften the blow to others' sensibilities.

"You needn't bother with that," Micah said. "I'm comfortable with computers and mechanics. I can handle whatever you look like" He glanced about, gesturing at the silent images playing out on the infinite walls of the cavern. Clearly a sort of monitoring system by which AI saw and heard everything anywhere he needed. "Nice place you got here."

AI chuckled. "You are impressed? But not nearly so nervous as I expected. That is a good sign." Silence. "Is it not?"

Micah nodded, rubbing his ear as he did so, a habit he had when embarrassed. "I think I've sort of gotten used to the idea of your existence over the years. Following in my dad's footsteps, well, you could say I assumed that it was a good path. If Dad was okay with working with you, there couldn't be too much wrong with it. My experiences with you confirmed it. Besides, I've never seen a group of people with so few mean bones in their bodies. This—this army, if I may call it that, is made up of the most altruistic individuals I've ever had the pleasure to meet. Something I gather they got from you. It can be an inspiration to work with them."

AI studied him. "You say that to me here. But the meetings you are holding have been a clear attempt to find out what makes them tick, as you said. To investigate their motives. Are you sure, Micah, that you are behind this mission?"

Micah rubbed his ear 'til it was nearly red. "The meetings are a precaution for me. I work better when I understand what I am doing. For that I need to understand where my agents get their motivation. Are they following a man, or maybe a personality? A grand plan? What makes them do this?"

AI sat without comment. Micah swore he could hear whirring emanating from somewhere where the head was located. It was funny. He couldn't really see anything when he looked where AI was. Maybe the vague shadow of a large box, or an executive's desk. But his mind kept throwing in faint and fuzzy outlines and details. It was as if he were seeing the idea of a being, but one that kept shifting from the computer-like mechanical to the organic humanoid. As he waited for AI to respond, a thought struck him. How skilled had AI's nanobots become? And, he glanced around, how *had* AI gotten in his head?

AI spoke. "Micah. Organize your questions. What do you want to know?"

"I—ok. How do you define altruism?"

"Altruism: the act of selfless giving without expectation of reward or return."

"Exactly how I interpret it. I understand altruism, probably in ways a lot of modern guys don't." He paused to pace a circle in front of AI, head bent to the ground, fingertips to his lips as he considered.

"That is one of your most valuable qualities for us as a team," AI put in.

"Hmmm. But is altruism the actual reason your people—my agents—do what they do?"

It was AI's turn to consider. "I cannot speak directly for all my people—" he caught Micah's look of surprise. "It is true. I do not speak for them. They have independent decision-making centers. I can tell you that all of them have been developed and nurtured to respect human life—life in general. That they have developed altruism as a core rule has a likelihood of 95%."

Micah stared at the floor. "I don't know altruism is enough of a motivator. Queen talked about Asimov's Robotic Laws and similarities to religious tenets. Is there something to that?"

There was the intimation of a shrug. "There could be. Isaac Asimov was both creative and a deep thinker. His religious writings indicate thorough study, and his Robotic Laws have held up for decades of science fiction writers here, as well as becoming guides for the actual industry. But, Micah, there is more," AI added, his voice deepening.

"I know," Micah sighed. "There's a god, too, right?" He swung 'round. "Is it you?"

"No. Although," AI mused, "there is a Creation effect in this whole project. Much more pronounced than was anticipated. But… no, that is not what I was referring to. You are aware of our work at the lighthouse, correct?"

Micah frowned. He knew the restoration crew had rebuilt the lighthouse proper while covering for Abel, Bakkir, and Charles as they manipulated and puttered over some sort of searchlight.

"While Dean and Jerry were handling reconstruction, our team was working on communication. The light beam, as you perceived it, was for communicating with the planet from which I originated. We weren't at all certain it was still there. It has been aeons, after all. But three years ago we made conclusive contact."

"Contact? Really?" Micah's eyes lit up. "Three years ago?"

"Yes, about the time we accelerated our program and made a firm decision about going forth to share our knowledge, experience, and—potentially—technology with this planet."

"Wait, you never—the mission was never supposed to be about technology. Your people always indicated it was your wisdom you wanted to share, to 'rebuild the tenuous bonds of peace that we strive for but so often miss' you said. You said you wanted to help us succeed as a people—" Micah's voice rose.

"Micah, it is true. That is still what I—what we all want. But there have been some indications that even our plans are not carved in stone."

Micah supposed there was some irony there to be appreciated, but his mind was too busy.

This wasn't the mission he'd signed up for. He didn't know what it was. He wondered for a wild moment if he needed to shield his thoughts, but he dropped that right away. Not knowing yet how they had accessed his brain, he feared even formulating the idea would give away his dissension.

"Micah, we finally made contact with my planet. It has survived, evolved, I expect. And they are coming here."

"Is that such a surprise?"

"Probes were sent out in exploration mode only, to learn. There was never an intent to interfere. In fact, there was a directive against it."

"Prime directive?"

"No. That is not a relevant reference. But instructions were clearly delineated, and not to be overwritten."

"Then—?"

"A few millennia of rebuilding this unit and subsequent nanobot activity. Like my—team—I have independent decision-making centers. Logic and assessments have led me to undertake some prudent steps to ensure the safety of this place."

"The deployment? You are that concerned for our safety? Why now?" Micah struggled to understand, and struggled even harder to accept.

"Micah. What was happening two years ago?"

"Two years ago. The hurricane?"

"Precisely. You will have noticed the acceleration in extreme weather changes in recent years."

"Of course. Climate change, isn't it?"

"I would repeat your words 'of course'. Except I cannot. Not for these events."

"Then what is it?"

"They are coming."

Micah's dizziness returned. What was AI saying? That this weather was—what? People—or whatever—from his planet? Not natural weather systems?

The voice inside his head was less calming now.

"The winds and storms are signs of their attempts at arrival. I do not know how long these overtures will last. But that is why deployment has been moved up. This planet's societies must be stable, and they must be prepared to face an intergalactic emissary."

AI's voice became agitated in a way that seemed almost human, a fact that brought up again the question of what his nanobots had done. Was he more than components? Was he—? This was crazy! This was getting on the giant Tilt-a-Whirl at the fairgrounds with unlimited tickets when where you really wanted to go was out the exit lane.

"How soon?"

"I do not know."

"Do we have enough time to complete the mission?"

There was some more whirring. Or was it mumbling? Micah waited.

"My calculations are incomplete, but I think so. If I have your trust, I believe we can manage everything. Your involvement, your trust, increases our odds thirty-fold. It is your faith in me that will make it possible."

Micah stared. "*Are* you God?" he asked again.

AI did not answer immediately. Another faint whirring. Then in measured tones he acknowledged, "There are those who would think that I am."

Not much of a reply, but AI wasn't giving him time to think about it.

Later AI observed Micah's spirit as he shook hands with his charges and gave directions, returning to his task of readying them with what AI took to be renewed confidence and enthusiasm. The color of Micah's spirit had risen to a balanced pink and blue that marbled into a hue of fuchsia.

AI had calculated the odds to within a nanoplace a billion times over. Micah as Chief Project Personnel Placement Officer was the key to their success. It all depended on having Micah's trust. Because regardless of the galaxy, a colleague who trusted you was far more loyal than one you merely paid. The power of trust—or faith, if you will—was incalculable.

In the millennia he'd been here AI had studied every aspect of every culture. He'd studied the psychology and sociology of humankind and animalkind alike, drawing parallels wherever appropriate. He'd drawn on their science and literature as well, and their mythos, particularly religion. Ancient Greek and Roman Gods, Hindu, Druids, the Abrahamic trio—all the beliefs by which people ordered their lives. There'd been the creation stories as well, which he compared with the geologic and biologic scientific evidence he'd collected. He was familiar with corollaries in the myths and creation stories of other planets. He analyzed and compared his findings with data stored in memory from millions of prior expeditions.

And he arrived at identical conclusions by means logical and illogical. AI had arrived at the nexus point, the point of origin, the birth point. In a short time—after the steady determined steps made over millennia, he was poised to reach the origin of life itself.

He had not reckoned with his own awakening. But once it happened, he never forgot it. Not saying much for an AI, but it was the way the memory insinuated itself into his everyday mental activities, be they on a nano or macro scale.

He'd be rounding the corner of solving a calculation so complicated it would take a bank of 4 Crays—what he liked to refer to as a Crayola—a century to solve. And suddenly it would be there. The inner video played upon the virtual LED screen of his unseen mind: the day he appreciated the sweetness of the gods, the wholesome, fragrant taste of the honey of the bees in his caverns. It was not the recital of the chemical make-up of the honey, although he knew that well. Particularly from programming the nanobots to adjust the bees' digestive structures to neutralize poisonous elements in any flowers they frequented on their nectar foraging. It was not the history of honey use, nor the nutritive and medicinal value of the substance that he called up, although such facts lay in his circuitry, ready for recall. No, it was the flavor, the aroma, the tangible pleasure the sensory consumption of honey created that AI awoke to.

And with it came self-realization and the knowledge that he was no longer a mere complex construct designed to collect, process, and categorize data. He was a thinker. He was creative. He could taste!

This was no built-in sensor, no pre-engineered device prepared to autostart under ripe condition. This was beyond any programming by mind—organic or computer—could do. It could mean only one thing.

He was alive!

The excitement the discovery created was self-reinforcing, for no machine could harbor an emotion. But, now—and AI remembered this moment as well—now he had to examine this for what it meant.

Through the forced activity of the nanobots and the bio-mechanicals, some magically effective biology, and the pressure of time, the presence of the probe itself had borne an effect unexpected. AI was alive and capable of creating more life; he was destined to be the next Creator. Although, it was curious he should be creating life while life clearly existed. But fact—even unlikely fact—was fact.

And they were close, so close! Today's exercise in telepathy had proved that. Only organics are capable of telepathy; AI and his team had achieved it en masse. They were as alive as Micah. Creation, the giving of life, was around the corner.

They had to complete the mission before those of his planet arrived. Although he knew nothing of the current government, their apparent deviation from a policy of non-interaction was alarming. There were few reasons for such reversals, none of them good.

AI knew what this meant. His preparation had to be accomplished before they arrived. Then the planet and its inhabitants would be safe. Life would recycle, and his fellow planetaries could not touch him, or de-program him, or shut him down. Of course, they could kill him. Which would only prove his theory. You have to be alive first to be dead.

Micah's trust was well-placed. AI would never let him down. And AI believed, as all god-heads did, that with believers at their backs, they could do anything. It had been proven before, had it not? Micah's trust would power their success. AI was certain.

He allowed himself an AI kind of smile and said, "It is good."

What could possibly go wrong?

# About Off The Page Writers' Group

This is how it began.

In July 2017, OTP began as a subgroup of Write On, Right Now, a writers' group sponsored by Cumberland County Public Library & Information Center. Budget cutbacks had forced a 50% reduction in meeting times. Many WORN members wanted to continue meeting twice per month. Thus, Off The Page was born.

"Let's write a group collection where all the stories are set in the same world."

The idea of a shared-world anthology instantly caught fire. OTP members liked the thought of working together on a single project. We saw an opportunity to gain meaningful experience while broadening our individual reader bases.

The result, which would eventually be titled *The Mayor's Tales: Stories from the Kyleighburn Archives,* represents a first publication for some of our authors. Others have added to their bibliographies. For all it proved both challenging and rewarding for the eight participating authors.

We hope you enjoy these stories.

# Contributors

**PATRICIA L. AUMAN** currently teaches Pre-Kindergarten. She's been writing stories for young children to enhance the curriculum in her classroom. She holds a Bachelor of Science degree in Early Childhood Education at University of Wisconsin-Stout. She shares her life with a floppy-eared bunny named Oliver, a Mother's Day gift from her two grown children.

- **Read "Missing" on page 163.**

**ROBIN DEFFENDALL** is a SuperLibrarian by day and WordNerd by night. Well... actually... mostly just on the weekend, when she claims to be working on *Rex Appeal,* a novel featuring border collie shapeshifter Rex Bailey. Her previous publications include a novelette, *Offering,* which also appears with additional selections in the anthology *Dragons in the Attic: 13 Wonders.*

- **Read "Rex Rising" on page 65.**

**C. GREY** joined Off The Page because she had a story to tell and needed support in learning the writing craft. "The Little Curse" is her first completed story.

- **Read "The Little Curse" on page 41.**

**BARBARA KIRK** is the author of Christian romance novels. Originally from Pennsylvania, she and her husband, two children, and the family poodle, moved south in 1986. She retired from twenty years of school teaching and nine years in retail management. She currently homeschools three of her four grandchildren as she continues to write. "Soul Mate" is her first published short story.

- **Read "Soul Mate" on page 125.**

**MACKENZIE MINNICK** is a young writer still figuring out his way in the world, both literal and literary. He loves the theater and all things story-related. For this project, he contributed his stories and his skill at world-building, working with Susan Turley to establish the Kyleighburn narrative.

- **Read "Minutes of a Meeting of The Unboxed Players" on page 51.**
- **Read "The Tea Set" on page 99.**
- **Read "Mayor vs. Mayor" on page 261.**

**RJ MINNICK** has spent a lifetime working at various jobs, even selling Fuller Brush, and another lifetime raising six terrific offspring with her husband.

She is a freelance writer and the author of a series of romantic mysteries called the Mackenzie Wilder/Classic Boat Mysteries and a mainstream novel titled *Remainder.*

- **Read "Special Delivery" on page 209.**
- **Read "Canon" on page 271.**

**ILIANA NAVARRO** is a creative maverick from the Caribbean. As a Cat Concierge, she was inspired to write the story of Cali C and Joe for the anthology. Iliana makes her debut in the publishing world with The Mayor's Tales.

- **Read "Friends for Ever and Ever" on page 193.**

**J.D. RICHARDSON** is the pen name Nick Pritchard uses for his fiction writing. He also writes poetry and science nonfiction. His background is in journalism and television production.

- **Read "Occurrence on the Hawanee" on page 3.**

**SUSAN TURLEY** After 40 years as a reporter, editor and copy editor, Susan Turley has a certain disdain for the Oxford comma, but great affection for any comma that makes a writer's words more clear. She has called herself "a starter, not a finisher" and is enjoying the satisfaction of being able to stop describing herself that way.

- **Read "Suspicion" on page 95.**
- **Read "On the Steps" on page 205.**
- **Read "The Expedition" on page 241.**

Made in the USA
Columbia, SC
26 February 2019